CUTTING EDGE

THIRD EDITION

INTERMEDIATE TEACHER'S RESOURCE BOOK

WITH RESOURCE DISC

DAMIAN WILLIAMS

SARAH CUNNINGHAM PETER MOOR

CONTENTS

TEACHER'S RESOURCE BOOK

Introduction

Teacher's notes

TEACHER'S RESOURCE DISC

Extra Resources

Tests

STUDENTS' BOOK CONTENTS

Pronunciation	Task	Language live/ World culture	Study, Practice & Remember
Sentence stress in questions Using intonation to show interest	Discuss the way you spend your time **Preparation:** Listening and reading **Task:** Speaking	**Language live** **Speaking:** Keeping a conversation going **Writing:** An informal email	Study & Practice 1, page 132 Study & Practice 2, page 132 Remember these words, page 134 Study tips, page 134
Past simple *-ed* endings	Describe a personal memory **Preparation:** Listening and vocabulary **Task:** Speaking **Follow up:** Writing	**World culture** **Video and research:** Flashbulb memories	Study & Practice 1, page 135 Study & Practice 2, page 136 Remember these words, page 137 Study tips, page 137
Stress and /ə/ sounds in comparative phrases Sentence stress in polite questions	Provide an insider's guide **Preparation:** Listening **Task:** Speaking	**Language live** **Speaking:** Travel problems **Writing:** A travel blog	Study & Practice 1, page 138 Study & Practice 2, page 139 Remember these words, page 140 Study tips, page 140
Strong and weak forms of *have* Linking in time phrases	Nominate someone for an award **Preparation:** Listening **Task:** Speaking **Follow up:** Writing	**World culture** **Video and research:** Charles Dickens: Writer and campaigner	Study & Practice 1, page 141 Study & Practice 2, page 142 Remember these words, page 143 Study tips, page 143
Word stress in word families Polite intonation in questions	Choose who to hire or fire! **Preparation:** Reading and listening **Task:** Speaking and listening	**Language live** **Speaking:** Making a formal telephone call **Writing:** A CV	Study & Practice 1, page 144 Study & Practice 2, page 145 Remember these words, page 146 Study tips, page 146
Hearing the difference between Past simple and Past perfect in connected speech	Retell a story **Preparation:** Listening and vocabulary **Task:** Speaking and listening **Follow up:** Writing	**World culture** **Video and research:** A story that rocked the world	Study & Practice 1, page 147 Study & Practice 2, page 148 Remember these words, page 149 Study tips, page 149

STUDENTS' BOOK CONTENTS

Pronunciation	Task	Language live/ World culture	Study, Practice & Remember
Word stress Sentence stress	Talk about a show you love or hate **Preparation:** Vocabulary and listening **Task:** Speaking	**Language live** **Speaking:** Making a social arrangement **Writing:** A review	Study & Practice 1, page 150 Study & Practice 2, page 150 Remember these words, page 152 Study tips, page 152
Polite intonation in requests	Give tips on how to behave **Preparation:** Listening **Task:** Speaking **Follow up:** Writing	**World culture** **Video and research:** Addicted to games	Study & Practice 1, page 153 Study & Practice 2, page 154 Remember these words, page 155 Study tips, page 155
Stress in compound nouns	Talk about things you couldn't live without **Preparation:** Reading **Task:** Speaking	**Language live** **Speaking:** Buying things **Writing:** A short thank-you message	Study & Practice 1, page 156 Study & Practice 2, page 157 Remember these words, page 158 Study tips, page 158
Shifting stress in word families *'ll* or *'d* in connected speech	Balance the budget **Preparation:** Listening **Task:** Speaking	**World culture** **Video and research:** In orbit	Study & Practice 1, page 159 Study & Practice 2, page 160 Remember these words, page 161 Study tips, page 161
Modal verbs in connected speech	Discuss new laws **Preparation:** Reading and listening **Task:** Speaking	**Language live** **Speaking:** Expressing and responding to opinions **Writing:** An opinion essay	Study & Practice 1, page 162 Study & Practice 2, page 163 Study & Practice 3, page 163 Remember these words, page 164 Study tips, page 164
Past modal forms in connected speech	Discuss dilemmas **Preparation:** Reading **Task:** Speaking **Follow up:** Writing	**World culture** **Video and research:** Life in a new country	Study & Practice 1, page 165 Study & Practice 2, page 166 Remember these words, page 167 Study tips, page 167

CUTTING EDGE
THIRD EDITION
INTERMEDIATE
STUDENTS' BOOK
WITH DVD-ROM
SARAH CUNNINGHAM PETER MOOR AND JONATHAN BYGRAVE
PEARSON
ALWAYS LEARNING
CUTTING EDGE
THIRD EDITION
WORKBOOK
WITH KEY
JANE COMYNS CARR FRANCES EALES AND DAMIAN WILLIAMS
PEARSON
CUTTING EDGE
THIRD EDITION
TEACHER'S RESOURCE BOOK
WITH RESOURCE DISC
DAMIAN WILLIAMS
WITH SARAH CUNNINGHAM PETER MOOR
PEARSON

CUTTING EDGE
THIRD EDITION
INTERMEDIATE
DVD-ROM
PEARSON
CUTTING EDGE
THIRD EDITION
INTERMEDIATE
ACTIVETEACH
PEARSON
CUTTING EDGE
THIRD EDITION
INTERMEDIATE
TEACHER'S
RESOURCE DISC
PEARSON

MESSAGE FROM THE AUTHORS

"

Do you remember the first time you sent a text message? Or when you started checking information online? These things may seem like centuries ago or only yesterday, but one thing is for sure, in the last twenty years or so we have lived through a period of unprecedented technological change. Change which has affected all of our personal and working lives. Change that will not go away but will continue in ways that we haven't yet imagined.

Cutting Edge Third Edition, while retaining its most popular features, has changed to reflect and embrace the digital age. We have done this through new texts, enhanced features and design along with a whole suite of new digital components. We've added richer and more varied video content in the *Language live and World culture* lessons. These also deepen learners' knowledge and understanding of global issues, direct them to purposeful, focused research on the internet and guide them to summarise their findings through guided writing tasks.

The new *Share your task* feature encourages learners to film and compare their work with other *Cutting Edge* users. The fully revised *MyEnglishLab* for *Cutting Edge Third Edition* has a wide variety of interactive exercises to motivate and engage learners along with the gradebook so you can keep track of your learners' progress in an instant.

Grammar rules, vocabulary lists and test scores all play their part in language learning, but that's not the whole story; in the end, language learning is about connecting people. *Cutting Edge Third Edition* provides a window on the world with dramatic video clips, information-rich texts and engaging tasks. These provide a springboard for learners to engage in meaningful speaking and writing activities that reflect the reality of the 21st century.

We hope that you and your learners will enjoy using *Cutting Edge Third Edition* and we would like to thank you for the invaluable input you have given us over the years. We look forward to continuing and widening our ongoing dialogue with *Cutting Edge* users all over the world.

"

Sarah Cunningham and Peter Moor

OVERVIEW OF COMPONENTS

STUDENTS' BOOK

- Twelve units with 90 to 120 hours of teaching material
- A comprehensive Study, Practice & Remember section
- Audio scripts of the class audio

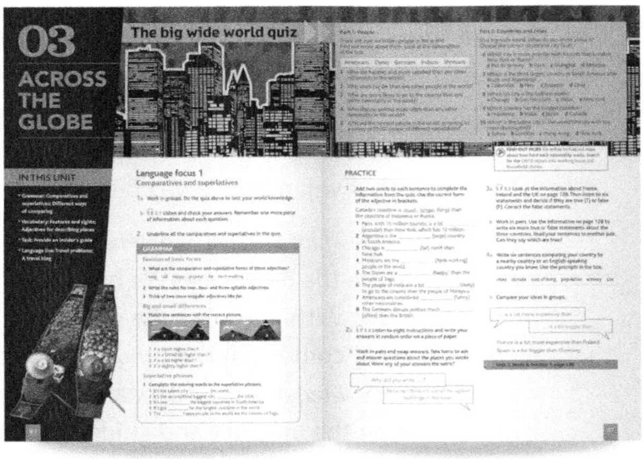

DVD-ROM

- Audio material for use in class
- DVD content (World culture and Language live)
- Audio and video scripts
- Digital Mini Dictionary

WORKBOOK

- Additional grammar, vocabulary and pronunciation exercises to complement the Students' Book
- Additional functional language practice exercises
- Extra listening and reading material
- Extra writing practice

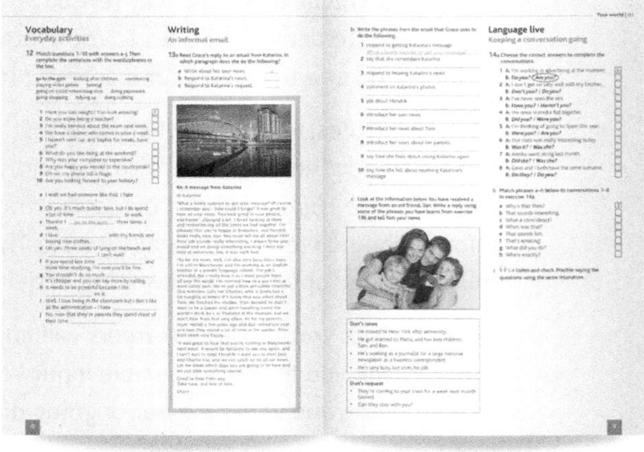

WORKBOOK AUDIO

- Audio material to practice listening, pronunciation and functional language
- Visit **www.english.com/students/cuttingedge3e** to download the audio

MYENGLISHLAB

Learning Management System that provides:

- Interactive workbook with instant feedback
- Extra practice in grammar, vocabulary and the four skills
- Unit, Mid-course and End of course tests
- Extra videos with interactive exercises

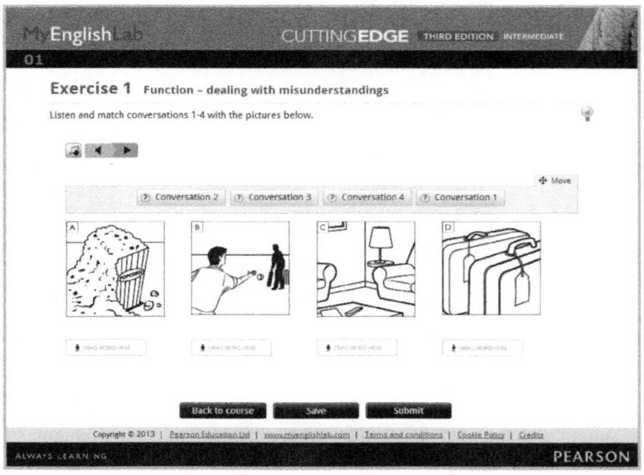

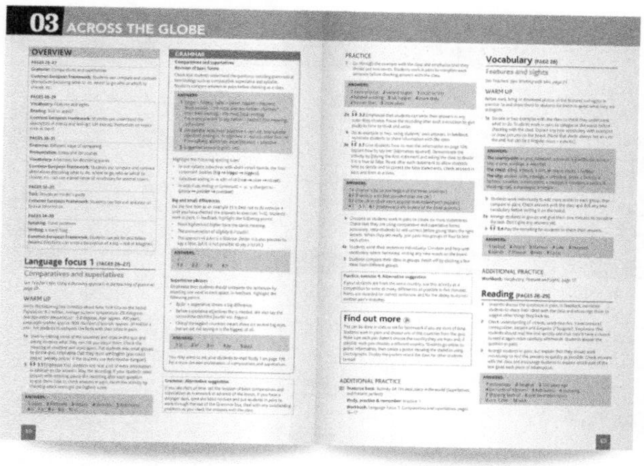

TEACHER'S RESOURCE BOOK

- Teacher's notes for every unit with alternative suggestions, culture notes and answer keys
- Generic teaching tips on useful areas such as: grammar, lexis, pronunciation, using video etc.

TEACHER'S RESOURCE DISC

- Class audio scripts and video scripts
- Photocopiable worksheets to provide additional practice of key language
- Editable and printable tests
- Test audio, audio scripts and answer keys

ACTIVE TEACH

Software for classroom use to help teachers get the most out of the course featuring:

- Answer reveal feature
- Integrated audio and video content
- Test master containing all course tests
- Large extra resources section
- Grammar and vocabulary review games
- A host of useful tools

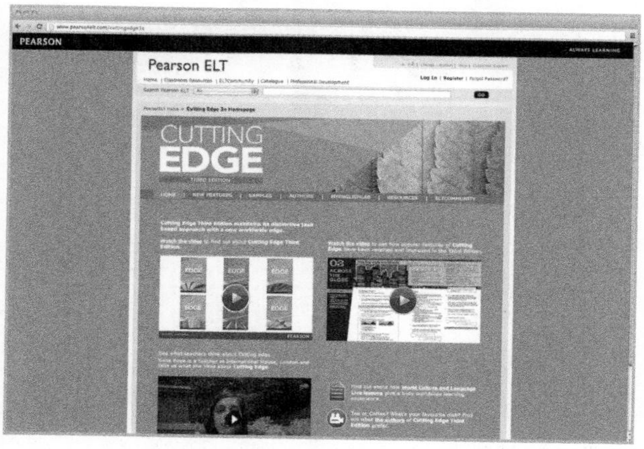

WEBSITE

- Information about the course
- Sample materials
- Placement test
- A range of free downloadable worksheets

www.pearsonELT.com/cuttingedge3e

THE STUDENTS' BOOK

1 Key language highlighted at the start of each unit.

2 'Discovery' approach to grammar engages learners and helps them remember rules.

3 Plenty of form-based and communicative practice of key language.

4 Cross-referencing to *Study, Practice & Remember* sections for additional explanations, exercises and *Study tips*.

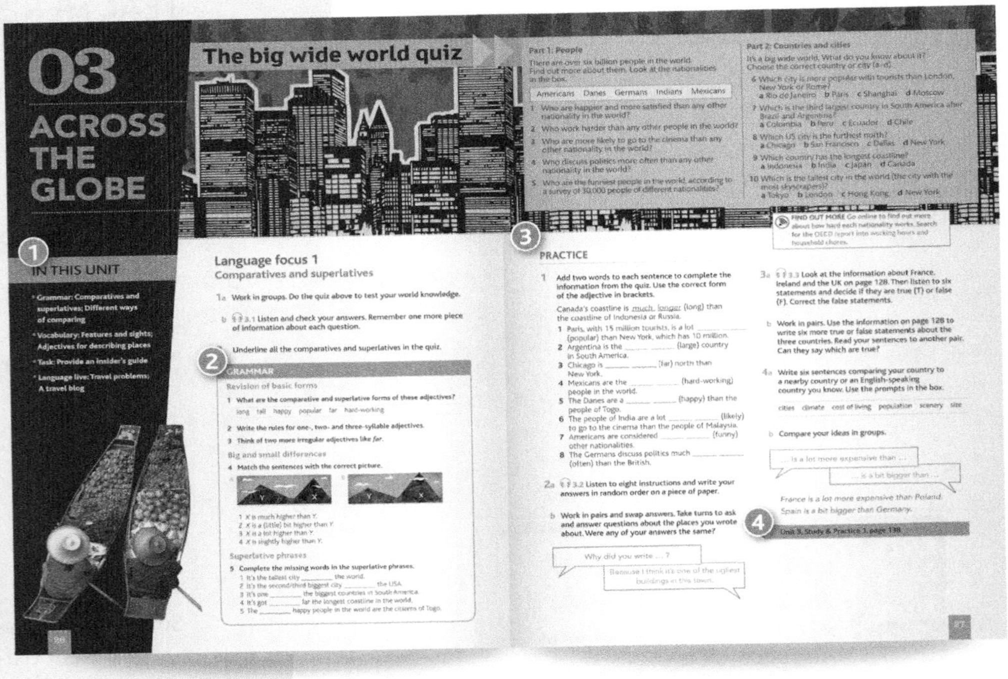

5 Topic-related vocabulary and focus on high-frequency, useful words and phrases.

6 Personalised speaking activities recycle vocabulary and encourage learners to draw on their own knowledge and experience.

7 Information-rich texts reflect learners' interests and experience.

8 A variety of pre and post-reading activities are provided to get the most out of reading texts.

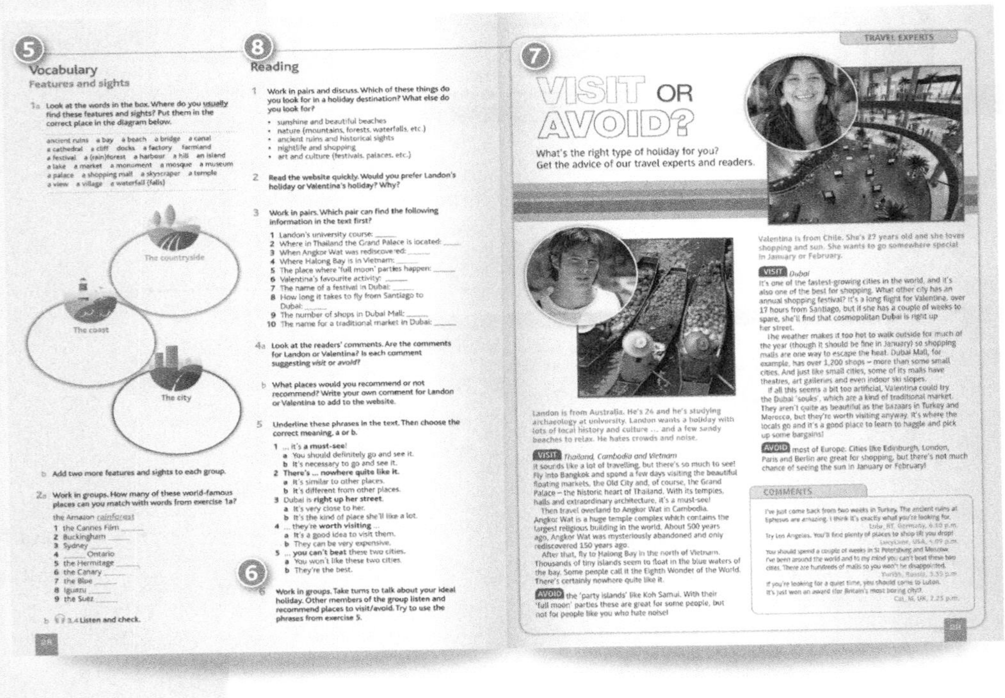

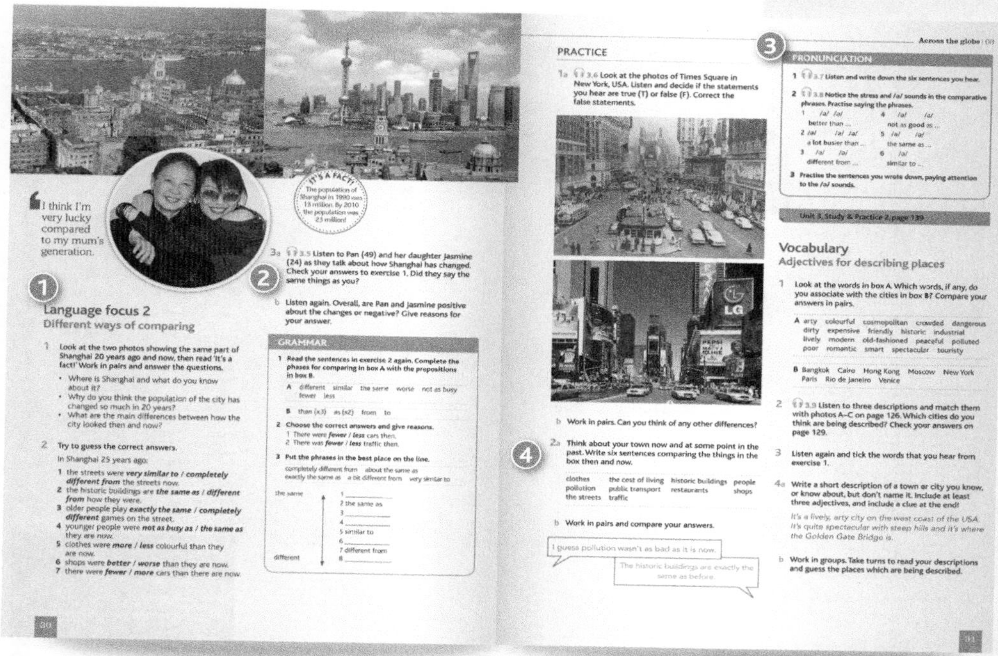

1 Grammar presented in context through listening and/or reading texts.

2 Learners are encouraged to learn more about the world and other cultures.

3 Special *Pronunciation* boxes focus on stress, weak forms and intonation.

4 Speaking and writing activities are integrated throughout to extend and consolidate language covered in the unit.

5 A model or stimulus is provided to show learners what they are expected to do.

6 Structured speaking tasks help learners to achieve a particular goal or outcome.

7 Learners are encouraged to think and prepare before they do the task.

8 *Useful language* boxes help learners find the right expressions.

9 *Share your task* activities encourage learners to reflect and perfect their performance.

THE STUDENTS' BOOK

1 *Language live* spreads focus on functional language and writing.

2 Key functional language is presented through light-hearted DVD clips.

3 Pronunciation is integrated throughout.

4 Writing sections focus on particular genres of writing e.g. blogs, emails etc. as well as practising particular sub-skills e.g. drafting.

5 *Can do* box at the end of the unit highlights what learners have achieved in the unit.

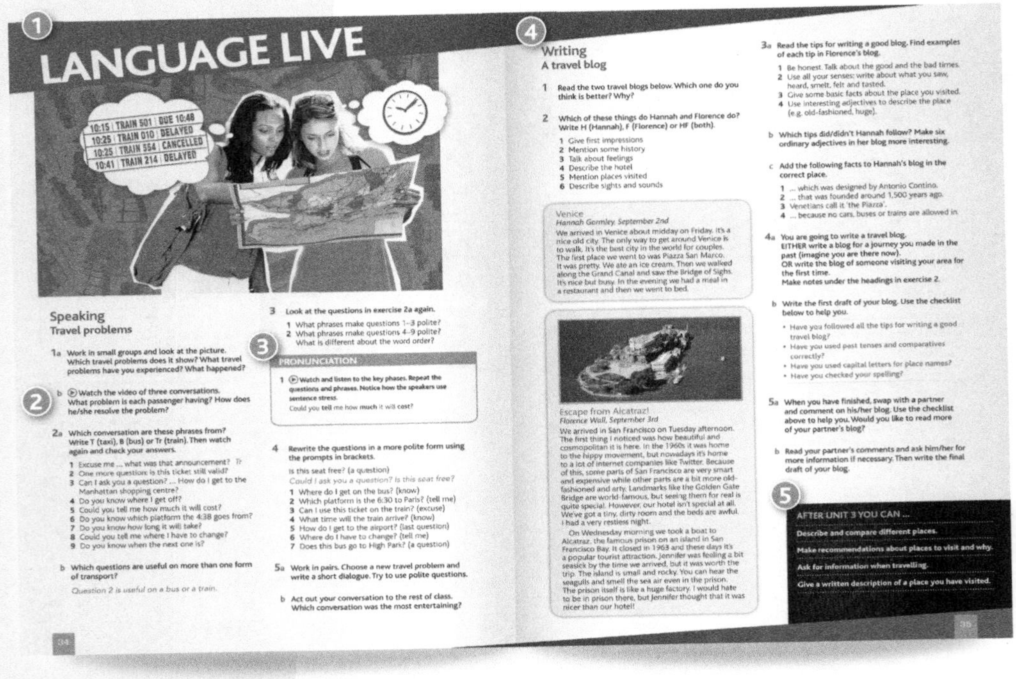

6 *World culture* spreads explore contemporary issues of global interest.

7 Topics are introduced through authentic, documentary-style clips from TV programmes and other sources.

8 *World view* sections encourage learners to share ideas and experiences.

9 *Find out first*/*Find out more* sections develop online research skills.

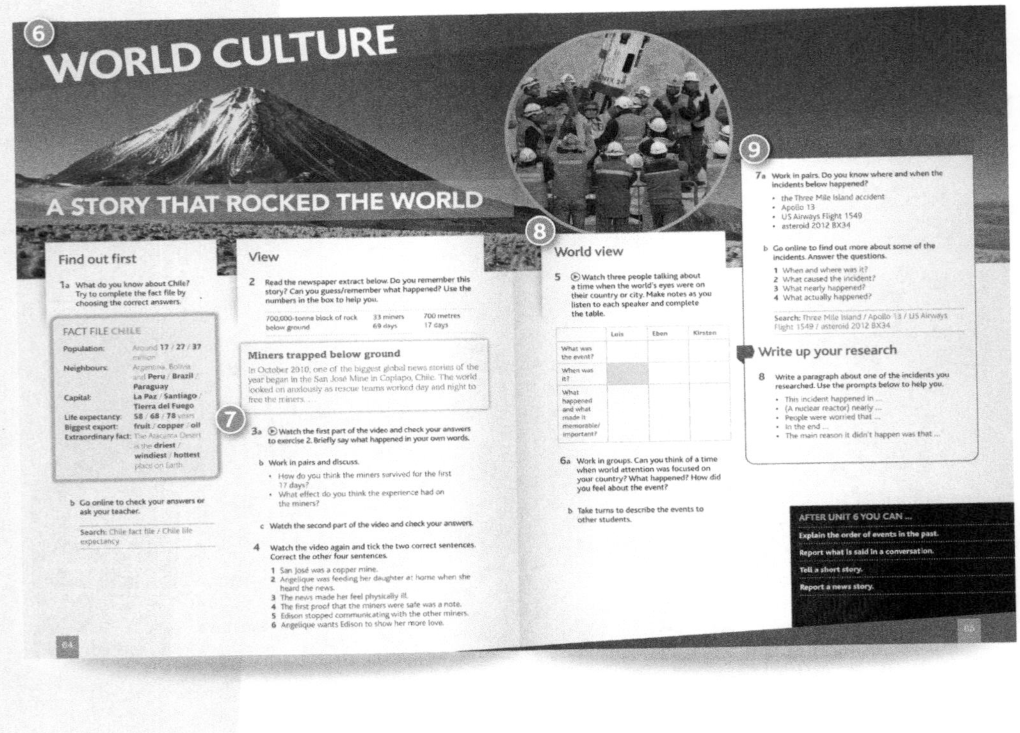

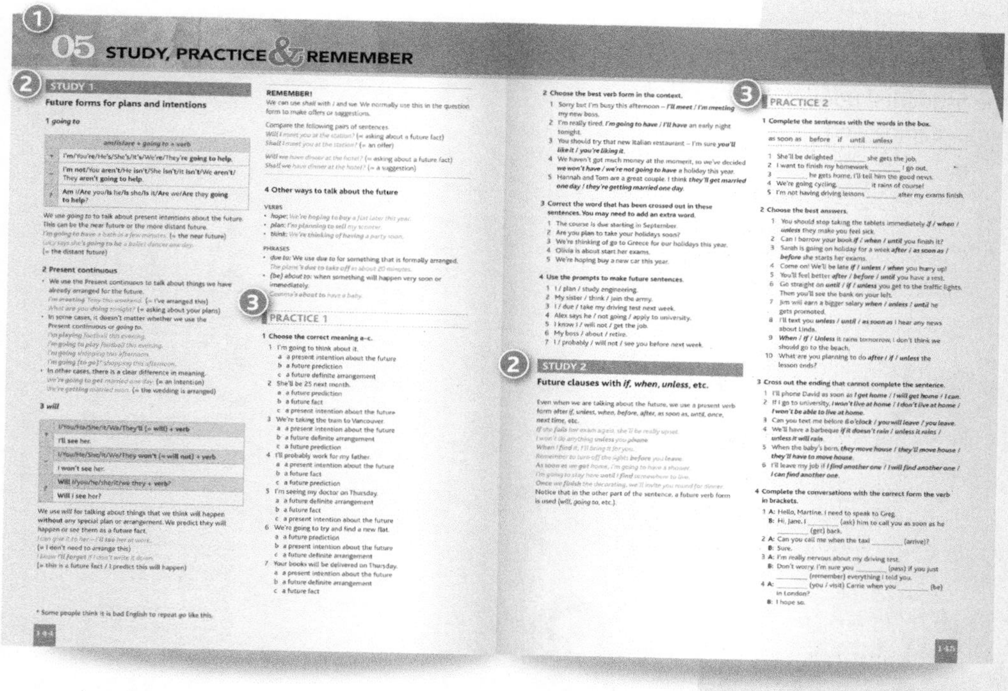

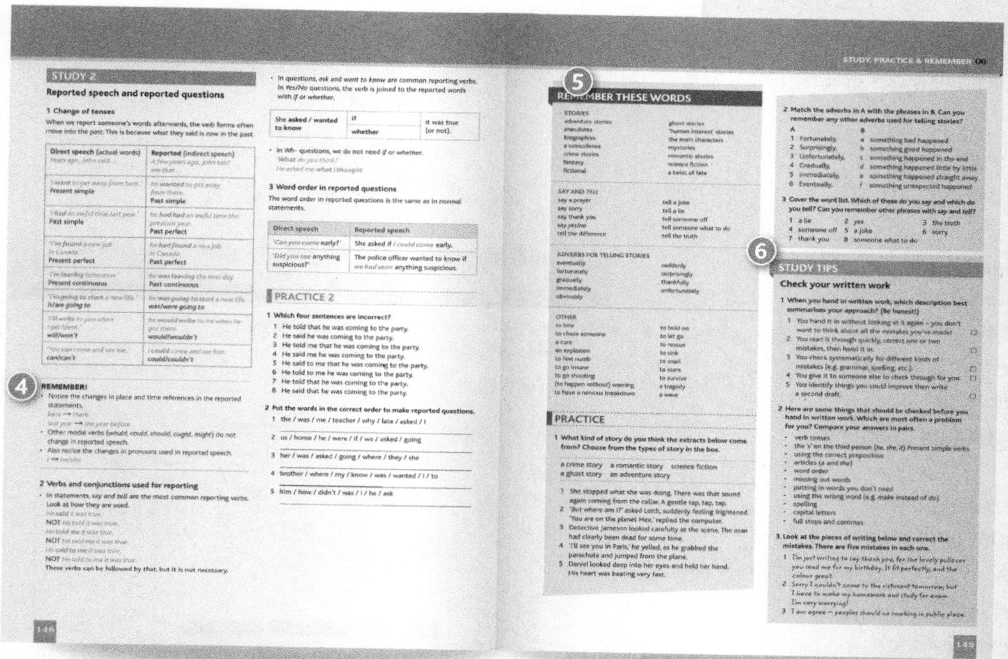

1 *Study, Practice & Remember* sections at the back of the Students' Book ensure systematic consolidation of new language.

2 *Study* sections provide a comprehensive overview of language covered in the unit.

3 Practice exercises can be used in class or set for homework.

4 *Remember!* boxes alert learners to key rules.

5 *Remember these words* sections provide a list of the most important words and phrases covered in the unit.

6 *Study tips* sections draw attention to important study skills and learning habits such as keeping vocabulary notes, using English outside the classroom etc.

THE SUPPORT COMPONENTS

WORKBOOK

The Workbook contains a wide variety of grammar, vocabulary and functional language exercises that review all the areas studied in the Students' Book. It also features additional listening, reading and writing practice.

1 *Listen and read* sections encourage learners to develop listening skills using the accompanying audio files.

2 The workbook contains regular listening practice using the accompanying audio files.

3 Writing exercises offer further practice of the genres covered in the Students' Book.

4 A variety of functional language practice activities consolidate areas covered in the Students' Book.

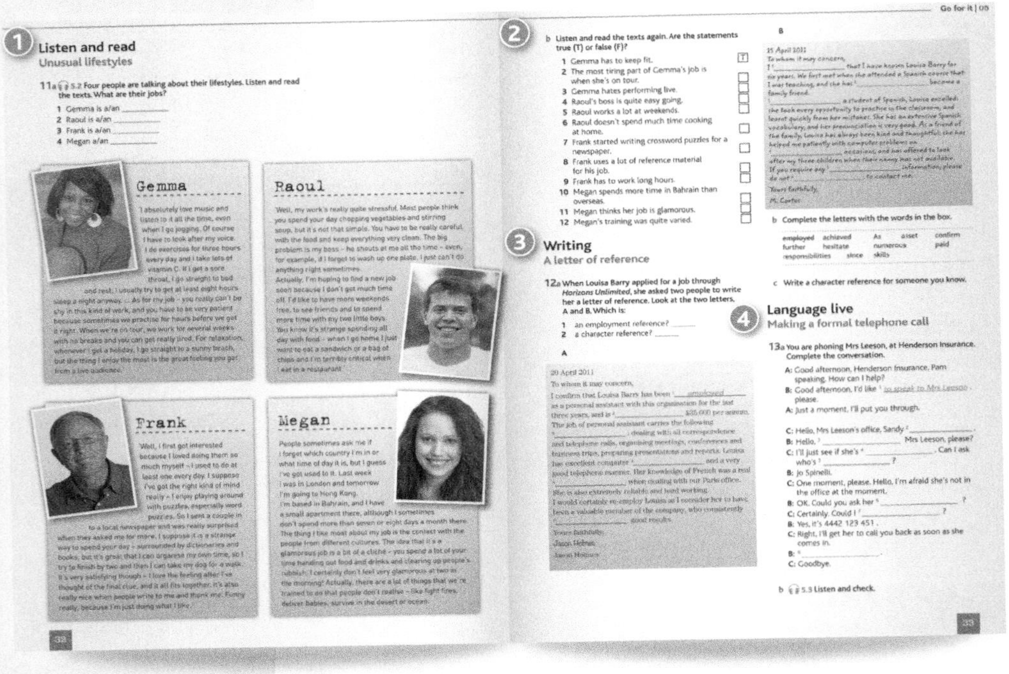

MYENGLISHLAB

MyEnglishLab provides a blended and personalised learning environment with materials that can be assigned at the touch of a button.

- Interactive workbook exercises with instant feedback and automatic grade book.
- Common error report that highlights mistakes that learners are making.
- Tips and feedback that direct learners to reference materials and encourage them to work out answers themselves.
- Mid-course and end of course tests.
- Extra video with interactive exercises for every unit.

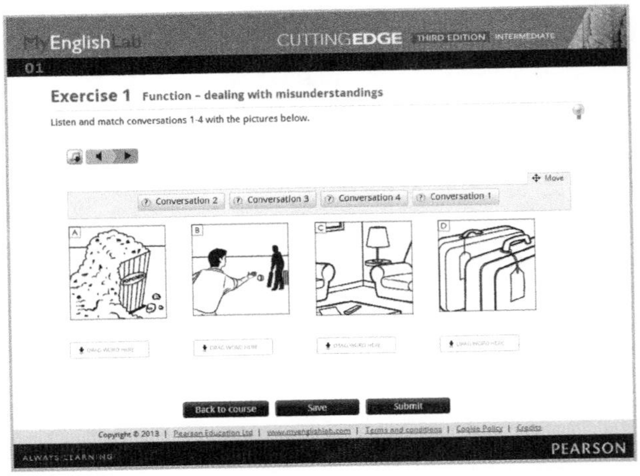

ACTIVETEACH

Cutting Edge Third Edition ActiveTeach contains everything you need to make the course come alive. It includes integrated whiteboard software that allows you to add notes, embed files, save your work and reduce preparation time.

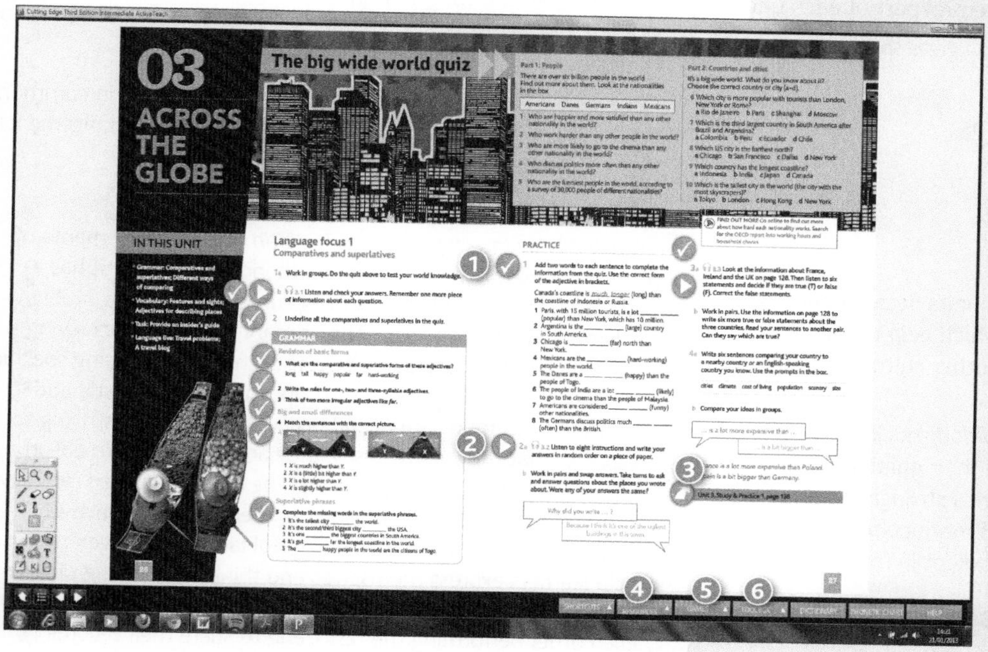

1. Answers to exercises are revealed at the touch of a button.
2. Audio and video content fully integrated with time-coded scripting.
3. Shortcuts to the relevant pages of the *Study, Practice & Remember* sections.
4. Extra resources section with photocopiables, teacher's notes, editable audio and video scripts, editable tests and more.
5. Grammar and vocabulary games for warm up and review activities.
6. Useful tools include a regular/phonetic keyboard, a stopwatch and a scorecard.

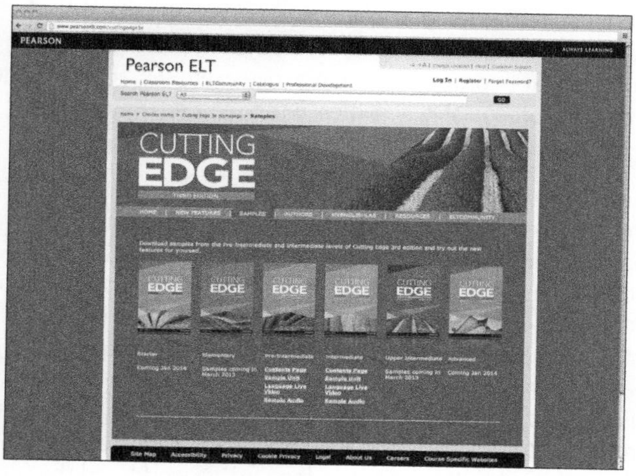

WEBSITE

The *Cutting Edge Third Edition* website provides a wealth of information and additional material to support the course.

- Information about the course, its components and the authors.
- Introductory author videos.
- Sample materials and free downloadable worksheets.
- A placement test.

www.pearsonELT.com/cuttingedge3e

COURSE RATIONALE

The thinking behind Cutting Edge Intermediate Third Edition

Overview

Cutting Edge Intermediate Third Edition has a multilayered, topic-based syllabus which includes thorough and comprehensive work on grammar, vocabulary, pronunciation and the skills of listening, reading, speaking and writing. Structured speaking tasks form a central part of each unit.

Cutting Edge Intermediate Third Edition gives special emphasis to:

- communication
- the use of phrases and collocations
- active learning and research skills
- recycling and revision.

Topics and content

We aim to motivate learners with units based around up-to-date, globally relevant topics which help them gather information about the world and other cultures through the medium of English.

Cutting Edge Intermediate Third Edition provides learners with many opportunities to share their opinions about the topics in focus and personalisation is strongly emphasized throughout. The differing needs of monocultural and multicultural classes has also been kept in mind throughout.

Approach to grammar

Learners are encouraged to take an active, systematic approach to developing their knowledge of grammar, and to use new language in a natural, communicative way.

Typically, there are two *Language focus* sections in each unit, in which grammar is presented using reading or listening texts. Each *Language focus* has a *Grammar* box which focuses on the main language points, and encourages learners to work out rules for themselves.

The *Language focus* sections are followed up thoroughly through:

- a wide range of communicative and written practice exercises in the *Students' Book*
- the opportunity to use new grammar naturally in the speaking tasks (see below)
- the *Study, Practice & Remember* sections which consolidate learning and clarify any remaining problems
- further written practice in the *Workbook* and interactive exercises in the fully revised *MyEnglishLab*.

(See *Teaching tips: Using a discovery approach to grammar* on page 20, and *Using the Study, Practice & Remember* sections on page 25.)

Approach to vocabulary

A wide vocabulary is vital to communicative success, so new lexis is introduced and practised at every stage in the course. Particular attention has been paid to the selection of high-frequency, internationally useful words and phrases, using information from the British National Corpus.

Vocabulary input is closely related to the topics and tasks in the units, allowing for plenty of natural recycling. Further practice is provided in the *Study, Practice & Remember* sections at the end of each unit and in the *Workbook*.

Fluent speakers make extensive use of 'prefabricated chunks' of language. *Cutting Edge Intermediate Third Edition* gives particular emphasis to collocations and fixed phrases which are integrated throughout in:

- topic-based vocabulary lessons
- the *Useful language* boxes in the speaking tasks
- *Language live* lessons, which focus on phrases used in common everyday situations such as telephoning or making arrangements.

(See *Teaching tips: Working with lexis* on page 21.)

The speaking tasks

Cutting Edge Intermediate Third Edition integrates elements of a task-based approach into its methodology. Each unit has a structured speaking task including surveys, mini-talks, problem-solving and narrative tasks. The primary focus is on achieving a particular outcome or product, rather than on practising specific language. The tasks provide the opportunity for realistic and extended communication, and because learners are striving to express what they want to say, they are more likely to absorb the language that they are learning. The tasks are graded carefully in terms of difficulty and, in order for them to work effectively, a model or stimulus is provided, useful language is given to help learners express themselves and thinking/planning time is included. Learners are also encouraged to record themselves or each other performing the tasks, and to share their recording with other learners through the new *Share your task* feature, thus providing extra motivation for rehearsal and accurate production.

(See *Teaching tips: Making tasks work* on page 23, and *Teaching intermediate learners* on page 26.)

In addition to the extended speaking tasks, *Cutting Edge Intermediate Third Edition* offers many other opportunities for speaking, for example, through the discussion of reading and listening texts, communicative practice exercises, and the wide range of photocopiable activities in the *Teacher's Resource Disc*.

World culture

The *World culture* pages are a new feature of *Cutting Edge Intermediate Third Edition* and are designed to deepen learners' knowledge and understanding of global issues. This is done through the use of authentic video clips which act as a stimulus for internet-based research around the issues raised in the video. Learners are guided through the necessary steps to make their research focused and productive, and are given guidance on how to summarise their research through a guided written follow-up. The emphasis throughout is on creating a link between the classroom and the outside world, and the development of research skills which will prove of lasting value.

Language live

Language live pages are another new feature of *Cutting Edge Intermediate Third Edition*. The main purpose of these pages is to help learners with the functional language they need to deal with everyday situations such as telephoning, shopping and making social arrangements. Learners are presented with key language through the medium of light-hearted DVD clips which provide an immediate and motivating context. They are then given the opportunity to practise the language further through roleplay activities, and to develop their writing skills through a related writing task.

Other features of *Cutting Edge Intermediate Third Edition*

Listening

Cutting Edge Intermediate Third Edition places strong emphasis on listening. Listening material consists of:

- short extracts and mini-dialogues to introduce and practise new language
- words and sentences for close listening and to model pronunciation
- longer texts (interviews, stories and conversations), many of which are authentic, often in the Preparation section as a model or stimulus for the Task
- regular *Listen and read* sections in the *Workbook* to further develop learners' confidence in this area.

Speaking

There is also a strong emphasis on speaking, as follows:

- The tasks provide a regular opportunity for extended and prepared speaking based around realistic topics and situations.
- Much of the practice of grammar and lexis is through oral exercises and activities.
- The topics and reading texts in each unit provide opportunities for follow-up discussion.
- There is regular integrated work on pronunciation.
- Most of the photocopiable activities in the *Teacher's Resource Disc* involve extensive speaking practice.

Reading

There is a wide range of reading material in the *Students' Book*, including newspaper and website articles, factual/ scientific texts, stories, quizzes, forms, notes, letters, blogs and emails. These texts are integrated in a number of different ways:

- extended texts specifically to develop reading skills
- texts which lead into grammar work and language analysis
- texts which provide a model or stimulus for tasks and models for writing activities.

Writing

Regular and systematic work on writing skills are developed in *Cutting Edge Intermediate Third Edition* through:

- *Language live* pages in the *Students' Book*, which focus on writing e-mails and letters, writing narratives and reviews, drafting and redrafting, use of linkers, etc.
- *Writing* sections in the *Workbook*, which expand on the areas covered in the *Students' Book*
- written follow-up sections to many of the speaking tasks.

Pronunciation

Pronunciation work in *Cutting Edge Intermediate Third Edition* is integrated with grammar and lexis and there are special pronunciation boxes in every unit. The focus is mainly on stress, weak forms and intonation. A range of activity types are used in the *Students' Book*, including discrimination exercises and dictation, and an equal emphasis is placed on understanding and reproducing.

Learning skills

Cutting Edge Intermediate Third Edition develops learning skills in a number of ways:

- The discovery approach to grammar encourages learners to experiment with language and to work out rules for themselves.
- The task-based approach encourages learners to take a proactive role in their learning.
- The *Study tips* in the *Study, Practice & Remember* sections focus on useful learning strategies, such as keeping notes and revision techniques. Learners are encouraged to share ideas about the most effective ways to learn.

Learning skills

Recycling is a key feature of *Cutting Edge Intermediate Third Edition*. New language is explicitly recycled through:

- speaking tasks which offer constant opportunities for learners to use what they have studied in a natural way, and for teachers to assess their progress and remind them of important points.
- extra practice exercises in the *Study, Practice & Remember* sections. These are designed to cover all the main grammar and vocabulary areas in the unit. After trying the exercises, learners are encouraged to return to any parts of the unit that they still feel unsure about to assess what they have (and have not) remembered.

(See *Teaching tips: Making tasks work* on page 23 and *Using the Study, Practice & Remember* sections on page 25.)

TEACHING TIPS

How to get the most out of Cutting Edge Intermediate Third Edition

Using a discovery approach to grammar

Cutting Edge Intermediate Third Edition often uses a 'discovery' approach to grammar input because:

- we believe that learners absorb rules best if they work them out for themselves.
- learners of this level often have some previous knowledge of the language.

This knowledge is often difficult for the teacher to predict. The 'test-teach' exercises and *Grammar* boxes are designed so that learners can utilise this knowledge, and so that teachers can adjust their approach to take account of it.

1 Get to know the material available

Every unit of *Cutting Edge Intermediate Third Edition* has two *Language focus* sections, which include:

- a short text or 'test-teach' type introductory material.
- a *Grammar* box focusing learners on the main language points.
- a *Study* section (part of the *Study, Practice & Remember* section) at the back of the *Students' Book* providing more detailed information about what is covered in the *Grammar boxes*.
- oral and/or written practice exercises.

These language areas are recycled through the *Study, Practice & Remember* sections at the back of the *Students' Book*.

The *Workbook* includes additional practice material.

The *Teacher's Resource Disc* also contains a number of photocopiable activities designed to further consolidate the grammar areas covered.

2 Be prepared to modify your approach

It is unlikely that you will discover that all learners are using the target language perfectly and need no further work on it. However, you may realise they only need brief revision, that you can omit certain sections of the *Grammar* box or go through some or all of it very quickly. Alternatively, you may decide to omit some of the practice activities, or set them for homework.

On the other hand, you may discover that many learners know less than you would normally expect at this level. In this case, spend more time on the basic points, providing extra examples as necessary, and leave more complex issues for another day.

3 Encourage learners to share what they know and make guesses

It is useful to do 'test-teach' exercises (for example, *Language focus 2*: exercises 1a and b on page 68 of the *Students' Book*) in pairs or groups. In this way, stronger learners can help weaker ones, and you do not have to provide all the input. If neither learner knows, encourage them to guess – sometimes they have internalised rules without realising. This can be checked as you go over the answers together.

4 Give learners time to adjust

The idea of such exercises is that learners form their own hypotheses about new rules, which they then check and refine. Learners not used to this approach may take time to adapt, but this does not mean that they will never get used to it. Some learners get anxious if they do not have things explained immediately. In such cases, do not leave them to become more frustrated – either answer their questions briefly on an individual basis, or make it clear that you will be dealing with them later.

If there are language areas that you think your class will be unable to tackle without previous input, you can change the whole approach, presenting the rules at the beginning of the *Language focus* and setting the 'test-teach' exercises as controlled practice activities:

5 Use Grammar boxes in different ways

Questions in the *Grammar* boxes can be tackled in different ways, depending on the ability/confidence of your learners and the relative difficulty of the language point in question. Here are some possible approaches:

- **Answer the questions individually / in pairs, then check them together as a class:**
  This is a good way of encouraging learners to have a more independent attitude. Make sure that they understand what they have to do for each question, and monitor carefully to see how they are coping – if they are obviously all stuck or confused, stop them and sort out the problem. As you check answers, write up examples to highlight any important problems of form, meaning, etc. The *Study* section at the back of the *Students' Book* can be read at the end, either individually or as a class.
- **Answer the questions together as a class:**
  With weaker classes, or for areas that you know your learners will find difficult, it may be best to read out questions to the whole class and work through them together, with examples on the board. Alternatively, set more straightforward questions for learners to answer in pairs, and do more complicated ones together as a class. As learners gain more confidence, you can set more and more questions for them to do on their own.
- **Learners work through the questions individually / in pairs, then check the answers themselves in the *Study* section:**
  Stronger, self-sufficient learners may be able to take most of the responsibility for themselves. Most classes should be able to do this with the simpler *Grammar* boxes. It is still important that you monitor carefully to make sure that there are no major problems, and check answers together at the end to clear up any remaining doubts.

Working with lexis

1 Become more aware of phrases and collocations

Thousands of phrases and collocations make up the lexis in English, along with the traditional one-word items. Learners should know about the importance of such phrases. They may look at a phrase such as *leave home* and assume that they know it (because the two constituent words look 'easy'), although in fact they are unable to produce the phrase for themselves when appropriate. Such phrases also blur the boundaries between 'vocabulary' and 'grammar'. In teaching these phrases you will be helping learners with many problematic areas that are traditionally considered to be grammar, from the use of articles and prepositions, to the use of the passive and the Present perfect.

The following list of phrase types shows how common these 'prefabricated chunks' are in all types of English:

- **collocations** – common word combinations – including:
  nouns + verbs (*work long hours, have a drink*)
  adjectives + nouns (*old friends, good news*)
  adverbs + verbs (*work hard, will probably*)
  verbs + prepositions/particles, including phrasal verbs (*think about, grow up*)
  adjectives + prepositions (*famous for, jealous of*)
  other combinations of the above (*go out for a meal, get to know*)
- **fixed phrases** (*Never mind! On the other hand ..., If I were you ..., Someone I know*)
- **semi-fixed phrases** – phrases with variations (*a friend of mine/hers/my brother's, both of us/them/my parents, the second/third/tenth biggest in the world*)
- **whole sentences which act as phrases** (*How are you? He's gone home. I'll give you a hand. I agree to some extent.*)

2 Keep an eye on usefulness and be aware of overloading learners

It is easy to 'go overboard' with collocations and phrases as there are so many of them. However, to avoid overloading your learners, limit your input to high-frequency, useful phrases. As you teach lexis, ask yourself questions such as: *How often would I use this phrase myself? How often do I hear other people using it? Do my learners need it? Is it too idiomatic, culturally specific or complex to bother with?*

3 Feed in phrases on a 'little but often' basis

To avoid overloading learners and ensure that your lexical input is useful, teach a few phrases relating to particular activities as you go along. For example, in a grammar practice activity, instead of simple answers such as *Yes, I do* or *No, I haven't*, feed in phrases such as *It depends, I don't really care, I would probably ...* . The same is true of discussions about reading/listening texts and writing activities.

4 Point out patterns in phrases

Pointing out patterns will help learners to remember phrases. Many do not fit into patterns, but you can often show similar phrases with the same construction, like this:

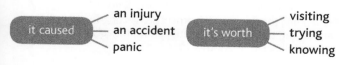

it caused – an injury / an accident / panic

it's worth – visiting / trying / knowing

5 Answer learners' questions briefly

One possible problem with a more lexical approach is that learners may ask a lot of questions beginning *Can you say ...?*, *What about ...?*, etc. Although learners should be encouraged to ask questions, there is obviously a danger of overload – and it may also be the same learner who is asking all the questions! Unless you feel that it is really important, answer briefly *yes* or *no*, and move on quickly. If you are not sure, the best answer is probably *I've never heard anyone say it myself*. If the learner is still not satisfied, say that you will give them an answer the following lesson.

6 Make the most of emerging language

One simple way to make your learners more aware of collocation is to get into the habit of writing word combinations on the board wherever appropriate, rather than just individual words. The more learners see these words together, the more likely they are to remember them as a unit. Rather than just writing up shopping or crime, write up do the shopping / go shopping (and explain the difference) or commit a crime. Remind learners to write down the collocations too, even if they 'know' the constituent words.

7 Reinforce and recycle phrases

This is particularly important with phrases which, for the reasons given above, can be hard to remember. Most revision games and activities teachers do with single items of vocabulary can be adapted and used with phrases. You may find the following useful in addition:

- **Make a phrase bank:**
  Copy new words and phrases from the lesson onto slips of card or paper (large enough for learners to read if you hold them up at the front of the room) and keep them in a box or bag. This is a good record for you, as well as your learners, of the phrases that the class has studied – do this frequently at the start and end of lessons to recycle the phrases often. Hold them up and ask learners to give you (choose as appropriate):
  – an explanation of the phrase
  – a translation of the phrase
  – synonyms
  – opposites
  – the pronunciation
  – situations where they might say this
  – a sentence including the phrase
  – the missing word that you are holding your hand over (for example, *on* in the phrase *get on well with*)
  – the phrase itself, based on a definition or translation that you have given them.
- **Have learners create their own review materials:**
  Take several small strips of paper into class, enough for a few for each learner. Ask them to look back over their notes (or in the *Remember these words* sections at the back of the book) and choose 3-4 phrases they've learnt recently and write each one on a strip of paper. Circulate and check learners have formed the phrases correctly. Learners then tear each strip into separate words, shuffle them all together and give them to a partner, to put in order.

TEACHING TIPS

How to get the most out of Cutting Edge Intermediate Third Edition

Helping learners with pronunciation

1 Aim for intelligibility

It is worth remembering that in today's world there are more speakers of English as a foreign or second language than there are native speakers, and so no-one can really say they 'own' the language or speak the most 'correct' form. It is therefore best to encourage learners to make themselves understood rather than aim for 'perfect' pronunciation, whatever that might be. Consonants (particularly at the beginning and end of words) are probably more important than vowels here. Use any tips you know for helping learners to reproduce them. You might focus them on a similar sound in their own language and then help them to adapt it, or use a trick like starting with /u…/ to get learners to produce the /w/ sound. Anything that works is valid here! Sometimes it is useful to contrast the problem sound with the one that learners are mistakenly producing, via a 'minimal pair' such as *best* and *vest*. Say the pair of words several times, and then ask learners to say which they can hear, before asking them to produce the words themselves.

2 Little and often is the key … and be realistic

There are regular *Pronunciation* boxes in the *Students' Book* but you should aim to integrate pronunciation work whenever learners have a problem. 'Little and often' also applies here.

On the other hand, think about what you want to achieve: clarity and confidence are what most learners need, rather than perfection in every detail. Individuals vary widely in what they can achieve, so don't push too much when a particular student is getting frustrated or embarrassed. Leave it and come back to it again another day. A humorous, light-hearted approach also helps to alleviate stress!

3 Drill in different ways, depending on the language

Choral and/or individual repetition is the simplest pronunciation activity to set up and possibly the most effective. It can help to build confidence by giving learners valuable practice in a 'safe' environment, as long as you don't overdo it (see above). There are different ways to drill language, and it's important to vary the way we do it. Here are some tips to remember:

- **When drilling longer phrases:**
  Establish a rhythm and start by drilling only the stressed syllables. For example, for the phrase *What do you usually do at the weekend?* Start with *What – us – do – week*. Keeping the same rhythm, 'cram' in the other syllables, pronouncing them naturally. This helps learners feel how we use weak forms and sentence stress in English.
- **Drill the phrase backward to keep it sounding natural:**
  With longer words and phrases, start from the end and drill backwards. For example, with the word *comfortable*, work backwards *–ble – table – comfortable*. This allows you to isolate difficult parts of the word or phrase, but keep a natural-sounding pronunciation.
- **Vary your voice:**
  This can be a simple way to add variety to drills, by e.g. shouting or whispering. It also gives learners different ways to practise saying the language.

4 Focus consistently on stress

This is an easy area in which to correct learners effectively. Get into the habit of focusing on word and sentence stress whenever you teach a new word/phrase with potential problems. If learners have problems, try one of the following ideas when you drill:

- Exaggerate the stress.
- Clap or click your fingers on the stressed syllable.
- Mumble the stress pattern, before saying the word: *mm-MM-mm attention*.
- Isolate the stressed syllable first, and then add the other syllables.

Don't forget to mark stressed syllables when you write new words on the board, by underlining or writing a blob over them, and encourage learners to do the same when they write in their notebooks.

5 Make learners aware of weak forms and word linking

As learners become more advanced, these features will also contribute to comprehensibility and fluency, and at any level they are important for the purposes of listening. As you teach new phrases and structures, draw learners' attention to weak forms and word linking as appropriate, and give them the opportunity to practise them, such as by using rhythm when drilling (see above). However, do not worry too much if they do not produce the weak forms and word linking spontaneously – this is more likely to come naturally when learners are more fluent.

6 Make learners aware of intonation

Intonation is a source of worry to many teachers and, consequently, learners. Teachers worry that their learners (or they themselves) cannot hear it, and that whatever they do their learners don't seem to 'learn' it. In reality, there are few situations in which wrong intonation leads to serious misunderstanding. Where problems do occasionally occur is in the area of politeness, and sounding sufficiently enthusiastic (although, even here, in real life many other factors – such as facial expression – can counteract 'wrong' intonation!).

In *Cutting Edge Intermediate Third Edition*, we focus on these limited areas for intonation work. You shouldn't expect your learners to produce perfect intonation, but instead aim to raise awareness of it when appropriate. If learners have problems hearing and reproducing the intonation patterns that you choose to focus on, try some of the following ideas:

- Exaggerate the intonation pattern, before returning to a more normal model.
- Hum the intonation pattern before repeating the words (incidentally, this is very useful for hearing intonation patterns yourself, if you have difficulty).
- Use gestures to show the intonation pattern (rather like a conductor).
- Mark the intonation on the board using arrows.

Remember, though, that if learners are getting frustrated, or cannot 'get' the correct intonation, it is probably best to leave it and come back to it another time.

Making tasks work

1 Treat tasks primarily as an opportunity for communication

Some of the tasks in this course may be familiar; the difference is in how they are treated. The main objective is for learners to use the language that they know (and, if necessary, learn new language) in order to achieve a particular communicative goal, not to 'practise' specific language. Although it is virtually impossible to perform some of the tasks without using the language introduced in the module, in others learners may choose to use this language only once or twice, or not at all. Do not try to 'force-feed' it. Of course, if learners are seeking this language but have forgotten it, this is the ideal moment to remind them!

2 Make the task suit your class

Learners using this course will vary in age, background, interests and ability. All these learners need to find the tasks motivating and 'doable', yet challenging at the same time. In *Cutting Edge Intermediate Third Edition*, the tasks include more stages than in previous editions, in order to provide learners with the support necessary to make the most of the tasks. However, do not be afraid to adapt the tasks to suit your class if this helps.

The Teacher's notes contain suggestions on how to adapt certain tasks for monolingual and multilingual groups, learners of different ages and interests, large classes, and weaker or stronger groups. There are also ideas for shortening tasks, or dividing them over two shorter lessons. We hope these suggestions will give you other ideas of your own on how to adapt the tasks.

3 Make the most of the *Useful language* boxes

As learners are preparing, it is important that they are able to ask you about language queries, so that when they perform the task they can say what they personally want to say. Although the task should not be seen as an opportunity to 'practise' discrete items, there may be specific language that would be useful in order to perform the task successfully.

Each task is accompanied by a *Useful language* box containing phrases which can be adapted by individual learners to express different ideas and opinions, as well as an opportunity to listen to the phrases used by speakers doing a similar task. The idea behind this is twofold: firstly, learners can hear how the phrases are used in context, and secondly this also helps draw their attention to the phrases in case they want to use them during the task. Some ideas for varying the way you do this include:

- Give learners a minute or two to say the phrases quietly to themselves so they know what to listen for before they listen.
- Have different learners listen for phrases under different sections of the *Useful language* box, then share their answers afterwards.
- After doing the exercise, have learners think of possible endings for the phrases, then read out their endings for their partner to guess the phrase.

4 Give learners time to think and plan

Planning time is very important if learners are to produce the best language that they are capable of. It is particularly useful for building up the confidence of learners who are normally reluctant to speak in class. Once learners have planned, discourage them from reading from notes. Give them time to look at their notes, and then ask them to close their notebooks. With certain learners this may have to be a gradual process.

5 Make notes for further input

Before or during the performance of the task, you may notice errors and gaps in learners' knowledge that you want to look at. It is usually best not to interrupt the flow of the task, but to make a note of points to cover later on.

6 Use the *Share your task* box

All the tasks in *Cutting Edge Third Edition Intermediate* have a *Share your task* box which can either be done completely in class or as a combination of homework and classwork. These offer learners the opportunity to repeat or carry out a similar task and film or record it, enabling them to consolidate what they have learnt, and put into practice any suggestions and corrections that you have discussed. This is also an opportunity for learners to practise 'perfecting' what they say when reporting on the task, in order to record a version of themselves using English to a high standard, which should be motivating. Some ideas for filming/recording include:

- learners create a video/audio montage of themselves doing the task.
- learners create a TV/radio programme with a 'presenter' who introduces different people doing the task.
- depending on the task, learners could act out part of a narrative as a short film.
- encourage learners to add music or other background noise/visuals, and to film in different locations to make their recordings more realistic.
- if learners are comfortable doing so, encourage them to post their recording on a blog or social networking site, then collect comments to share with the class.
- learners watch/listen to other learners' recordings, or show them to another class, and choose the best one.
- after learners have filmed/recorded themselves, collect in the recordings and plan a 'find someone who' task. Give learners a list of things which appear in their classmates' tasks and ask them to discuss whose task each thing appears in. They then watch/listen and check their answers.
- learners watch/listen to their classmates' tasks and then write a summary report.

See the *Teacher's notes* for further suggestions on how to use each *Share your task* box.

TEACHING TIPS

How to get the most out of Cutting Edge Intermediate Third Edition

Using video material in class

The video lessons are a new feature of *Cutting Edge Intermediate Third Edition*, and are intended to be modern, engaging ways of consolidating and extending some of the topics covered in the units. The video lessons occur at the end of every unit, and half the units have a *World culture* lesson, while the other half have a *Language live* lesson.

World culture lessons:
The *World culture* lessons contain two clips per unit: part of a TV programme and *World view* clips, which are short 'talking heads' style interviews, where people give their opinions on the topics covered in the programme. They are intended to encourage learners to explore contemporary topics and develop the important 21st century skill of online research.

Language live lessons:
The *Language live* lessons contain two clips per unit: part of a story, used to introduce functional language and a *Key phrases* clip, where the functional language from the lesson is repeated in isolation. They are intended to introduce functional language in a light-hearted way and develop learners' writing skills through structured support.

1 Using video in class

Video can be an excellent way to study language as it is not only motivating but also illustrates the importance of non-verbal aspects of communication. In many respects, it is the 'next best thing' to observing real life. In order to get the best out of it though, observe the following guidelines:

- **Watch the clip yourself beforehand:**
  It is important to know what to expect so you can help learners understand the humour in the *Language live* clips (see below).
- **Do something visual first**:
  The exercises in *Cutting Edge Intermediate Third Edition* are designed to go from easier to more challenging, but sometimes, with stronger classes, you might find that they will benefit from first just watching the clip to get a general idea of what it is about, before watching again and doing the exercises in the *Students' Book*.
- **Don't replay the clip too many times**:
  Learners may become demotivated if they really can't understand something in the clip. Instead, make the most of the subtitles or time-coded scripts (see above). Always give learners a chance to comprehend by viewing only first, but if they run into difficulties with a particular part of the clip, use the subtitles/scripts to pinpoint the difficult language and explain as necessary.
- **Vary how you use it**:
  There are many different ways of using video in class, with different purposes. For example, learners can sit in pairs, one facing the screen and the other with their back to it. Play the clip with the sound off, and the learner facing the screen describes what happens to the other learner, who then watches afterwards and checks. You'll find more suggestions in the teacher's notes for each lesson, and it's a good idea to vary the way you use the video material in class to keep it interesting.

2 Exploit the humour in the Language live clips

The *Language live* clips introduce functional language in a light-hearted way, which helps maintain learners' interest and make learning more enjoyable overall. A lot of the humour is visual and can be seen through the actors' expressions, but sometimes it will be useful to draw learners' attention to features in the clips, to get the most out of them. This is where it's important to watch the clip beforehand, and think about how you can draw learners' attention to these aspects with the use of guiding questions. For example, in Unit 2 you could ask *What's wrong with the announcement? Do you have this problem when listening to announcements?* or in Unit 7 you could ask *Where are they?* at the beginning.

3 Doing online research

The *World culture* lessons involve two opportunities for learners to do online research. Firstly, in the *Find out first* section where they collect background information on the topic of the video, and secondly after the *World view* section when they find out about further things related to the topic of the video. This is an important 21st century skill for learners to master in English, and so the following ideas may help:

- **Make the most of available technology**:
  If learners have smartphones, they can use them to do the research. If not, you can set it for homework: before the class for the *Find out first* sections and after class for the research later in the lesson.
- **Vary the way in which learners do research:**
  In one lesson learners can research alone then compare answers in pairs, and in the next lesson they could research in pairs, then pool ideas as a class or in groups. Vary the way in which learners research, too, so rather than just using the same search engine, different learners could enter the search terms into different encyclopedia sites, forums, etc., and compare results.
- **Be on hand to help**:
  Since there are very few limits as to what's available online, circulate and be available to help with language, and also to step in in the case of inappropriate search results.
- **Encourage learners to prioritise information**:
  Part of being a good researcher is not just obtaining results but also prioritising the most important points. Encourage learners to do this by asking them to find no more than three facts, for example, or only noting down facts which they can find on more than one website.
- **Encourage learners to be critical thinkers:**
  There is a lot of information available on the internet, and not all of it is always reliable! Encourage learners to question information they find, and corroborate it with other learners. How reputable is the website where they found the information? Whether they can prove what they've found clearly is perhaps not as important as encouraging them to question everything.

Using the *Study, Practice & Remember* sections

The *Study, Practice & Remember* sections are a new feature of *Cutting Edge Intermediate Third Edition* and can be found at the back of the *Students' Book*. Each unit has a *Study* section which provides a summary of key language as well as review and extension exercises. There are also comprehensive *Study tips* for each unit which provide useful advice on an aspect of learning English and an opportunity for learners to share ideas on how they approach each aspect.

The *Study, Practice & Remember* sections and the *Study tips* have the following main aims:

- to ensure systematic consolidation of new language before learners move on to the next unit.
- to recycle vocabulary through recording and practice.
- to encourage learners to take responsibility for and keep a record of their own progress.
- to encourage learners to share best practice on ways of studying.

1 Use the *Study, Practice & Remember* sections to consolidate learning

The *Study sections* provide a comprehensive overview of each language point covered in the main unit. These can be used in different ways. For example:

- learners read the *Study* section before focusing on the *Grammar* box in the main unit.
- after clarifying the language in the lesson, give learners a few minutes to read the *Study* section to consolidate what they have learnt, and think of questions to ask you.
- learners read the *Study* section for homework, either before or after the class, and think of questions they would like to ask.
- if you think your learners need additional practice before attempting the more communicative activities in the main units, you could select one or two of the *Practice* activities to do in class first.

2 Use the different activities as warmers and fillers

The activities in the *Study, Practice & Remember* sections can be used when you have ten or fifteen minutes to spare. For example, you could do the *Study* section at the end of one lesson, and do the exercises in the *Practice* sections in another lesson.

3 Make the most of the *Remember these words* sections

These sections aim to provide learners with a list of the most important words and phrases from each unit. However, it is important for learners to 'take ownership' of these lists, by adding to them, providing translations, example sentences, definitions, etc. Encourage learners to experiment with different ways of doing this and finding out what works for them.

You can also use these lists towards the end of each unit to plan recycling activities (see *Teaching tips: Working with lexis* above).

4 Use the Study tips to discuss the best ways to learn and to set targets

The *Study tips* draw learners' attention to a number of important study skills such as using English outside the classroom, recording or filming themselves, taking notes, etc. Learners often look at a list of suggestions and discuss which ideas they feel would work best for them. They are also asked to contribute ideas of their own. This should be an open discussion, but at the end it would be useful to pin down a particular suggestion or suggestions that the learner is going to try (for example, to speak more during pair and group work), and set this as a clear target. You could get them to stick a note on the front of their *Students' Book* reminding them of this target. It is very useful to return to these targets a few weeks later to discuss how well they are getting on. This will help learners measure and see the progress they make.

5 Set homework based on these sections

If you are short of time in class, the *Practice* section could easily be set as homework. If you do this, it might be useful to explain in class where learners should look in the *Study* section if they need to do further revision.

6 Set aside time for learners' questions

If you set the *Study* or *Practice* sections for homework, in the next lesson set aside some time for learners to ask any questions they have. You could encourage learners to discuss their questions in small groups before answering them with the whole class.

7 Encourage learners to take responsibility for their own progress

The approach in the *Study, Practice & Remember* section is to encourage learner independence and personal responsibility for progress. By using these sections frequently and in different ways, you will provide opportunities for learners to reflect on their learning and experiment with different ways of studying.

TEACHING TIPS

How to get the most out of Cutting Edge Intermediate Third Edition

Teaching intermediate learners

Teaching intermediate learners comes with its own unique set of challenges and benefits. Learners at this level have by now met most of the main areas of grammar, but still have a long way to go in terms of fluent, natural use. Learners will have already tried lots of different ways of learning and hopefully discovered a few ways which work well for them. At this stage of their learning they can start to make more sense of authentic language use and so make the most of the language around them. There are a few things to bear in mind when teaching intermediate learners:

1 Help learners see their progress

At intermediate level, it can be more difficult for learners to be aware of their progress than it is at lower levels, since they already have a wide language base to build on. This doesn't mean that they aren't making as much progress as they were at lower levels, just that it's more difficult to see clearly. You can help learners see their progress with frequent recycling of the language that they have studied in a unit, for example, and encouraging them to set themselves clear targets when using the *Study* tips. Also giving regular feedback on examples of good language use after speaking activities will help. This will ensure learners stay motivated.

2 Encourage learners to notice and use English outside class

It is important for learners to stay in contact with English, and not just during class time. Setting homework is useful, but you can also encourage learners to pay attention to English outside the class. This could be through internet research (see *Teaching tips: Using the video material in the classroom*), or watching films/TV programmes in English with or without subtitles. Encourage learners to make a note of any interesting phrases or uses of language and bring them to class to share or ask you about. Learners who take an active approach to their own learning are far more likely to succeed than those who expect the teacher to do it all for them.

3 Provide a challenge, but don't overwhelm learners

At this level it is important to provide enough challenge for learners in order for them to feel as if they are progressing. For example, stronger learners can help weaker ones in class, and early finishers can come to the board to write the answers to an exercise for a class.

Similarly, in *Cutting Edge Intermediate Third Edition*, there is a wealth of material in the different components for you to use with your learners. Don't feel you have to use everything, all of the time. The idea is that you have a variety of material to choose from, and in doing so you can choose the most appropriate activities for your learners.

4 Be responsive to your learners' needs, but do not get sidetracked

It is important that you encourage learners to take an active approach to their learning by asking questions and noticing language outside the class. However, one danger of this approach is that a teacher may get sidetracked by dominant individuals who want all their attention, leading to frustration and irritation among others. If you feel that this is happening, tell these individuals that you will answer their questions later, and move quickly on. Keep a 'bird's-eye' view of the class, moving in to help learners if they need it rather than spending too much time with one pair/group/individual.

5 Have strategies for dealing with questions you cannot answer

If you have access to the internet in the classroom, have a window open on a dictionary site where you look up words or phrases as a class. Alternatively, if learners have smartphones, ask them to look up a new word or phrase – you could do this as a 'race' to increase motivation. If learners ask for idioms and expressions, make sure you keep it simple – in most cases you will be able to come up with an adequate phrase even if it is not precisely the phrase the learner wanted. Finally, if all else fails, promise to find out for the next lesson – but make sure you remember to do so as the learner who asked invariably will!

6 Note down important language points to be dealt with later

Note any important language points that come up during tasks and discussions, and build in time to go over these later. Write the errors on the board, and invite learners to correct them / think of a better word, etc. It is important that you treat these as 'class errors' so as not to single out any individual learners. Remember it is motivating (and instructive) to include examples of good language used as well as errors, and this will also help intermediate learners see their progress. Feedback slots can either be at the end of the lesson, or at the beginning of the next. Learners are more likely to retain a few well-chosen points in these correction slots rather than a long list of miscellaneous language points. The following are useful things to bear in mind.

- **Usefulness:**
  Many items may only be of interest to individual learners – only bring up general language with the whole class.
- **Quantity/Variety:**
  Try to combine one or two more general points with a number of more specific/minor ones, including a mixture of grammar, vocabulary and pronunciation as far as possible.
- **Level:**
  Be careful not to present learners with points above their level or which are too complex to deal with in a few minutes.
- **Problems induced by learners' mother tongue:**
  Correction slots are an excellent opportunity to deal with L1-specific errors (false friends, pronunciation, etc.) not usually mentioned in general English courses.
- **Revision:**
  The correction slots are a very good opportunity to increase learners' knowledge of complex language covered previously, as well as to remind them of smaller language points.

TEACHER'S NOTES INDEX

OVERVIEW

PAGES 6–7

Grammar: Questions and short answers

Pronunciation: Stress in questions

Common European Framework: Students can ask and answer questions and exchange ideas and information on familiar topics in everyday situations.

PAGES 8–9

Grammar: Present simple and Present continuous

Vocabulary: People around you

Common European Framework: Students can give a description of people; can give descriptions on a variety of familiar subjects.

PAGES 10–11

Reading and speaking: The myths that make you feel guilty

Vocabulary: Everyday activities

Common European Framework: Students can read factual texts on subjects related to their interests; can express themselves on topics pertinent to their hobbies and interests.

PAGES 12–13

Task: Discuss the way you spend your time

Common European Framework: Students can communicate with confidence on familiar routine matters; can exchange, check and confirm information.

PAGES 14–15

Writing: An informal email

Speaking: Keeping a conversation going

Common European Framework: Students can write personal letters describing experiences, feelings and events in some detail; can maintain discourse appropriately with effective turntaking.

Language focus 1 (PAGES 6–7)

Questions and short answers

See *Teaching tips: Using a discovery approach to grammar*, page 20.

WARM UP

Before the class, cut up some blank strips of paper, one for each student in the class. Ask students to think of a question they would like to ask their classmates (for example, *Why are you learning English? Where do you live?*) and write it on the strip of paper. Make sure they don't show anyone their question. Collect all the questions and redistribute them so that each student has someone else's question. Students walk around and ask that question to everyone else in the class. When they have finished, put them in groups to share the information they found out.

1a Focus students' attention on the photos and ask them to imagine who the people are and what they might be talking about. Go through the descriptions 1–3 and check that students understand *greeting*. Get students to work in pairs to match the descriptions to the photos, then go through the answers with the class.

ANSWERS:

1 C 2 B 3 A

b Elicit some ideas for questions, or give a few ideas to get the students started. Emphasise that there is no right or wrong answer. Students work in pairs or small groups to think of questions. Circulate to see what sort of questions they are thinking of. Note down any common problems you notice to help you choose what to emphasise when you clarify the grammar. If you have a weak class, for each photo, get students to think of one question each person might ask. In feedback, nominate students to share their answers with the class.

2a **1.1** The idea of this activity is to expose students to different types of questions before they study question forms. Play the recording for students to match the conversations with the situations in exercise 1a. Ask students to compare answers in pairs, then check answers with the class. Don't elicit what the questions were at this stage.

ANSWERS:

1 1 2 2 3 1 4 3 5 3 6 2 7 1 8 3 9 2

b Students work in pairs to make their lists. Monitor and help where necessary, noting any common problems to focus on in the grammar clarification. When they are ready, play the recording again for students to check their answers.

ANSWERS:

See the audio script for 1.1 for the questions.

GRAMMAR

Forming questions

All the tenses dealt with here are looked at in more detail later. Most students should at least be familiar with the form, but if there are serious difficulties with the use, it is probably best to leave this until the later modules where these are covered.

1 Check understanding of the question words. Students work in pairs to think of more question words. Elicit students' answers and write them on the board.

SUGGESTED ANSWERS:

Who? Why? Whose? When? How many? What time? (See Study 1 on page 132 of the Students' Book for more examples.)

2 Give students time to read the questions and cross out the incorrect word order. If you have a weak class, do this together and go over the rules for word order in most *wh-* questions.

ANSWER:

Question 1 is incorrect.

Short answers

3 Go over the example with the class. Students work alone to rewrite the answers. Monitor and help where necessary. Check answers with the class.

ANSWERS:

1 My parents do, but my sister doesn't. **2** No, he doesn't.

You may want to ask students to read Study 1 on page 132 for a more detailed explanation of questions and short answers.

PRACTICE

1a Read the example with the class. Students complete the questions and answers alone, then check answers in pairs. Check answers with the class.

ANSWERS:

1 What's your postcode, please?
2 Where exactly do you live?
3 How's your job going?
4 A: Do you speak any other languages apart from English?
B: No, I don't.
5 Do all your family speak English?
6 Could you tell me your date of birth?
7 A: Did you have a nice holiday?
B: Yes thanks, I did.
8 A: Have you got any brothers and sisters?
B: No, I haven't.

b Remind students of the situations in exercise 1a on page 6. If necessary, do the first one as an example with the class. Get students to work in pairs. Don't elicit any answers yet.

c **1.2** Students listen and check their answers. In feedback, check answers with the class and drill the questions and answers.

ANSWERS:

Example A
1 C **2** C **3** B **4** A/C **5** A **6** C **7** B **8** A/C

PRONUNCIATION

See *Teaching tips: Helping students with pronunciation*, page 22.

1 Give students a minute to read the examples and pay attention to which words are stressed. Drill the examples with the class.

2 Point out the stress in short answers.

3 **1.2** Focus attention on the questions and answers in exercise 1a. Students listen and underline the stressed words. Pause after each one to give students time to think and mark the stress. Check answers with the class, then play the recording again, pausing after each question for students to repeat.

ANSWERS:

1 What's your postcode, please?
2 Where exactly do you live?
3 How's your job going?
4 A: Do you speak any other languages apart from English?
B: No, I don't.
5 Do all your family speak English?
6 Could you tell me your date of birth?
7 A: Did you have a nice holiday?
B: Yes thanks, I did.
8 A: Have you got any brothers and sisters?
B: No, I haven't.

Pronunciation: Helping students with stress and weak forms

Focus on stress first – the following techniques might help the students to hear stress patterns:

- reading out the sentences yourself
- exaggerating the stressed syllables
- clapping/tapping on the stressed syllables as students listen and repeat
- mumbling the stress pattern like this: *mm-mm-MM-MM-mm*
- marking the stressed syllables on the board with blobs (••••), colours, etc.

Once you have established the stress pattern, move on to weak forms. Again, it helps to exaggerate, so model them as even weaker than they are on the recording. (Be careful that in drawing students' attention to weak forms you do not accidentally stress them!) If students are having difficulty, start with a stressed syllable and gradually build in the weak forms, like this: *live near here?* → *you live near here?* → *Do you live near here?* This technique is known as 'back-chaining'.

Don't go on for too long if students do not pronounce the sentences perfectly. Focus on this little and often, ideally whenever you introduce a new phrase or structure involving weak forms.

2 Give students a few moments to agree on a conversation and to think of questions to ask. Emphasise that they should not write the questions down. Students work in pairs to act out the conversations.

3a This exercise can be oral or written. If you have a large class, it is easier to keep track of students' ideas by asking each pair to write their suggested questions down.

b **1.3** When listening and checking answers, students may have difficulty catching the exact words used. Encourage them to listen again, more than once if necessary, before you elicit and write the answers on the board. This is very useful in developing their ability to listen closely to the language used.

ANSWERS:

1 What's the English word for this?
2 How do you pronounce this word?
3 How do you spell your name?
4 Which page are we on?
5 Could you explain that again, please?
6 Could you say that again, please?
7 What's today's homework?
8 Could you write it on the board, please?

4 In this activity, students practise asking questions. If they are not familiar with each other, tell them to work together in groups of three, with two new partners. If they know each other, encourage them to ask you questions. Whichever you choose, allow time for students to select and prepare the questions they will ask. Circulate as they ask and answer, so that you are aware of any problem areas. Focus on these with the class at the end of the activity if necessary.

ADDITIONAL PRACTICE

Resource bank: Activity 1A *Three-person snap* (Questions and short answers)

Study, practice & remember: Practice 1

Workbook: Language focus 1: *Questions and short answers*, pages 4–5; Pronunciation: *Sentence stress in questions*, page 5

Vocabulary (PAGE 8)

People around you

See *Teaching tips: Working with lexis*, page 21.

1a Students work in pairs to cross out the wrong word and move it to the correct group. Practise the words with a repetition drill, marking the stressed syllables on the board. The pronunciation of the following words may need particular attention: *relative* /ˈrelətɪv/, *grandchild* /ˈgræntʃaɪld/, *grandparents* /ˈgrænˈpeərənts/, *colleague* /ˈkɒli:g/, *niece* /ˈni:s/, *best friend* /ˈbesˈfrend/, *acquaintance* /əˈkweɪntəns/, *neighbour* /ˈneɪbə/, *cousin* /ˈkʌzən/.

ANSWERS:

Family	older sister, stepmother, relative, ~~stranger~~, grandchild, half-brother, grandparents, **niece, mother-in-law, cousin**
Work/school	classmate, boss, colleague, employee, ~~niece~~
Friends	best friend, old school friend, acquaintance, ~~mother-in-law~~
Other	neighbour, flatmate, ~~cousin~~, ex-girlfriend, **stranger**

Note: There may be some variations in your students' ideas. For example, they may have put *ex-girlfriend* as a friend. While this is an acceptable difference, it is not necessarily true for all people.

b When brainstorming other vocabulary to add to the table, discourage words that are too simple (*mother, father*, etc.) and focus on vocabulary that students may not know, for example, *nephew, godmother, manager, partner*. Note that *partner* has different meanings. In the context of family and friends, it is similar to *husband, wife, boyfriend, girlfriend*. In the context of work, it means 'someone you run a business with'. In the context of the classroom, it means 'the student you work with'. In feedback, elicit students' ideas and write them on the board, marking the stressed syllables.

2a **1.4** Explain that each instruction will tell students to 'choose a space' to write their answer in. Make sure they write their answers in random order in the spaces. Play the recording, pausing after each instruction to give students time to think and write.

b Look at the examples with the class, then do one or two examples with them before they do the activity in pairs. Ask one or two pairs to tell the class something they found out.

ADDITIONAL PRACTICE

Resource bank: Activity 1B *Vocabulary extension* (Phrases for talking about people around you)

Workbook: Vocabulary: *People around you*, page 5

Language focus 2 (PAGES 8–9)

Present simple and Present continuous

See *Teaching tips: Using a discovery approach to grammar*, page 20.

1a Focus students' attention on the photos and check that they understand the task. Students discuss the questions in pairs. Don't give any answers yet.

b **1.5** Play the recording and encourage students to compare answers in pairs before checking with the whole class.

ANSWERS:

Lydia: best friend; Tom and Saliba: old friends; Isabel: little sister; John: grandfather/grandpa; Luxmmi: old school friend; Joe: big brother; Pete: father/dad; Harriet: cousin; Andy: uncle

2 If you have a stronger class, ask them to do the exercise from memory before playing the recording again. Play the recording and check answers as a whole class.

ANSWERS:

1 Lydia is working in a DIY shop at the moment.
3 She's applying for lots of courses.
4 Isabel is getting big.
7 Luxmmi is training to be a doctor.
10 He really likes the city./He likes the city very much.

3a Write up the first examples of the Present simple and the Present continuous to illustrate the activity for the whole class. Students underline/circle the examples individually, then check answers in pairs and discuss how the Present continuous is formed.

ANSWERS:

1 Lydia is working in a restaurant at the moment.
2 She wants to become a social worker.
3 She's applying for lots of jobs.
4 Isabel is getting old.
5 She always pulls faces in photos.
6 Jess's grandparents go out a lot.
7 Luxmmi is training to be a dentist.
8 Joe is wearing sunglasses.
9 Joe's living in a student house at the moment.
10 He doesn't like the city very much.

Form of Present continuous: *am/are/is* + *-ing*

b Go over the examples in Grammar and answer any questions students have. Students work individually to find further examples, then check answers in pairs. Check answers with the class.

ANSWERS:

Present simple 1: She always pulls faces in photos./Jess's grandparents go out a lot. Present simple 2: She wants to become a social worker. Present continuous 1: Joe is wearing sunglasses. Present continuous 2: Luxmmi is training to be a dentist. Present continuous 3: Lydia is working in a restaurant at the moment. Present continuous 4: Isabel is getting old.

GRAMMAR

Present simple and Present continuous

Focus attention on the uses and examples. Although this should be revision, many students are unaware of their own lack of accuracy in this area and may need to be reminded of the following problems:

Present simple

- the use of the third person singular *-s* in the affirmative form: *She lives in the flat upstairs from us.*
- the use of *do/does* in the question form: *Does he live with your parents, too?*
- the use of *don't/doesn't* in the negative form: *She doesn't go out much.*

Present continuous

the use of the contracted form of the auxiliary verb *to be*: *He's enjoying the course* (= *he is enjoying*).

Potential problem with state and dynamic verbs

One of the examples in Present simple 1 shows a verb behaving as a state verb (*to live*). It can also be a dynamic verb:

She's living with her brother for a month. (a temporary situation)

If students are unclear about the difference between state and dynamic verbs, you can raise awareness with the following activity. Put students in pairs, As and Bs. A faces the board and B faces their partner, with their back to the board. Each turn, write the following verbs on the board for As to mime and Bs to guess, in this order: *eat, drive, have a shower, be, have a car*. Students will struggle with the last two. After the activity, ask students which verbs they found difficult to mime/guess and explain that these verbs describe states, not actions.

You may want to ask students to read Study 2 on pages 132 and 133 for a more detailed explanation of the Present simple and Present continuous.

Language focus 2: Alternative suggestion for the Present simple and continuous

A more task-based approach may be more challenging here (although it will require you to 'think on your feet' quite a lot during the lesson!).

Play the recording or give a short talk of your own about your family and friends. If possible, illustrate your talk with photos. Try to make it sound natural rather than scripted. Briefly check basic comprehension.

Move straight on to Practice, exercise 4, getting students to talk about their family/friends in the same way that you/Jess did. Do not do any specific input on present tenses, but emphasise that you want them to talk about these people's lives as they are at the moment. Write up the following prompts to encourage this: *their jobs/studies, where they live, anything else important in their lives at the moment.*

Give students time to plan what they will say and feed in any necessary vocabulary. Put students in small groups and get each one to give a short talk. Circulate and note down any errors you hear with the use of the Present simple and continuous (these can be errors of form, meaning or pronunciation – it may help to divide your notes into these three sections).

Write up the errors and get students to correct them. Go over the problems on the board yourself, or direct students to Study 2. Select exercises from the Students' Book (Practice, exercises 1, 2 and 3) or the Workbook on the areas they need to practise.

If you do not feel confident about selecting material on the spot like this, spread this approach over two lessons so you can analyse students' errors/needs more carefully.

PRACTICE

1 Students work individually before checking answers in pairs. Go through answers with the whole class, eliciting which explanation from Grammar, exercise 3 applies in each case.

ANSWERS:

1 is wearing, 's **2** plays **3** doesn't smoke, hates
4 don't like, do you think **5** is working

2a Do one or two examples with the class. Students work individually, then compare in pairs before checking answers with the class.

ANSWERS:

1 Do you like **2** Are you reading **3** Do you read
4 Are you studying **5** Do you prefer
6 Do you usually get up **7** Are you planning

b Practise a few example questions by repetition drilling. Do this exercise as a mingle drill, possibly making it into a competition to see who can find a 'yes' answer to each question first.

3 Check the meaning of *to lose weight* and *to go grey*. This may be a useful opportunity to feed in *to put on/gain weight*. Do an example about yourself with a student, eliciting a question, e.g. *Are you getting taller?* and a negative, e.g. *I'm not getting taller*. Let students compare their answers in pairs, then go through them with the class.

4a If students have mobile phones with photos of people they know on, ask them to find them. Otherwise, tell students to write the names of six people who are important in their lives.

b Give students time to make notes. Circulate and help where necessary.

c Put students in groups to do the activity. If possible, put them in groups with people they do not normally work with. Focus on the example and encourage them to ask each other questions.

ADDITIONAL PRACTICE

Resource bank: Activity 1C *Something in common* (Present simple and Present continuous)

Study, practice & remember: Practice 2

Workbook: Language focus 2: *Present simple and Present continuous*, pages 6–7

Reading and speaking (PAGES 10–11)

WARM UP

Write the following phrases on the board: *go to bed late, go to bed early, do exercise, play sport, use the internet, get stressed, sleep for eight hours*. Students discuss how often they do each of these things in pairs. In feedback, nominate students to share their answers with the class.

1a Students look at the photos and discuss the questions in small groups.

b Check the meaning of *multitasking*. Give students time to read the questions and advice, then discuss the questions in their groups. Ask two or three groups to tell the class what they said.

2a Check the meaning of *grumpy* and *an internet addict*. Explain that the text is about things which make us feel guilty about our lifestyle. Students read the article and complete the gaps in the text with the phrases from exercise 1b. Check answers with the whole class.

ANSWERS:

1 b **2** d **3** a **4** c

b Students discuss the question in pairs. Check answers with the class. If you have a stronger class, ask them to explain why each sentence is a myth, according to the article.

ANSWER:

They are all myths, according to the article.

3a Students work individually to answer the questions. Encourage them to compare their answers in pairs before checking with the class. When checking answers, ask students to cover the text to encourage them to give answers in their own words.

ANSWERS:

1 He feels guilty and a bit depressed.
2 Night owls are more productive ten hours after waking.
3 Top athletes who are now in their fifties had damage to their heart muscles.
4 45- to 54-year-olds spend most time online in the USA.
5 Older people are better at actually using the internet.
6 Yes, according to the author. You simply do each thing less well.

b Give students time to choose their paragraphs and think of reasons. Students share their ideas in pairs. Ask two or three students to share their ideas with the class.

4a Read the examples with the class. Students make their lists individually. Encourage students to think of different ideas to those in the article. Circulate and help with ideas and any specific vocabulary students ask you for.

b If you have a multilingual class, arrange students so they are working with partners from different countries. Students compare their lists in pairs and decide if each belief is a fact or myth. Ask two or three pairs to share their ideas with the class and ask if other students agree.

Find out more

This could be done in class or set for homework if you are short of time. Divide students into three groups: *early birds and night owls*, *Steven Nguyen* and *multitasking*. Within each group, students search individually online for these terms and find three interesting facts. When they have finished, arrange students in groups of three, with one person from each group to share their facts. Nominate a student from each group to share the most interesting ideas with the class.

Vocabulary (PAGE 11)

Everyday activities

See *Teaching tips: Working with lexis*, page 21.

1a Go through the phrases with the class and check that students understand *chatting, hanging out, doing paperwork, texting.* Students underline the activities individually.

b Read the examples with the class and point out the position of the adverb. Students compare their answers in pairs.

2 Focus students' attention on the categories and make sure they understand that some activities can go in more than one category. Students categorise the activities individually, then compare with a partner and add more activities to each category. In feedback, elicit the additional activities and write them on the board, marking the stressed syllables.

ANSWERS:

Sport/fitness: going to the gym **Social:** chatting to friends, hanging out with friends, going on social networking sites, going shopping (clothes, etc.), relaxing, texting **Domestic:** looking after children, doing paperwork, tidying up, going shopping (grocery), relaxing, doing the ironing **Personal care:** doing your hair, putting on make-up **Other:** doing paperwork, commuting, relaxing, doing nothing, playing video games (however, this could also be under 'Social', as many games are now played online)

3 Look at the example with the class, then get students to do the exercise individually and compare their answers with a partner before checking answers with the class.

ANSWERS:

2 e 3 a 4 b 5 c*

The present simple is used in each case.

**To be into* and *to be interested in* have the same meaning. *To be into* is more informal. It is possible to say *I'm really interested in* ... and *I'm not really into* ... .

4 Read the examples with the class and, if necessary, model a few whole sentences yourself. For example: *I'm really into going to the gym. I spend too much time commuting.* Give students time to write their sentences. Circulate and help with ideas and vocabulary where necessary.

5 Read the examples with the class. Students should try to use as many different starting phrases as possible. Ask two or three students to share information about their partner with the class.

ADDITIONAL PRACTICE

Resource bank: Activity 1D *Who am I?* (Expressing likes and dislikes)

Workbook: Vocabulary: *Everyday activities*, page 8

Task (PAGES 12–13)

Discuss the way you spend your time

See *Teaching tips: Making tasks work*, page 23.

Preparation (PAGE 13)

Listening and reading

1a Focus attention on the introduction to the questionnaire on page 12 and give students time to answer the question before checking the answer with the class.

ANSWER:

The survey is trying to find out if we spend our free time doing things that really matter to us.

b Give students time to read the statements and find the ones that are true for them. Don't elicit any answers yet.

2a **1.6** Emphasise that students do not need to understand everything at this stage. Play the recording, pausing after each conversation to give students time to think, write and compare in pairs. Play the recording again, if necessary, before checking answers with the class.

ANSWERS:

Speaker 1: statement 7
Speaker 2: statement 8
Speaker 3: statement 5
Speaker 4: statements 13 and 15
Speaker 5: statement 12

b Check that students understand *on the go*. Focus attention on the Useful language box and give students time to read the phrases in part a. If you have a weaker class, drill the phrases so that students can get a feel for what they sound like. Students listen and tick the phrases they hear.

ANSWERS:

Speaker 1: I spend way too much time travelling. The whole journey takes about an hour and a half.

Speaker 2: I'm on the go the whole day long. There just isn't enough time!

Speaker 3: I spend quite a lot of time looking after my daughter.

Task (PAGE 13)

Speaking

1 Give students time on their own to prepare what they're going to say. Encourage them to use the phrases in Useful language a and ask you for any vocabulary they need.

2a Tell students that they are going to explain their answers to the questionnaire in more detail. Encourage them to refer to the phrases in Useful language b, but emphasise that they can add their own ideas if they want. Some students may feel more confident if they write down their questions, but emphasise that they do not have to stick to these if others seem more appropriate during the task.

b Explain that in the task they should try to find out as much as possible about each other. They should make notes to help them when they report back to the class. As they interview each other, feed in any language they need in an informal way and refer them to Useful language a and b if necessary. Do not correct at this stage unless absolutely necessary, as this will interrupt communication. Note down errors with language from the unit for analysis at the end of the task.

3 Give students time to plan how they are going to report their partner's information to the class and encourage them to use the phrases in Useful language c. When they are ready, students tell the class about their partner. If you have a very large class, you could divide students into two groups for this stage.

Share your task

Some additional ideas could include:

- Students film themselves doing some of the activities they spoke about in the lesson and create a video montage.
- Students record themselves talking about the activities they don't enjoy, for other students to watch/listen and give advice on how to make better use of their time.
- Students imagine they are a famous person and give a talk about how they spend their time.
- Students watch/listen to the recordings and decide who makes the best use of their time.
- Students watch/listen to the recordings and write a report on the most common activities in the class.

Language live (PAGES 14–15)

Writing (PAGES 14)

An informal email

1 Check students understand *online social networks* by eliciting examples that they use. Students discuss the questions in groups. Ask two or three groups to share their ideas with the class.

2 Ask students to read the message, ignoring the gaps. Students read individually before checking answers as a whole class.

ANSWERS:

They know each other from university. Katarina wants to meet up with Grace when she's in Manchester.

3 Give students time to read the phrases first, then work in pairs to do the exercise. Go through the answers with the class.

ANSWERS:

1 d 2 f 3 c 4 i 5 a 6 g 7 h 8 b 9 e*

**PS* is Latin and stands for *Post Script*. We use this to add more information after we have signed off, usually as an afterthought.

4 Look at the example and point out that there are a lot of questions in this paragraph. Students match the other topics and paragraphs individually before checking answers with the class.

ANSWERS:

1 c 2 a 3 d 4 b

5a Give students an example from your own life and write it on the board. Give students time to think of their own examples.

b Demonstrate the activity by adding notes to your own example on the board. Give students time to note down their own ideas. Circulate and help with ideas and vocabulary where necessary.

6 While students are writing their drafts, go round and feed in any language they need in an informal way, being careful not to interrupt the 'flow' of their writing. When they are ready, go through the questions in the checklist and give students time to check their writing.

Writing, exercise 6: Alternative suggestion

Do this as a speed-writing activity. Tell students that you are going to give them five minutes only to write a first draft. As they are writing, be strict about the time and count down after each minute. After five minutes, tell students to stop writing, even if they haven't finished. Students now have one minute to check what they've written, using the checklist in exercise 6.

7a Students swap drafts and check each other's work.

b Encourage students to be sensitive when discussing each other's work, and be ready to answer any questions they have. When they have written their final drafts, attach them to the walls and ask students to walk round and read the messages before choosing the best one.

Speaking (PAGE 15)

Keeping a conversation going

See *Teaching tips: Using the video material in the classroom*, page 24.

WARM UP

Write the following topics on the board: *my home town, my studies, a holiday, the weather in my country, someone I met recently*. Students play *Just a minute* in groups. Each turn, a student chooses a topic and speaks for one minute about it. If they have difficulty, other students in the group can help by asking them follow-up questions.

1 Focus students' attention on the photo and ask them to imagine who the people are and what situation they might be meeting in for the first time. Students discuss the questions in pairs. Explain that in this lesson they are going to learn how to keep a conversation going.

2 Check students understand that these are the people mentioned in the *message* on page 14. Students listen, then check their answers in pairs before checking with the whole class.

ANSWERS:

how they met Katarina, university, a holiday in the past

3 If you have a stronger class, they could do this activity from memory before watching again to check. Otherwise, students watch and match, then check answers in pairs before checking with the whole class.

ANSWERS:

1 e 2 c 3 g 4 a 5 f 6 b 7 h 8 d

PRONUNCIATION

1 Students watch again and repeat the phrases as they hear them. Listen to how students use intonation and, if necessary, drill the phrases again with the class.

Potential problem with intonation

In informal conversation, it's important that we use intonation to sound friendly and inviting. How we say things is sometimes more important than what we actually say. If students don't vary their intonation, they can sound bored and uninterested. On the other hand, if students use unusual intonation, they can sound strange. The following techniques might help students notice intonation patterns:

- mimicking the intonation used by native/proficient speakers, either in real life or on video
- using arrows on the board to show patterns, e.g. *Do you?*
- using gestures to show the direction of intonation when we drill phrases

Do not insist on 'perfect' intonation if students have difficulty. The most important thing is to raise awareness where it's relevant.

4 Model the activity by asking two stronger students to read out the example to the class. Students take turns to read out the sentences and respond in pairs. When they have finished, ask them to swap roles and practise the responses again. Monitor and watch how students are pronouncing the responses, modelling further where necessary.

ANSWERS:

(Note these are auxiliary questions for starting off responses only.)
1 Are you? **2** Has he? **3** Are you? **4** Do they?
5 Was he/she? **6** Have you?

5a Give students time to read the situations and ask if anyone has ever been in these or similar situations. Students practise the conversations in pairs. If any pairs finish early, get them to swap roles and practise the situations again.

b Join the pairs into groups of four. If you don't have the right number of students, you could have one or two groups of three and circulate the roles, with one 'monitor' each time. Circulate and be ready to answer any questions the students have, but be careful not to interrupt their conversations. If possible, students can record the conversations on their mobile phones, then play them back when giving feedback to each other.

ADDITIONAL PRACTICE

Resource bank: Activity 1E *Wordspot:* have *and* have got (Collocations with *have* and *have got*)

Workbook: Writing: *An informal email*, pages 8–9; Language live: *Keeping a conversation going*, page 9

Study, practice & remember

(PAGES 132–134)

See *Teaching tips: Using the Study, practice & remember sections*, page 25.

Practice 1

ANSWERS:

1
1 do **2** has **3** didn't **4** haven't **5** were **6** doesn't **7** is

2
1 Where **2** How **3** What time **4** are **5** What colour
6 What kind of **7** Whose **8** How often

3
1 Do the rest of your family speak English?
2 How many children do your aunt and uncle have?
3 Which gym does your brother go to?
4 What time do you and your friends go out?
5 Where were your brothers and sisters born?
6 Which university are you applying to?

Practice 2

ANSWERS:

1
1 Tomas doesn't usually speak much in class.
5 I don't know your brother.
6 Harry has six older sisters.
8 I understand the Present continuous perfectly.

2
1 gets **2** Do you like **3** is having **4** is getting
5 think **6** spend

3
1 dream **2** knows **3** stands **4** don't forget
5 leave **6** wait **7** is becoming **8** remains **9** pay

Remember these words

ANSWERS:

1
1 ex-girlfriend **2** stepmother **3** a stranger **4** niece
5 father-in-law **6** boss **7** flatmate **8** an employee **9** cousin
10 my/a neighbour **11** my/a classmate **12** my/a relative

2
1 go **2** going **3** going **4** doing **5** put, do **6** looks **7** do
8 tidy **9** doing **10** playing **11** relax **12** going

Study tips

These exercises can be done in class or at home. If done for homework, students can bring them to the next class and have a discussion based on their answers.

1 Emphasise that students should be honest when selecting their answer. Students compare their answers in pairs and give reasons.

2 Go over the sentences with the class, then give students time to think about their answers and tick the things they do before comparing answers in pairs.

3 Go through the sentences and elicit the benefits of each one. Allow the discussion to develop naturally and write any other tips the students have on the board.

4 Remind students of the classroom questions they learnt on page 7. In pairs, students discuss which they can remember before checking their answers with the audio script on page 168.

OVERVIEW

PAGES 16–17

Reading and speaking: The secrets of your memory

Common European Framework: Students can recognise significant points in articles on familiar subjects; can give personal views and opinions in discussing topics of interest.

PAGES 18–19

Grammar: Past simple and Past continuous

Pronunciation: Regular past tense verb endings

Common European Framework: Students can communicate with reasonable accuracy in familiar contexts.

PAGES 20–21

Listening and vocabulary: Childhood and upbringing

Grammar: *used to* and *would*

Vocabulary: Remembering and forgetting

Common European Framework: Students can use a range of vocabulary for most general topics; can describe events.

PAGES 22–23

Task: Describe a personal memory

Common European Framework: Students can narrate a story; can give detailed accounts of experiences, describing feelings and reactions.

PAGES 24–25

World culture: Flashbulb memories

Common European Framework: Students can understand most TV news and current affairs programmes; can describe experiences and events.

Reading and speaking (PAGES 16–17)

WARM UP

Ask students to think of two interesting facts about themselves and write them down. Circulate and help with vocabulary where necessary. When they are ready, students walk around and share their facts with other students in the class. After about five minutes, arrange them in small groups and ask them to make a list of as many facts as they can remember about other students in the class. In feedback, ask each group to read out their lists to check what they remember and award a point for each correctly remembered fact. The group with the most correct answers wins.

1a Check that students understand *pin numbers*. Give students time to read the question, then discuss in pairs.

b Students discuss the question in pairs, then use their partner's answers from exercise 1a to see if they agree. In feedback, nominate pairs to share their answers with the class.

2 Give students time to read the comments, then discuss any similar memories they have in pairs before sharing ideas with the class.

3 Check understanding of *photographic memory* and *pi*. Explain that students shouldn't try to understand every word and that they'll have a chance to read the text again more carefully afterwards. Set a time limit of three minutes for students to read the text and match the paragraphs with the comments in exercise 2. Encourage students to check answers in pairs before checking with the class.

ANSWERS:

1 c **2** extra para **3** d **4** b **5** a

Reading and speaking, exercise 3: Alternative suggestion

If your students need help with reading quickly for gist (skimming), then ask them to close their books while you give instructions for the activity. Do exercise 3 as a race. The first student to correctly match the comments and paragraphs wins.

4 Get students to read the statements and answer any which they can remember. Then they should read the text again to complete the task. Put them in pairs to compare their answers before checking as a class. Ask students to locate the part of the text in which each answer is found.

ANSWERS:

1 T **2** F (Retelling events helps to fix them in our memories.)
3 F (He is good at remembering particular things for a limited time.)
4 F (not yet proved)
5 F (Each piece of information is connected to many other pieces.)
6 F (Our memory starts to get worse after the age of 25 and is significantly worse by middle age.)
7 F (Recent research shows that some people can remember being a baby.)

5 Students discuss their ideas in pairs before sharing them with the whole class.

Find out more

Arrange the class in two large groups: *Daniel Tammet* and *Stephen Wiltshire*. Within their groups, students search individually online to find out as much information as they can. When they are ready, arrange students in pairs, with one student from each of the previous groups. Students then take turns to imagine they are these people and interview each other. Ask students to share any interesting information they found out with the whole class.

6 Give students time to read the tips, then compare their answers in pairs before checking with the class. When going through the answers, ask students to explain why they chose that answer in their own words.

ANSWERS:

doing crossword puzzles R lack of sleep F doing new things R imagining strange pictures R short, regular revision R oxygen going to your brain R asking yourself questions R

7 Students discuss their ideas in pairs before sharing them with the class.

Language focus 1 (PAGES 18–19)

Past simple and Past continuous

See *Teaching tips: Using a discovery approach to grammar*, page 20.

1 Before students discuss the questions in small groups, check any unknown vocabulary in the quiz questions. Circulate during the discussion and nominate groups to report back on any interesting information you have heard.

2 **2.1** Emphasise that students don't need to understand every word and that they'll have a chance to listen again more carefully afterwards. Play the recording, pausing after each speaker to give students time to check answers in pairs. Check answers with the class.

ANSWERS:

Speaker 1: question 6 **Speaker 2:** question 1 **Speaker 3:** question 2
Speaker 4: question 4 **Speaker 5:** question 8

3a Ask students to complete the sentences from memory, then check answers in pairs.

b Play the recording again, pausing after each speaker to allow students time to write and encourage them to compare ideas in pairs. Check answers with the class at the end.

ANSWERS:

1 white **2** thirteen, aunt **3** football **4** hair, eyes, eyes
5 shop window, assistant

4a Students work individually, then check answers in pairs before checking with the class.

ANSWERS:

2 was (irregular, be), appeared (regular), walked (regular)
4 had (irregular, have), wore (irregular, wear)
5 saw (irregular, see), went (irregular, go), asked (regular)

b Students work individually, then check answers in pairs before checking with the class. As you elicit answers from the students, write up the full form of the Past simple and Past continuous using an example verb (see Study 1 on page 135). Students should have studied these forms before and so be able to recognise the different forms. If they clearly have no idea, give the answers and move on to highlighting how the Past simple and Past continuous are formed. Highlight the following:

- that in the Past simple, regular verbs are followed by *-ed*.
- that irregular verbs have to be learnt individually (point out that there is a list on page 175).
- that questions and negatives are formed with *did* and *didn't* in all persons, that the question and negative forms in both cases are with the 'bare' infinitive (*Did they start?* not *Did they started?*, *We didn't start* not *We didn't started*).
- that the form of the Past continuous is the same as the Present continuous, except that *was/were* is used.

ANSWERS:

1 was wearing **2** was walking, were holding **3** was watching
5 was shopping, was happening, was talking
Form of Past continuous: *was/were + -ing*

GRAMMAR

Past simple and Past continuous

1 Students work individually to choose the correct alternative in the rules, then compare answers in pairs. Check answers with the class, referring to the timeline where necessary.

ANSWERS:

1 Past simple **2** Past continuous **3** while

2 Focus attention on the example and remind students of the rule from Language Focus 2 in Unit 1. You may want to ask them to read Study 1 on page 135 for a more detailed explanation of the Past simple and Past continuous.

PRACTICE

1a Check the meaning of *traffic jam, mate* and *bang my head*. Explain that students shouldn't choose the alternatives yet, just read the three answers quickly to answer the question. Check answers with the class.

ANSWERS:

1 question 2 **2** question 8 **3** question 1

b Students work individually, then check answers in pairs. When checking answers with the class, ask students to tell you why they chose each answer, referring back to the rules in the Grammar box.

ANSWERS:

1 was sitting, was driving, missed
2 always watched, came, switched on, weren't showing, was showing, didn't understand
3 was sitting, was cooking, was cutting out, fell, banged, took

2 🎧 **2.2** Ask students if they know how their parents or grandparents met. Students work individually, then check answers in pairs. When they are ready, play the recording, pausing after each verb to check students' answers.

ANSWERS:

1 met **2** were travelling **3** was **4** started **5** discovered
6 had **7** were **8** were training **9** were going **10** was snowing
11 stopped **12** wasn't **13** fell **14** decided **15** reached **16** took

PRONUNCIATION

See *Teaching tips: Helping students with pronunciation*, page 22.

1a 🎧 **2.3** Go through the example with the class first, drilling the verb and counting the syllables. Students listen to the recording and write the number of syllables, then check answers in pairs.

ANSWERS:

started 2, discovered 3, stopped 1, decided 3, reached 1

b Students discuss the question in pairs before checking with the class.

ANSWERS:

-ed is pronounced as a separated syllable in *started* and *decided*. This is because we pronounce the *-ed* ending after the sounds /t/ and /d/.

2 🎧 **2.4** Put the students in pairs to discuss this, then play the recording to check answers, pausing after each one and getting students to repeat it.

ANSWERS:

/d/: arrived, remembered, studied, offered, travelled
/t/: asked, hoped, watched, worked, noticed
/ɪd/: invited, expected, visited

Potential problem with -*ed* endings

Many students find these endings difficult to pronounce, since they are used to seeing them written rather than hearing them spoken. If your students find the pronunciation of -*ed* endings difficult, then raise awareness of how we pronounce them with the following:

Write the following letters on the board:

ay m n v z g
f k ch sh s
t d

Ask students to repeat the first line after you, resting their finger on their throat. Repeat the procedure for the second line and ask students what they notice. They should notice that with the first line their throat vibrates and with the second it doesn't. Now ask them to do the same, but add a 'd' after each one. Explain that with the first line, the second sound sounds like a /d/ sound and with the second line, it sounds like a /t/ sound. With the second line, it's almost impossible to say and so we add a syllable: /ɪd/. Explain that this is what happens when we pronounce regular past simple verbs. How we pronounce the -*ed* ending depends on whether the sound before it is voiced or unvoiced.

Another way of showing how they are pronounced is to write the following sentences on the board:

He ask tif I hope tit would be sunny.
We travel dall night and arrive din the morning.

Practise saying them with the class, then point out that this is how we pronounce these verbs in the past simple.

3a Students work individually to write the questions. Circulate and help where necessary, checking students are forming the questions correctly. When you check answers, drill the questions chorally and individually.

ANSWERS:

1 Where did you meet?
2 What was happening in your life at that time?
3 What was happening in your friend's/partner's life at that time?
4 What was the first thing you noticed about him/her?
5 What did you talk about?
6 What did your friend/partner look like then?
7 What was he/she wearing?
8 Was anyone else there?
9 How did you feel after you first met?
10 How did you meet again?

b Students discuss the questions in pairs. While they are working, make a note of students' problems with the use and form of the Past simple and Past continuous. If there are a lot of problems, write some examples on the board and then try to correct their mistakes as a class.

Practice, exercise 3b: Alternative suggestion

Students can either answer the questions truthfully or make up a story and give false answers. Their partner then decides if it was a true or false story.

ADDITIONAL PRACTICE

Resource bank: Activity 2A: *Past tense pelmanism/What about you?* (Irregular past simple forms), Activity 2B: *Alibi* (Past simple and Past continuous)

Study, practice & remember: Practice 1 and 2

Workbook: Language focus 1: *Past simple and past continuous*, pages 10–11; Pronunciation: *Past tense forms*, page 11

Listening and vocabulary (PAGE 20)

Childhood and upbringing

WARM UP

Write the following topics on the board: *songs, games, TV programmes, family rules, toys, friends*. Ask students to think of an example of each that they can remember from their early childhood. When they are ready, students share their ideas in groups and find out if they have any answers in common.

1 Students read the descriptions, then discuss the question in pairs. In feedback, elicit their ideas and write them on the board.

2 **2.5** Check the meaning of *pocket money, sleepovers, tell me off* and *praise*. Give students time to read the phrases, then play the recording for them to answer the questions. Encourage students to check answers in pairs before checking with the class.

ANSWERS:

Rafael: 1 c 2 b 3 a 4 a 5 a
Mi-Sun/Emily: 1 b 2 b 3 b 4 c 5 c

3 Students discuss what they can remember in pairs. If necessary, play the recording again for them to check their answers.

4 If you have access to dictionaries, distribute them for students to use. Alternatively, students can use their mobile devices. Circulate and help where necessary and write any new words on the board. Students first check the meanings in pairs, before deciding who said each sentence. When they are ready, play the recording again, pausing after each sentence for students to check their answers.

ANSWERS:

1 R 2 R 3 M 4 R 5 M 6 M 7 R 8 R 9 M

5 Read the examples with the class, then put students in pairs to discuss the questions. Circulate and encourage students to use the words in exercise 4. In feedback, nominate students to share their ideas with the class.

ADDITIONAL PRACTICE

Workbook: Vocabulary: *Childhood and upbringing*, page 11

Language focus 2 (PAGES 20–21)

used to and *would*

See *Teaching tips: Using a discovery approach to grammar*, page 20.

1 With weaker classes, elicit the first example and write it on the board (*We used to practise*). Students work individually, then check their answers in pairs before checking with the class.

ANSWERS:

We used to practise, I used to feel, we used to play, I used to love, my dad would tell me off, we'd (we would) go inside

GRAMMAR

used to* and *would

1 Give students time to work individually before checking answers with the class. Highlight:

- the forms of *used to* and *would: used to/would* + infinitive without *to* for all persons.
- the question form of *used to*: *Did you use to … ?*
- the negative form of *used to*: *I didn't use to*.
- the pronunciation of *used to*: /ˈjuːstə/.
- that there is no equivalent present form of *used to* with the same meaning (this is particularly important where there is an equivalent present form in students' own language, for example, Spanish). However, we can use the adverb *usually* with the same meaning in the present.

ANSWERS:

1 We used to practise for two hours every day / we used to play in the street / my dad would tell me off / we'd go inside and play games
2 I used to feel very ashamed. / I used to love hanging out in town with my friends.
3 Occasionally, I argued with my mum / I thought I was really cool!

2 Focus attention on the examples and highlight that:

- *anymore* always comes after the verb
- *still* comes before most verbs, but after *be*: *They still live in the same house. He is still at school.*

You may want to ask your students to read Study 2 on page 136 for a more detailed explanation of *used to* and *would*.

PRACTICE

If you think your students need more controlled practice before doing these exercises, they could do Practice 2 on page 136 first.

1 Students work individually to complete the sentences about themselves. Circulate and check students are using *used to* and *would* correctly.

2 Students discuss the questions in pairs. Finish the activity by asking students to report on any surprises.

Practice, exercise 2: Alternative suggestion

Ask students to work in pairs with somebody they know or have worked with before. Individually, they should try to complete the sentences in exercise 1 so they are true for their partner. They then compare answers to see if their guesses were correct.

3 Give students a few minutes to think about what they are going to write. Explain that they don't have to include any topics they don't want to. Encourage them to ask for any language they need. Go round checking and correcting if necessary as students write their descriptions.

ADDITIONAL PRACTICE

Resource bank: Activity 2C *School reunion* (*used to, would, still, not … any longer/not … anymore*)

Study, practice & remember: Practice 2

Workbook: Language focus 2: *used to* and *would*, page 12

Vocabulary (PAGE 21)

Remembering and forgetting

See *Teaching tips: Working with lexis*, page 21.

1 Check that students understand the instructions and go through the example with the class. Students work individually, using dictionaries if available, before comparing in pairs. As you check answers with the class, elicit/write up examples of full sentences with the correct forms, highlighting possible constructions, using the examples.

ANSWERS:

b to do something **c** of something **d** to do something

2 Emphasise that students should only add a word if they think it is necessary. You could demonstrate this by doing the first two items as examples with the class. Encourage the use of dictionaries if available, as this is an important dictionary skill for students to practise.

ANSWERS:

1 – **2** to **3** when **4** to **5** – **6** – **7** to **8** –

3 Allow time for students to select and prepare the questions they will ask. Circulate as they ask and answer, so that you are aware of any problem areas. Focus on these with the class at the end of the activity if necessary. Get stronger students to ask and answer all the questions.

ADDITIONAL PRACTICE

Resource bank: Activity 2D *The best days of your life?* (Vocabulary extension: childhood and upbringing)

Workbook: Vocabulary: *Remembering and forgetting*, page 14

Task (PAGES 22–23)

Describe a personal memory

See *Teaching tips: Making tasks work*, page 23.

Preparation (PAGE 22)

Listening and vocabulary

1a Focus attention on the pictures and elicit what memories students think they show. Students work in pairs to find the things in the box in the pictures before checking with the class.

b Students check the meaning of the words and phrases, using dictionaries if available. Check understanding of the phrases with the class, especially:

- *to be tame* – when an animal has been trained to live with humans
- *to get tangled* – when a cord gets caught up in something
- *to perch* – how a bird sits on something
- *to black out* – to become unconscious
- *to get choppy* – when it gets windy at sea and causes big waves

Students work in pairs to match the verbs and phrases in the box to the words in exercise 1a. Check answers with the class.

ANSWERS:

to be tame = a budgie to fall off = a branch/a swing
to fly off = a budgie to float = a sailing boat
to get tangled = an anchor to perch = a budgie
to black out = a branch/a swing to get choppy = a sailing boat
to rescue = a sailing boat

2 2.6 Emphasise that students do not need to understand everything at this stage. With stronger classes, ask them to guess the titles using the vocabulary in exercise 1 before they listen. Play the recording, pausing after each story to give students time to think and compare in pairs. Play the recording again if necessary, before checking answers with the class.

ANSWERS:

Story 1: A story about a childhood pet
Story 2: A childhood accident
Story 3: A time I was really frightened/A day when everything went wrong

3 Ask students to answer the questions from memory in pairs. Play the recording again for students to check before checking answers with the class.

SUGGESTED ANSWERS:

Story 1
1 when speaker was eight or nine **2** first pet, called Ollie, named after the Olympics, very tame (would sit on bed while boy did homework, jump onto plate during dinner, etc.) **3** mother left back door open and budgie flew off; they never found her. **4** a bit sad

Story 2
1 in garden at parents' house when speaker was 11 or 12 **2** parents were having a party, there was a swing on a cherry tree, her father made it when she was little **3** speaker jumped on the swing, but the branch the swing was attached to fell off the tree; the swing hit her on the head and she blacked out for a few moments
4 embarrassed

Story 3
1 in Sicily on holiday about two years ago **2** they hired a boat, the sun was shining, they were sunbathing **3** they dropped the anchor, but it got tangled up in the engine and the engine stopped working; the boat floated out to sea and at the same time the weather changed and the sea got choppy; the radio didn't work and water started to come in the boat; speaker's girlfriend managed to phone the people who gave them the boat and they rescued them
4 very worried and very scared

4 Focus attention on the Useful language box on page 23 and give students time to read through the phrases. Play the recording for students to tick the phrases they hear. Students check answers in pairs before checking with the whole class.

ANSWERS:

Story 1: I remember when ... ; I used to (come home from school) ... ; One day ... ; Then ... ; It was a bit (sad).
Story 2: This is the story of something that happened to me when (I was about 11).; It was so (embarrassing)
Story 3: It was about (two) years ago.; The sun was shining.; Then ... ; At the same time ... ; At the time we were very (worried).; In the end ...

Task (PAGE 23)

Speaking

1a Explain that students are now going to describe a memory of their own. Remind students of the titles in exercise 2 on page 22 and give them time to choose one.

b Refer students to the Useful language box, sections a–d. Encourage them to make notes about what they are going to say. Circulate and help with vocabulary where necessary, writing any new words/phrases on the board.

2a When they are ready, arrange students in pairs or small groups to share their memories.

b Refer students to the Useful language box, section e. Encourage students to ask questions and show interest as they listen to each other's stories. Finish the activity by asking students to report back any surprising information.

Follow up (PAGE 23)

Writing

1 Students use their notes from exercise 1b to write a short paragraph about their memories on a piece of paper. Circulate and check their work, helping where necessary. When they have finished, display their paragraphs around the class and ask them to walk around and read the texts in order to choose their favourite one.

Task: Speaking: Alternative suggestion

When students tell their stories in exercise 2a, ask them not to say which title from exercise 2 on page 22 they chose. Other students listen to their story, then guess which title they chose.

Share your task

Some additional ideas could include:

- Students film themselves acting out each story in small groups, with each student playing a different character from their story.
- Students compile their recordings into a class radio programme/podcast.
- Students add music to their recordings to add atmosphere.

ADDITIONAL PRACTICE

Workbook: Writing: *A story*, pages 14–15

World culture (PAGES 24–25)

Flashbulb memories

Culture notes

The Beijing Olympic Games: These were held in the summer of 2008, with 11,028 athletes competing from 204 countries. China won the most gold medals (51), while the USA won the most medals altogether (110). US swimmer Michael Phelps broke the record for most gold medals in one Olympics.

The Berlin Wall coming down: The Berlin Wall started being demolished on 9th November 1989. The wall had long been seen as the main symbol of the divisions of the Cold War between the capitalist West and the socialist East, and its fall was seen as a victory for the west.

The death of Diana, Princess of Wales: On 31st August 1997, Princess Diana was involved in a car crash with her partner, Dodi Fayed, in which she died. At first it was thought that the crash was caused by the actions of the paparazzi, but a later investigation found that the crash was caused by the driver, who was drunk at the time. The public reaction to the news was huge, with her funeral watched on TV by an estimated 2.5 billion people.

The assassination of John F. Kennedy: President Kennedy was assassinated on 22nd November 1963, while travelling with his wife Jacqueline in an official Presidential motorcade in Dallas, Texas. The initial investigation found that Lee Harvey Oswald was responsible, though he was killed before he could stand trial. Over the last 50 years the assassination has continued to be an issue for discussion and has created a range of conspiracy theories.

The first person on the moon: On 21st July 1969, the American Neil Armstrong became the first man to walk on the moon, when he said the famous words, 'That's one small step for (a) man, one giant leap for mankind.' He had travelled there as part of the Apollo 11 space mission. Neil Armstrong died on 25th August 2012, at the age of 82.

Find out first (PAGE 24)

1a Focus attention on the photos and the title of the section, and ask students what they think *flashbulb memories* are. Students match the photos with the events in pairs before checking answers with the class.

ANSWERS:
(clockwise, starting from the background) the Beijing Olympic Games, the first person on the moon, the Berlin Wall coming down, the assassination of John F. Kennedy, the death of Diana, Princess of Wales

b Students work in pairs. Don't check any answers yet.

c If you have access to the internet, students can research the events individually, then check in pairs. Otherwise, check answers with the class.

ANSWERS:
assassination of J. F. K.: 1963; first person on moon: 1969; Berlin Wall coming down: 1989; Diana's death: 1997; Bejing Olympics: 2008

Find out first, exercise 1c: Alternative suggestion

Put students in five groups and allocate one of the events to each group. Write the following prompts on the board: *Where? When? Main people involved? Main events? Other interesting information?*

Students go online to research the events using the prompts on the board. When they are ready, each group presents its information to the rest of the class.

View (PAGE 24)

See *Teaching tips: Using the video material in the classroom*, page 24.

2a Students match the words and meanings individually, then check answers in pairs before checking with the whole class. Drill the words/phrases with the class and check the pronunciation of *psychologist* /saɪˈkɒlədʒɪst/, *amygdala* /əˈmɪgdələ/ and *idiosyncratic* /ɪdiːəʊsɪŋˈkrætɪk/.

ANSWERS:
1 d 2 e 3 f 4 b 5 g 6 c 7 a

b Explain that students shouldn't worry if they don't understand every word in the video, they should just watch for the main ideas this time. Refer students back to the events in exercise 1, then play the DVD for them to watch and check. Students check answers in pairs before checking with the class. Elicit which other events are mentioned.

ANSWERS:
The assassination of John F. Kennedy, the death of Diana, Princess of Wales, the Berlin Wall coming down; John Lennon's and Jimi Hendrix's deaths are also mentioned.

3a Students discuss the questions in pairs. When they are ready, play the DVD again for them to check their answers. With weaker classes, pause the DVD after each relevant point to allow students to write their answers.

b Students compare answers in pairs before checking with the whole class.

ANSWERS:
1 You can remember exactly when and where you were and what you were doing at the time. **2** years afterwards **3** to deal with emotion **4** relatively few **5** highly emotionally charged events **6** Unexpected public deaths bring to an end important cultural themes.

World view (PAGE 25)

4a Focus attention on the table and make sure students understand what to watch for. Play the DVD for students to watch and complete the table. If necessary, play it a second time.

World view, exercise 4a: Alternative suggestion

In order to contextualise before students attempt the exercise, ask students to close their books and watch the video once, before asking them what they can remember about each person. Don't correct any of their ideas yet.

When they are ready, focus attention on the table and play the DVD again in order for students to complete it.

b Students compare their notes in pairs before checking answers with the class.

ANSWERS:

	The public event	The personal associations
Sion	the death of Whitney Houston	He (and his girlfriend) had been listening to her the day before.
Anna	the fall of the Berlin Wall	She crossed out the borders in her school atlas.
Martin	the ash cloud causing air traffic chaos in Europe	He was unable to fly to a conference.

5a Personalise this exercise by sharing your own answers to the questions with the class first. Students discuss the questions in small groups.

b Discuss the questions as a class.

Find out more (PAGE 25)

6a Write *memory* on the board and ask students if they think they have a good memory. Students discuss the questions in pairs. In feedback, nominate students to share their ideas with the class and write them on the board.

b Students choose one of the topics to research online and take notes. Focus on the search terms given to help them. Circulate while they are online and help with any vocabulary where necessary.

Write up your research

7 Go through the prompts with the class and elicit ways to finish each sentence as an example. Students write their paragraphs individually, using their notes from exercise 6b. Circulate and help where necessary, and write any new words/phrases on the board. When they have finished, students swap paragraphs with other students who researched a different question. In feedback, nominate students to share any new information they discovered with the class.

Students can now do Unit test 1 on the Teacher's Resource Disc.

Study, practice & remember

(PAGES 135–137)

See *Teaching tips: Using the Study, practice & remember sections*, page 25.

Practice 1

ANSWERS:

1

1 c **2** a **3** d **4** e **5** b

2

2 we arrived **3** the doorbell rang **4** we didn't want **5** I heard **6** I liked

3

1 saw, were playing **2** were arguing **3** walked, stopped **4** lasted

4

1 e: My sister broke her leg while she was skiing.
2 d: I met my best friend when we both worked at a sandwich bar.
3 c: The sun was shining when I woke up this morning.
4 a: It was raining this morning so my husband gave me a lift to work.
5 b: The police stopped him because he was driving too fast.

Practice 2

ANSWERS:

1

1 would believe **2** Did you would **3** use to encourage **4** didn't would do **5** Would you

2

1 used **2** use **3** any **4** more **5** still

3

1 I used to spend a lot of time playing video games.
2 Ali never used to do any exercise as a child.
3 Did Phil use to be interested in art?
4 It used to be quiet here, but it isn't any longer.
5 I didn't use to have enough time to relax.
6 Where did you use to go on holiday?
7 He used to have a beard, but he doesn't any more.
8 I used to be frightened of spiders and I still am.

Remember these words

ANSWERS:

1

1 a, c **2** b, c **3** a, b **4** b, c **5** a

2

1 remember **2** reminds **3** remember **4** recognise **5** remember **6** recognise **7** forgot **8** remind **9** remember **10** forget

Study tips

1 Go over the sentences with the class, then give students time to think about their answers and tick the things they do. Note that for 6, it's important that students check their translation is correct first, in order to avoid learning a 'false friend'. For example, *nervous* in many languages means *angry*, not *anxious* or *worried*.

2 Students compare their answers in pairs. In feedback, go through the sentences and elicit the benefits of each one. Allow the discussion to develop naturally and write any other tips the students have on the board. Highlight that:

- there are many ways to help remember new lexis.
- the key is to interact with new words as often as possible.
- there is no 'correct' way to do this, but it's important that students find methods that work for them and stick to them.

OVERVIEW

PAGES 26–27

Grammar: Comparatives and superlatives

Common European Framework: Students can compare and contrast alternatives discussing what to do, where to go, who or which to choose, etc.

PAGES 28–29

Vocabulary: Features and sights

Reading: Visit or avoid?

Common European Framework: Students can understand the description of events and feelings; can express themselves on topics such as travel.

PAGES 30–31

Grammar: Different ways of comparing

Pronunciation: Stress and /ə/ sounds

Vocabulary: Adjectives for describing places

Common European Framework: Students can compare and contrast alternatives discussing what to do, where to go, who or which to choose, etc.; can use a good range of vocabulary for general topics.

PAGES 32–33

Task: Provide an insider's guide

Common European Framework: Students can find out and pass on factual information.

PAGES 34–35

Speaking: Travel problems

Writing: A travel blog

Common European Framework: Students can ask for and follow detailed directions; can write a description of a trip – real or imagined.

Language focus 1 (PAGES 26–27)

Comparatives and superlatives

See *Teaching tips: Using a discovery approach to grammar*, page 20.

WARM UP

Write the following key statistics about New York City on the board: *Population: 8.2 million; Average summer temperature: 29.4 degrees; Average winter temperature: -2.8 degrees; Age: approx. 400 years; Languages spoken: approx. 800; Number of tourists: approx. 50 million a year*. Ask students to compare the facts with their cities in pairs.

1a Start by naming some of the countries and cities in the quiz and asking students what they can tell you about them. Check the meaning of *coastline* and *skyscrapers*. Put students into small groups to do the quiz. Emphasise that they must use English (you could deduct 'penalty points' if the students use their mother tongue!).

b 🎧 **3.1** Emphasise that students will hear a lot of extra information in addition to the answers. Play the recording. If your students need support with listening, pause the recording after each question to give them time to check answers in pairs. Finish the activity by checking which team got the highest score.

ANSWERS:

1 Danes **2** Mexicans **3** Indians **4** Germans **5** Americans
6 b **7** b **8** a **9** d **10** c

GRAMMAR

Comparatives and superlatives

Revision of basic forms

Check that students understand the questions, including grammatical terminology such as *comparative*, *superlative* and *syllable*. Students compare answers in pairs before checking as a class.

ANSWERS:

1 longer – longest; taller – tallest; happier – happiest; more popular – the most popular; further – furthest*; more hard-working – the most hard-working
* It is also possible to say *farther – farthest*. The meaning is the same.
2 one-syllable adjectives: adjective + *-er/-est*; two-syllable adjectives ending in *-y*: adjective + *-er/-est*; other two- or three-syllable adjectives: *more/the most* + adjective
3 (suggested answers) good, bad

Highlight the following spelling rules:

- In one-syllable adjectives with short vowel sounds, the final consonant doubles (*big* → *bigger* → *biggest*).
- Adjectives ending in -e add *-r/-st* (*nice* → *nicer* → *nicest*).
- In adjectives ending in consonant + *-y*, *-y* changes to *-ier/-iest* (*pretty* → *prettier* → *prettiest*).

Big and small differences

Do the first item as an example. (It is best not to do exercise 4 until you have checked the answers to exercises 1–3.) Students work in pairs. In feedback, highlight the following points:

- *Much higher/a lot higher* have the same meaning.
- The pronunciation of *slightly* is /ˈslaɪtli/.
- The opposite of *a lot* is *a little bit*. (*Note*: it is also possible to say *a little*, but it is not possible to say *a lot bit*.)

ANSWERS:

4
1 B **2** A **3** B **4** A

Superlative phrases

Emphasise that students should complete the sentences by inserting one word in each space. In feedback, highlight the following points:

- *By far* + superlative shows a big difference.
- Before superlative adjectives *the* is needed. We also say *the second/the third/the fourth/*etc. *biggest*.
- *One of the biggest countries* means there are several big ones, but we are not saying it is the biggest of all.

ANSWERS:

5
1 in **2** in **3** of **4** by **5** least

You may want to ask students to read Study 1 on page 138 for a more detailed explanation of comparatives and superlatives.

Grammar: Alternative suggestion

If you are short of time, set the revision of basic comparatives and superlatives as homework in advance of the lesson. If you have a stronger class, omit the basic revision and put students in pairs to work through the rest of the Grammar box. Deal with any outstanding problems as you check the answers with the class.

PRACTICE

1 Go through the example with the class and emphasise that they should use two words. Students work in pairs to complete each sentence before checking answers with the class.

ANSWERS:

1 more popular **2** second largest **3** much further
4 hardest-working/most hard-working **5** lot happier
6 more likely **7** funnier than **8** more often

2a 🎧 **3.2** Emphasise that students can write their answers in any order they choose. Pause the recording after each instruction to give students time to think and write.

b Do an example or two, using students' own answers. In feedback, nominate students to share information with the class.

3a 🎧 **3.3** Give students time to read the information on page 128. Explain how to say *km²* (kilometres squared). Demonstrate the activity by playing the first statement and asking the class to decide if it is true or false. Pause after each statement to allow students time to decide and to correct the false statements. Check answers in pairs and then as a class.

ANSWERS:

1 F (France is by far the largest of the three countries.)
2 F (France is a lot less crowded than the UK.)
3 F (The UK is much more popular with tourists than Ireland.)
4 T **5** T **6** F (Heathrow is the busiest of the three airports.)

b Circulate as students work in pairs to create six more statements. Check that they are using comparative and superlative forms accurately. Help students to self-correct before giving them the right answer. When they are ready, join pairs into groups of four to test each other.

4a Students write their sentences individually. Circulate and help with vocabulary where necessary, writing any new words on the board.

b Students compare their ideas in groups. Finish off by eliciting a few ideas from different groups.

Practice, exercise 4: Alternative suggestion

If your students are from the same country, use this activity as a competition to write as many differences as possible in five minutes. Points are awarded for correct sentences and for the ability to correct another pair's mistakes.

Find out more

This can be done in class or set for homework if you are short of time. Students work in pairs and choose one of the countries from the quiz. Make sure that each pair doesn't choose the country they are from and, if possible, that each pair chooses a different country. Students go online to gather information, then create a poster showing the statistics using charts/graphs. Display the posters round the class for other students to read.

ADDITIONAL PRACTICE

Resource bank: Activity 3A *The best place in the world* (Superlatives and Present perfect)

Study, practice & remember: Practice 1

Workbook: Language focus 1: *Comparatives and superlatives*, pages 16–17

Vocabulary (PAGE 28)

Features and sights

See *Teaching tips: Working with lexis*, page 21.

WARM UP

Before class, bring or download photos of the features and sights in exercise 1a and show them to students for them to guess what they are called in English.

1a Do one or two examples with the class to check they understand what to do. Students work in pairs to categorise the words before checking with the class. Explain any new vocabulary with examples or draw pictures on the board. (Note that *docks* always has an *-s* on the end, but can be a singular noun – *a docks*.)

ANSWERS:

The countryside: a bridge, a canal, farmland, a festival, a (rain)forest, a hill, a lake, a view, a village, a waterfall (falls)
The coast: a bay, a beach, a cliff, docks, a harbour, an island
The city: ancient ruins, a bridge, a cathedral, docks, a factory, a harbour, a market, a monument, a mosque, a museum, a palace, a shopping mall, a skyscraper, a temple

b Students work individually to add more words to each group, then compare in pairs. Check answers with the class and drill any new vocabulary before writing it on the board.

2a Arrange students in groups and give them two minutes to complete the task. Don't give any answers yet.

b 🎧 **3.4** Play the recording for students to check their answers.

ANSWERS:

1 Festival **2** Palace **3** Harbour **4** Lake **5** Museum
6 Islands **7** Mosque **8** Falls **9** Canal

ADDITIONAL PRACTICE

Workbook: Vocabulary, *Features and sights*, page 17

Reading (PAGES 28–29)

1 Students discuss the questions in pairs. In feedback, nominate students to share their ideas with the class and encourage them to suggest other things they look for.

2 Check understanding of *sandy beaches, crowds, travel overland, cosmopolitan, bazaars* and *bargains* (/ˈbɑːɡɪnz/). Emphasise that students should read the text quickly and that they'll have a chance to read it again more carefully afterwards. Students answer the question in pairs.

3 Arrange students in pairs, but explain that they should work individually to find the answers as quickly as possible. Check answers with the class and encourage students to explain which part of the text gives each piece of information.

ANSWERS:

1 archaeology **2** Bangkok **3** 150 years ago
4 the north of Vietnam **5** Koh Samui **6** shopping
7 shopping **8** over 17 hours **9** over 1,200 **10** souk

4a Go through the first comment with the class as an example. Students work individually, then check answers in pairs before checking with the class.

ANSWERS:

Lulu_RT: Landon; visit **LucyLane:** Valentina; visit
Yuri55: Valentina; visit **Cal_M:** Landon; avoid

b Remind students of the introductory information for Landon and Valentina and give them time to think of suggestions and write their comments. Circulate and help with vocabulary if necessary. When they have finished, students share their comments with the class.

5 Students work individually, then check answers in pairs. Check answers with the class and give further explanations/examples where necessary.

ANSWERS:

1 a **2** b **3** b **4** a **5** b

6 Give students time to prepare what they are going to say individually. Circulate and help with vocabulary, writing any new words/phrases on the board. When they are ready, arrange students in groups to share their ideas.

Reading, exercise 6: Alternative suggestion

Ask students to write short descriptions of their ideal holiday on a piece of paper and make sure they leave space at the bottom of the paper. Circulate and encourage students to use the phrases from exercise 5. When they have finished, display the descriptions around the class and ask students to walk around, read the descriptions and write comments below each text.

Language focus 2 (PAGES 30–31)

Different ways of comparing

See *Teaching tips: Using a discovery approach to grammar*, page 20.

1 Focus attention on the photo and *It's a fact!* Students discuss the questions in pairs before sharing their ideas with the class. There are no correct answers here, so encourage students to share as many ideas as possible.

SUGGESTED ANSWERS:

Shanghai is in China. The population has grown since the 1990s, when the city was redeveloped on a massive scale. This attracted foreign investment and large numbers of migrant workers. Life expectancy also increased significantly. The main difference is that there were fewer/no tall buildings.

2 Students work individually, then check answers in pairs. Circulate and note how students are using the language. This will give you an idea of how much to focus on in the Grammar box.

ANSWERS:

1 completely different from **2** the same as **3** exactly the same
4 not as busy as **5** less **6** worse **7** fewer

3a 🎧 **3.5** Play the recording for students to check their ideas. Encourage students to check their answers in pairs before checking with the whole class.

b Play the recording again, then students discuss the question in pairs. Check answers with the class and ask students to give reasons why.

SUGGESTED ANSWER:

Overall, they are positive. Jasmine is more positive than Pan.

GRAMMAR

Different ways of comparing

1 Students match the adjectives and prepositions in pairs. If you have a weak group, refer them to the sentences in exercise 2, where each adjective–preposition combination can be found.

ANSWERS:

different from, similar to, the same as, worse than, not as busy as, fewer than, less than

2 Students work individually before checking answers with the class. Highlight that:

- *fewer* is used with countable nouns.
- *less* is used with uncountable nouns.

ANSWERS:

1 fewer **2** less

3 Check that students understand that the line is a scale from one extreme to the other. Students work individually before going through the answers with the class.

ANSWERS:

1 exactly the same as **3** about the same as
4 very similar to **6** a bit different from
8 completely different from

Potential problem with prepositions

Prepositions are notoriously problematic for learners of English, as they vary so much and there are very few rules governing their use. In order to make them less problematic for students:

- always record any new words with the prepositions that they are used with on the board and encourage students to do the same.
- test students regularly (and ask them to test each other) by asking them to complete phrases which you call out, e.g. *the same … (as), similar … (to)*, etc.

Highlight the fact that comparisons can also be made using the following forms:

- *not as* + adjective + *as*: this does not mean *is not the same as*. It means *less … than*. This may be different in the students' own language and difficult for students to understand.
- *fewer … than/less … than*: they mean the same, but *less* is used with uncountable nouns, whereas *fewer* is used with countable nouns.

You may want to ask students to read Study 2 on page 139 for a more detailed explanation of different ways of comparing.

PRACTICE

If you think students need more controlled practice before doing these exercises, they could do Practice 2 on page 139 first.

1a 🎧 **3.6** Focus attention on the photos. After looking at the photos for a few minutes, students listen and answer *true* or *false*.

ANSWERS:

1 F: Times Square in the 1950s looks different from Times Square now. **2** F: The adverts then were a bit different from modern ones. **3** T **4** T **5** F: The taxis then were completely different from the taxis now. **6** F: The traffic then was about the same as the traffic now. **7** F: The pollution then was worse than the pollution now. **8** T

Practice, exercise 1a: Alternative suggestion

If you have time, allow students a few minutes to study the photos. Then ask them to close their books. In small groups, they try to answer *true* or *false* from memory as they listen. In feedback, find out which group had the most correct answers.

b Emphasise that students should use the phrases from the Grammar box, and also those from Language focus 1, to express more differences as precisely as possible. The focus here is on accuracy, so go round checking and correcting sentences. In feedback, check that the meaning is also correct by referring to the photos.

2a Give students a few minutes to think about similarities and differences between their town now and at a time in the past. Go round the class supplying any vocabulary that students need, for example, adjectives.

b Put students into pairs to compare answers.

PRONUNCIATION

See *Teaching tips: Helping students with pronunciation, page 22.*

1 **3.7** Play the recording as many times as necessary, pausing after each sentence for students to write. Alternatively, read out the sentences yourself. (Keep to a natural speed, with natural use of weak forms and linking – maintain this speed no matter how many times students ask you to repeat the words.)

ANSWERS:

1 The restaurants are better than before.
2 The streets are a lot busier than they were.
3 The clothes are different from before.
4 Public transport is not as good as it was.
5 The historic buildings are the same as before.
6 The streets were similar to the way they are now.

2 **3.8** Make sure that students are familiar with the schwa sound. Read out the phrases, exaggerating the /ə/ sounds slightly and getting students to copy. Alternatively, play the recording, pausing to allow the students to repeat. Replay the recording several times.

3 Refer students back to the sentences they wrote in Practice, exercise 2a. Ask them to decide where the schwa sounds are, before they practise saying each sentence with their partner. Go round the class to check that students are using the schwa sounds correctly.

Pronunciation: the schwa /ə/ sound

The schwa sound is the most common sound in English and it is unique in that it is never stressed. You can demonstrate how the sound is produced by asking students to completely relax their mouth and 'push' themselves lightly in the stomach.

ADDITIONAL PRACTICE

Resource bank: Activity 3B *Spot the differences* (Vocabulary extension: Features and sights)

Study, practice & remember: Practice 2

Workbook: Language focus 2: *Different ways of comparing*, page 19; Pronunciation: *Stress and /ə/ sounds in comparative phrases*, page 20

Vocabulary (PAGE 31)

Adjectives for describing places

See *Teaching tips: Working with lexis*, page 21.

1 Go through the adjectives with the class and encourage students to ask you about any they're not sure of. Students work in pairs to match the adjectives with the cities. Nominate students to share their ideas with the class and ask if others agree.

Vocabulary, exercise 1: Alternative suggestion

If you are in one of the cities, ask students to compare how they think foreigners would describe their city to how they describe it.

2 **3.9** Focus attention on the photos on page 126 and elicit which cities students think they show. Play the recording for students to check their answers.

ANSWERS:

1 C **2** A **3** B

3 Students listen again and tick the adjectives from exercise 1 they hear, before checking in pairs. Play the recording again if necessary, then check answers with the class.

ANSWERS:

1 romantic, historic, touristy **2** smart, modern, dangerous, expensive
3 colourful, modern, smart, poor, dirty

4a Read the example with the class and emphasise that students should use at least three adjectives and include a clue. Give students time to write their descriptions individually. Circulate and help where necessary.

b Arrange students in groups to read out their descriptions and guess the places.

Vocabulary, exercise 4a: Alternative suggestion

If students are all from the same city, ask them to write descriptions of a different city which they know.

ADDITIONAL PRACTICE

Workbook: Vocabulary: *Adjectives for describing places*, page 20

Task (PAGES 32–33)

Provide an insider's guide

See *Teaching tips: Making tasks work, page 23.*

WARM UP

Put students in teams to do a quiz about London. Read out the statements below and ask teams to decide if each one is true or false:

1 London was founded by the Romans. (True)
2 London is the largest city in the world. (False, though it was at the end of the 19th century.)
3 The average temperature in July is 35.5 degrees. (False, though that is the record highest temperature for July.)
4 The London Underground system is often called *the Tube*. (True)
5 There are 14 league football clubs in London. (True)
6 London has two airports. (False; it has six.)

Go through the statements and award points for correct answers. The team with the most points wins.

Preparation (PAGE 32)

Listening

1 Focus students' attention on the photos and ask if anyone has visited London. In feedback, go through the things shown in the photos, using the information in the Culture notes below.

Culture notes

The photos show:

Street performers: There are many street performers in London. Every day of the year (except Christmas Day) you can see street performers in Covent Garden, in Central London. People have been performing there for over 300 years and competition is tough – performers have to audition to be allowed to perform there.

Big Ben: The clock tower in Westminster, next to the Houses of Parliament. It is over 150 years old and fully functioning.

Tower bridge: This is a fully functioning drawbridge near the Tower of London, where it gets its name from. It is over 100 years old and opens up to allow boats to pass through.

The Sherlock Holmes museum: This is located in Baker Street, the home of the famous fictional detective, created by the writer Sir Arthur Conan Doyle.

A traditional red telephone box: These can be seen in various places around the city.

A deer: This photo shows Richmond Park, in South-West London. It is the largest royal park in London and the second largest urban park in Britain, and is famous for the over 600 deer who live there.

A chair: Shops selling retro fashion and designs are popular in Brick Lane.

Graffiti: Some of the graffiti along the South Bank is really interesting.

Fashion: Shops selling vintage fashion and individually designed clothes can be found in Brick Lane.

Ethnic food: This photo shows food from a Greek restaurant. In London, you can find restaurants that cook food from countries all around the world.

2 **3.10** Give students time to read the summaries before playing the recording. Check answers with the class.

ANSWER:

b

3 **3.11** Check understanding of *book stalls* and *an arty area*. Go through the ideas in the box, then play the recording for students to match the ideas with the places. Encourage students to check their answers in pairs before checking with the class.

ANSWERS:

1 theatres and concert halls, free exhibitions, street entertainers, a lively atmosphere **2** ethnic food, vintage stuff, individually designed clothes, clubs and nightlife **3** picnics, deer **4** the 19th century

4 Focus students' attention on the Useful language box and go through the phrases. Students listen and tick the phrases they hear. Check answers with the class, then drill the phrases.

ANSWERS:

a It's a great place to (watch people). It's famous for its (food). It's a great place to (eat food from all over the world). It's good for (clubs and nightlife/walking).
b I'd definitely recommend (going there). You should definitely go. You'll love it.
c What's it like? Which shops/restaurants/parks do you recommend?

5 Students discuss the questions in pairs. In feedback, nominate students to share their ideas with the class.

Task (PAGES 33)

Speaking

1a It is probably most motivating if students choose different places, so if you have a monolingual class, ask students to choose a city or region from their country rather than the country as a whole. Give students time to think of the places they are going to recommend. Encourage them to think of as many places as possible at this stage and refer them to the ideas in exercise 3 on page 32 for ideas.

b From the list they thought of in exercise 1a, students now choose the best five ideas. If several students have chosen the same area, ask them to work together to compare their lists.

2a Go through the example with the class, then encourage students to make notes on the places they chose in exercise 1b. Circulate, answering vocabulary questions and helping students to plan their recommendations. If necessary, ask prompt questions, for example, *How long do you think they should stay in …?*

b Remind students to look back at the phrases in the Useful language box, sections a and b, then plan what they are going to say. Circulate and help where necessary.

3 If possible, arrange students so they are working with a student who has chosen a different place to them. Remind students of the phrases in the Useful language box, section c, and encourage them to ask each other questions. Circulate as students work, noting down any errors or useful language for analysis at the end of the task. Students report back briefly to the whole class about what appeals/doesn't appeal about their partner's recommendations.

Task: speaking: Alternative suggestions

a If you want to provide a model yourself, it may be more motivating for students if you present a tour of an English-speaking country/region that you have visited. If you are a native speaker of English, students may be interested in your own region and town.

Plan briefly what you will say, incorporating useful phrases (*It's really worth visiting,* etc.). If possible, take a map of the city/area/country to refer to, marking the places you talk about with stickers. Encourage students to ask any questions they have as you present your tour.

b If you are short of time or have short lessons, do the model for the task (either the London model or your own) on one day, then set the planning stage (exercises 1 and 2) as homework. Students can talk through the task in the next lesson, after asking you for any vocabulary they need.

Share your task

Some additional ideas could include:

- Students film themselves giving recommendations, then compile them in the style of a travel programme.
- Students record themselves giving one recommendation each, then compile them as a travel podcast.
- Students share their recorded recommendations on a social networking site, then, a few days later, bring any comments to class to share.
- Students recommend places in the city where they live, then film themselves visiting those places.

ADDITIONAL PRACTICE

Resource bank: 3C *The City Language School* (Recommending and advising)

Language live (PAGES 34–35)

See *Teaching tips: Using the video material in the classroom*, page 24.

Speaking (PAGE 34)

Travel problems

1a Focus attention on the photo and elicit what problems it shows. Then students discuss which travel problems they have experienced in small groups. When they have finished, nominate students from each group to share their experiences with the class.

ANSWER:

train cancellations/delays

b Students watch the video and answer the questions in pairs, before checking with the class.

ANSWERS:

1 The driver will not tell the woman how much the taxi ride will cost. She asks him to turn on the meter.
2 The British man wants to know how to get to the Manhattan shopping centre. He asks the bus driver for directions. (The differences between American and British English also cause some confusion.)
3 The passenger cannot understand the announcement. He speaks to the information officer.

2a Students answer the questions from memory in pairs. Play the DVD for students to check their answers.

ANSWERS:

1 Tr **2** Tr **3** B **4** B **5** T **6** Tr **7** T **8** Tr **9** Tr

b Go through the example with the class. Students work in pairs, then check answers with the class.

ANSWERS:

2 bus/train **3** bus/train/taxi **4** bus/train **5** bus/train/taxi
7 bus/train/taxi **8** bus/train **9** bus/train

3 Students answer the questions individually, then check answers in pairs. Check answers with the class and highlight the fact that in indirect questions, the word order is the same as in a sentence, i.e. there is no inversion of the subject and the auxiliary.

ANSWERS:

1 Excuse me; One more question; Can I ask you a question?
2 Do you know; Could you tell me
In questions 1–3, the subject and verb are inverted because they are direct questions. In questions 4–9, the subject and verb are not inverted because they are indirect questions.

Potential problem with indirect questions

Students may have difficulty understanding that they don't need to invert the subject and auxiliary in indirect questions. If this is the case, write the following example on the board:
What's the time? ***Do you know*** *what the time is?*
The time is (3 o'clock).

Show students that the part of the indirect question in bold is actually the question form and the underlined part is the same as the answer.

PRONUNCIATION

See *Teaching tips: Helping students with pronunciation*, page 22.

1 Play the DVD, pausing after each question for students to repeat. Point out that when stressing words in a sentence, it is the important, content words that we stress. Write the stressed words from the example on the board (*tell much cost*) and ask if students can get a general idea of the question. Then write the unstressed words below (*Could you me how it will*) and ask the same question. Point out that when students are listening to natural speech, they should listen out for the stressed words to get the main idea.

4 Go through the example with the class. If you have a weaker class, do one or two more examples. Students rewrite the sentences individually, then check answers in pairs before checking with the class.

ANSWERS:

1 Do you know where I get on the bus?
2 Could you tell me which platform is the 6:30 to Paris?
3 Excuse me ... can I use this ticket on the train?
4 Do you know what time the train will arrive?
5 One last question: how do I get to the airport?
6 Could you tell me where I have to change?
7 Can I ask you a question? Does this bus go to High Park?

5a With weaker classes, students may need to write the dialogue first. With stronger classes, you could ask them to do the exercise orally. Circulate and check students are using the polite questions correctly.

b Emphasise that students need to choose the most entertaining conversation while they listen, in order to make sure they pay attention. Pairs take it in turns to perform their conversations for the class.

ADDITIONAL PRACTICE

Resource bank: Activity 3D *How do I get to ... ?* (Asking for and giving directions)

Writing (PAGE 35)

A travel blog

1 Check understanding of *the hippy movement, a restless night, seasick* and *seagulls*. Give students a time limit of three minutes to read the blogs quickly and choose the best one. When checking answers with the class, encourage students to give reasons for their opinion.

SUGGESTED ANSWER:

Florence's blog is better – this point can be made after exercise 2.

2 Give students time to read the blogs more carefully and answer the questions individually before checking in pairs. Check answers with the class and encourage students to highlight the parts of the blogs where they can find these things.

ANSWERS:

1 F **2** F **3** F **4** F **5** HF **6** F

3a Give students time to read the tips and check understanding. Students work individually, then check answers in pairs before checking with the class.

ANSWERS:

1 However, our hotel isn't special at all. We've got a tiny, dirty room and the beds are awful. I had a very restless night.
2 You can hear the seagulls and smell the sea air even in the prison.
3 In the 1960s it was home to the hippy movement, but nowadays it's home to a lot of internet companies like Twitter.
4 The first thing I noticed was how beautiful and cosmopolitan it is here.

b Remind students of the adjectives for describing places in exercise 1 on page 31. Students change the adjectives in Hannah's blog individually, then check answers in pairs. In feedback, nominate students to share their ideas with the class.

ANSWERS:

Hannah didn't follow tip 2 (using all her senses), tip 3 (basic facts) and tip 4 (using interesting adjectives).
nice → wonderful   old → historic   best → most romantic
pretty → beautiful   nice → spectacular   busy → crowded/touristy

c Students work individually, then check answers with the class.

ANSWERS:

1 ... the Bridge of Sighs, which was designed by Antonio Contino.
2 ... nice old city that was founded around 1,500 years ago.
3 ... Piazza San Marco. Venetians call it 'the Piazza'.
4 ... to get around Venice is to walk because no cars, buses or trains are allowed in.

4a Allow plenty of time for students to make notes. Circulate and help with ideas and vocabulary, writing any new words/phrases on the board.

b Give students time to write their blogs individually. Circulate and encourage students to use adjectives to describe places. When they have finished, go through the checklist with the class, then give students time to check their writing.

5a Encourage students to make both positive comments and suggestions, and to write them on the blog. Encourage them to follow the tips in the checklist in exercise 4b.

b Give students time to read the comments and discuss them with their partner. Students then write the final draft of their blog.

Writing, exercise 5: Alternative suggestion

If you have access to the internet, set up a free blog before class. In exercise 5a, instead of writing their blog posts on paper, students type them and add to the class blog. For homework, ask students to read their classmates' blog posts and leave comments. Show these comments in the next class.

ADDITIONAL PRACTICE

Workbook: Language live: *Travel problems*, page 20; Writing: *Postcards*, page 21

Study, practice & remember

(PAGES 138–140)

See *Teaching tips: Using the Study, practice & remember sections*, page 25.

Practice 1

ANSWERS:

1
1 is further than **2** the dirtiest part **3** worse than I expected **4** the most boring museum **5** are cheaper than buses **6** the furthest car park **7** the tiniest beach **8** the worst restaurant **9** It's hotter in the south **10** is uglier than

2
1 is a lot smaller than **2** is a bit further north **3** is a lot hotter than **4** Correct **5** a lot less populated **6** Correct **7** is slightly smaller than

3
1 one, in **2** slightly **3** lot **4** little **5** least **6** more **7** second, in **8** of

4
1 By far the worst **2** one of the tallest **3** by far the smallest **4** the second most populated **5** the least populated

Practice 2

ANSWERS:

1
1 similar to **2** about the same as **3** completely different from **4** not as big as **5** very different from

2
1 less **2** in **3** from **4** as **5** less **6** worst **7** fewer **8** exactly **9** to **10** from **11** than **12** further

Remember these words

ANSWERS:

1
1 bridge **2** palace **3** docks **4** ancient ruins

2
1 colourful **2** peaceful **3** touristy **4** arty **5** historic **6** crowded **7** polluted **8** industrial

3
1 d **2** b **3** e **4** a **5** f **6** c

4
1 seeing **2** in **3** on **4** for

Study tips

1 Go over the sentences with the class, then give students time to think about their answers and tick the things they do.

2 Students compare their answers in pairs. In feedback, go through the sentences and elicit the benefits of each one. Allow the discussion to develop naturally and write any other tips the students have on the board.

OVERVIEW

PAGES 36–37

Grammar: Present perfect and Past simple

Pronunciation: strong and weak/contracted forms of *have*

Common European Framework: Students can describe experiences and events; can relate details of unpredictable occurrences.

PAGES 38–39

Reading and speaking: Pushed too far?

Common European Framework: Students can scan longer texts to locate desired information in order to fulfil a specific task; can develop an argument well enough to be followed without difficulty.

PAGES 40–41

Vocabulary: Life events

Grammar: Present perfect simple and Present perfect continuous

Pronunciation: linking

Common European Framework: Students can highlight the personal significance of events and experiences.

PAGES 42–43

Vocabulary: Personal qualities

Task: Nominate someone for an award

Common European Framework: Students can give a clear, prepared presentation, giving reasons in support of a particular point of view.

PAGES 44–45

World culture: Charles Dickens: Writer and campaigner

Common European Framework: Students can understand spoken language on both familiar and unfamiliar topics; can find out and pass on straightforward factual information.

Language focus 1 (PAGES 36–37)

Present perfect and Past simple

See *Teaching tips: Using a discovery approach to grammar*, page 20.

WARM UP

Before class, write the following statements on pieces of paper and display them round the classroom.

1 *He/She once dressed as a giant chicken while working for a restaurant.*
2 *He/She has said he/she is difficult to work with.*
3 *He/She has been given the nickname 'The British Bulldog'.*
4 *His/Her surname is also the name of a small city in Japan.*
5 *His/Her family own a very successful online business.*

Focus attention on the photos on pages 36 and 37 and elicit the names of the people. Students walk around the classroom and guess who the statements refer to. Check answers with the class.

ANSWERS:

1 Brad Pitt **2** Shakira **3** Winston Churchill **4** Barack Obama **5** Kate Middleton

1 Go through the questions with the class, then write *achievements* in the middle of the board. Elicit possible achievements and create a mind map on the board (e.g. *appeared on TV, won a competition, passed an important exam*). Give students time to think of something they have achieved and prepare what they are going to say. When they are ready, arrange them in groups to discuss the questions. In feedback, nominate students from each group to share their experiences with the class.

2a Focus students' attention on the photos and elicit who the people are and what they are famous for.

b Students work in pairs to match the famous people with their achievements. Don't give any answers yet.

ANSWERS:

1 Barack Obama (President of the United States) **2** Winston Churchill (British prime minister) **3** Shakira (pop singer) **4** Brad Pitt (Hollywood actor) **5** Kate Middleton (Duchess of Cambridge)

c **4.1** Check understanding of *row* (*a boat*). Play the recording for students to check their answers. Encourage students to check in pairs and answer the question before checking answers with the class.

ANSWERS:

5 It was too dangerous because so many photographers were planning to follow her boat.

3 The aim of this exercise is to get an idea of how much students know about the Present perfect and Past simple before analysis in the next stage. While students are doing the exercise, monitor carefully to get an idea of how much detail you need to go into in the next stage. Students work individually, then check answers in pairs before checking with the class.

ANSWERS:

1 has published, wrote **2** painted, wrote, won **3** has founded, has also raised **4** has been, has designed **5** was, trained

GRAMMAR

Present perfect and Past simple

Language focus 1: Notes on the approach to the Present perfect

In many courses and student grammars, it has been customary to divide the Present perfect into several 'uses'. However, we believe that there is essentially only one 'use' of the Present perfect – that it connects the present and the past, so that the past action is still part of the present in some way. As such, it should be regarded as a present tense, not a past tense, and has much in common with other perfect forms which are studied later in the course. In the Grammar box and Study sections, although we have referred to rules that students may be familiar with, we have tried to draw them together so that students can see this overall pattern.

Students work individually or in pairs before discussing answers with the whole class. As well as checking meaning, it may be necessary to check form. In particular, highlight that:

- the Present perfect is formed with *have/has* + past participle.
- *have* and *has* are often shortened to *'ve* and *'s*.
- regular past participles are verb + *-ed*; irregular ones have to be learnt individually (see page 175 of the Students' Book).
- in questions, *have/has* and the pronoun are inverted.
- negatives are formed with *haven't/hasn't*.

Potential problem with the Present perfect

A similar form to the Present perfect exists in many languages, but it is often used differently, e.g. to refer to recent actions in the past or simply to refer to the past instead of linking it to the present. You can show how it's used to refer directly to the present with the following examples:

- *Where did you go on holiday?*
- *Italy.*
- *Oh, I've been to Italy!*

Here, the person uses the Present perfect because they really want to say, 'Let's have a conversation about it.'

- *Do you want to watch this film?*
- *No, I've seen it.*

Here, the person uses the Present perfect to mean, 'I don't want to watch it.' In both cases, the Present perfect has a present use rather than a past use.

ANSWERS:

1 The Present perfect simple is formed with the present tense of *have* + the past participle.
Regular: publish, paint, found, raise, design, train
Irregular: write, win, be

2
1 Present perfect (e.g. Brad Pitt has been interested in architecture since he was young.)
2 Present perfect (e.g. Barack Obama has published several books.)
3 Past simple (e.g. In 2008, he wrote a book for his two daughters.)

3 **Past simple:** in 2010, ten minutes ago, when, yesterday, when I was young
Present perfect: since 2005, so far, in the last ten years
You may want to ask students to read Study 1 on page 141 for a more detailed explanation of the Present perfect and Past simple.

PRACTICE

1 Write on the board: *Why is Toby's achievement surprising?* Give students one minute to read the text, ignoring the gaps, to find the answer (He has given away a lot of money, but he isn't rich.). Students work individually before checking answers in pairs. Go through the answers with the class, eliciting which explanation from Grammar, exercise 2, applies in each case.

ANSWERS:

1 decided **2** promised **3** has given **4** gave **5** found
6 realised **7** decided **8** have given **9** has bought

2a 4.2 Focus students' attention on the dialogue descriptions before playing the recording. Students compare answers in pairs before checking with the class.

ANSWERS:

1 c **2** b **3** e **4** a **5** d

b Explain that the sentences come from the five dialogues students have just heard. Students complete the gaps individually or in pairs.

c Play the recording, pausing after each sentence for students to check their answers in pairs.

ANSWERS:

1 've lost, Have, seen **2** 've changed **3** 've lost **4** 's, gone
5 's gone **6** Has, locked **7** 've finished **8** haven't finished
9 have, met

PRONUNCIATION

See *Teaching tips: Helping students with pronunciation*, page 22.

1 **4.3** Play the first dialogue, asking students to write down an example of each. Play the recording more than once if necessary.

ANSWERS:

1 Yes, I have. **2** Have you seen it anywhere? Have you seen it? Have you looked on the coffee table?
3 I've lost my mobile. I can't believe you've lost it again! OK, so I've lost it again. It's not there, I've looked.

Highlight the following about *have:*

- It is strong if it stands alone without a main verb.
- It is weak in the question form.
- It is often contracted in the affirmative if it is followed by a main verb.

2 Get students to repeat the phrases chorally and individually. Start with the stressed word in each phrase so students get the weak forms and contractions right. The other phrases can be 'back-chained' in a similar way.

3 In pairs, practise strong, weak and contracted forms of *have* using the audio script on page 170.

3 Check the question form for asking about a life experience by referring students to the example. Set this up as a competition. Students work in pairs to find six experiences they have had which their partner hasn't. Go through the example with the class. Emphasise that they can use the ideas on page 126 or their own ideas. The winner is the first person to find six differences.

Practice, exercise 3: Alternative suggestion

Before class, prepare a blank strip of paper for each student in the class. Give out one strip of paper to each student and ask them to write an experience they've had using the Present perfect. Emphasise that it doesn't need to be a surprising experience, but it should be one that they haven't already used in this lesson. Circulate and check students are forming the Present perfect correctly. When they have finished, collect all the strips of paper, shuffle them, then redistribute them to students, making sure they have someone else's sentence. Students walk around and try to find the person who wrote the sentence, by asking *Have you … ?* When a student is asked the question, they must lie and say *Yes, I have*. They then need to ask further questions using the Past simple to find out if the student they asked is lying.

ADDITIONAL PRACTICE

Resource bank: Activity 4A *Find someone who … lied!* (Present perfect simple for experience)

Study, practice & remember: Practice 1

Workbook: Language focus 1: *Present perfect and past simple*, pages 22–23; Pronunciation: *Linking in time phrases*, page 23

Reading and speaking (PAGES 38–39)

1 Students discuss the questions in small groups. When they have finished, nominate a student from each group to report their answers to the class.

2 Focus attention on the photos of Andre Agassi and elicit what students know about him, writing their ideas on the board. Students read the text and answer the question in pairs. Check answers with the class and tick any of the information on the board that was mentioned in the text.

ANSWERS:

Agassi is famous as one of the greatest tennis players of all time.
His father trained him intensively as a child.
He became one of the biggest stars in tennis.
He has suffered from drug and other personal problems.
He is married to Steffi Graf, one of the greatest female tennis players.
They have not taught their children to play tennis.

3 Students discuss the questions in pairs.

4 Check the meaning of *under my breath* and *whisper*. Give students two minutes to read the text quickly, then check answers in pairs. Go through the answers with the class.

ANSWERS:

1 He is remembering tennis practice as a child.
2 He hates tennis with all his heart.
3 He is scared of his father and feels he never listens, only shouts.
4 'The dragon' is a ball machine.

5 Emphasise that students should underline the part of the text that gives the answer to each sentence. Students work individually, then check answers in pairs. Go through the answers with the class and ask students to show you which part of the text gives the answers.

ANSWERS:

1 T (I'm talking to myself, because … I'm the only person who listens to me.)
2 F (At the moment my hatred for tennis is focused on the dragon.)
3 T (My father has deliberately made the dragon fearsome.)
4 T (He wants me to beat the dragon. The thought makes me panicky.)
5 F (The dragon is a lot like my father. Except my father is worse.)

6 Go through the example with the class. If students don't have different colour pens, ask them to circle the words related to tennis and underline the words related to Andre's feelings of fear. Students work individually, then compare answers in pairs. Go through the answers with the class, checking understanding of the words.

ANSWERS:

Tennis: a racket, a court, to chase, to bounce, to hit, unbeatable, to beat
Fear: horrifying, a terrifying roar, to flinch, fearsome, to yell, panicky

7 Students discuss the questions in pairs. In feedback, nominate students to share their ideas with the class and find out if other students agree.

8a Go through the statements with the class and check understanding. Students work in groups to decide if they agree or disagree. If they partially agree, get them to state which parts they agree/disagree with. Encourage them to take notes where appropriate.

b Rearrange students into new groups so they are working with other students. Students compare their ideas from exercise 8a.

Practice, exercise 8: Alternative suggestion

Arrange students in two groups. Get one group to think of ideas for each statement and the other group to think of ideas against. Circulate and help with ideas. When they are ready, arrange students in pairs, with one student from each of the previous groups. Students discuss their ideas for and against each statement and try to agree.

Find out more

This can be done in class, or set for homework if you are short of time. Divide students into two groups: 'Andre Agassi', and 'pushy parents'. Students search online and find as much information as they can. When they are ready, tell them that they are going to act out a meeting between Andre Agassi and a 'pushy' parent, using the information they found online. Give them time to prepare what they are going to say, then arrange them in pairs with one person from each of the previous groups. Students roleplay the meeting and share their information. In feedback, nominate pairs to share what they found out with the class.

Vocabulary (PAGE 40)

Life events

See *Teaching tips: Working with lexis*, page 21.

1a Students will be familiar with most of the words in the box, but may not be able to use the full phrases correctly. The pronunciation of the following may need drilling: *retire* /rɪˈtaɪə/, *get engaged* /ˈgetɪŋˈgeɪdʒd/, *get married* /ˈgetˈmærɪd/ and *get divorced* /ˈgetdɪˈvɔːst/. Students work in pairs to categorise the phrases. Circulate and help where necessary. Check answers with the class.

ANSWERS:

Love and relationships: fall in love, get divorced, get engaged, get married
Education: graduate, go to university, leave school, pass your exams, start school
Home and family: bring up your children, have children, leave home, move house, rent or buy a house
Career: change job, get a promotion, get a job, lose your job, make a lot of money, retire, quit your job

b Elicit ideas on the order in which these things usually happen. Emphasise that there are different possibilities. Students discuss the questions in pairs.

2 Emphasise that students should study the phrases before doing the quiz in pairs. If they have started to make vocabulary notes (Remember these words, page 143), this may help them to memorise the phrases. Set the quiz up as a competition. Check answers as a class and see which pair has the most points.

ANSWERS:

1
get a promotion, buy a house, get a job
2
children
3
1 g **2** c **3** b **4** f **5** e **6** a **7** d
4
1 to **2** with **3** to **4** from

ADDITIONAL PRACTICE

Workbook: Vocabulary: *Life events*, page 25

Language focus 2 (PAGES 40–41)

Present perfect simple and Present perfect continuous

See *Teaching tips: Using a discovery approach to grammar*, page 20.

WARM UP

Draw your own lifeline on the board, showing some of the key events in your life. Talk students through it and encourage them to ask you follow-up questions to find out more information.

1 **4.4** Focus students' attention on the photos and elicit what they think each one represents in Meltem's life. Ask one or two questions to check that they understand the concept of the 'lifeline', e.g. *Did she start learning English before or after she joined a band?* Students listen and complete the captions, then check in pairs before checking with the class.

ANSWERS:

3 English **4** 2002 **5** guitar **6** Business **7** 2010 **8** 2011 **9** uncle

2 Students work individually or in pairs before checking answers with the audio script. Students' choice of verb form here will help you to establish if they have noticed the use of the Present perfect continuous in the audio script.

ANSWERS:

1 12 **2** eight **3** answer depends on when students are doing the exercise **4** four **5** 2011 **6** answer depends on when students are doing the exercise **7** answer depends on when students are doing the exercise **8** 20 **9** flat

GRAMMAR

Present perfect simple and Present perfect continuous

1 Students work in pairs, looking back at the examples from Language focus 2, exercise 2 to help them.

ANSWERS:

Present perfect simple: 7, 8

Present perfect continuous: 2, 3, 5, 6, 9

Highlight the following:

- In the question form, only *have* is inverted; *been* doesn't change position.
- the negative form
- the use of *has/hasn't* in the third person singular
- the fact that *been* never changes form
- the contracted forms of *have/has*
- the weak form of *been*: /bɪn/
- The idea of long/repeated actions is one of the most important distinctions between the Present perfect simple and continuous.

2 Point out that *for* refers to a period of time and that *since* refers to a point in time.

ANSWERS:

1 for **2** since

You may want to ask students to read Study 2 on page 142 for a more detailed explanation of the Present perfect simple and Present perfect continuous.

PRACTICE

1 Students work in pairs before checking answers with the class. With weaker classes, it may be useful to do this exercise in two parts: first asking students to choose between *for* and *since* and checking answers before students write the verbs in the correct form.

ANSWERS:

1 has been learning, for, took, has been giving **2** has been studying, for, has passed **3** has been, for, got, since, has been working **4** worked, for, since, bought, has been trying

PRONUNCIATION

See *Teaching tips: Helping students with pronunciation*, page 22.

1 **4.5** Play the recording, pausing after each phrase to allow students to mark where the linking occurs.

ANSWERS:

1 a couple_of minutes_ago **2** since_April **3** for_a while **4** a long time_ago **5** since_eight_o'clock

2 Students practise saying the phrases. Listen carefully to how they are linking the sounds and if necessary, drill with the class, using the 'back-chaining' technique. Highlight that while it's not necessary for students to produce linking 'perfectly' when speaking, an awareness of when it occurs can help them distinguish words when listening to connected speech.

3 **4.6** Pause the recording after each sentence to allow students time to write. Play each sentence several times. Students check answers in pairs before checking with the class.

ANSWERS:

1 He passed his driving test about a year ago.
2 We haven't had a holiday since October.
3 They got married a few weeks ago.
4 They've been married for ages.
5 She hasn't been well for a long time.
6 He's been working here since about 2009.

2a **4.7** Stress that students only need to write a phrase as in the example, not a complete sentence. Pause the recording after each sentence, replaying if necessary.

b Use the recording to check answers and work on pronunciation as you go along. Insist on the correct use of the verb forms in the reconstructed questions.

3a Remind students of the kind of information on Meltem's lifeline and give them ten minutes to prepare their own.

b Circulate giving help, suggestions and vocabulary. To make the practice more controlled/accuracy-oriented, get students to write sentences about themselves similar to the ones in Language focus 2, exercise 2, on page 40. Check and correct them as you go round.

c Demonstrate the activity with a student. Circulate and note down both good and bad examples of the use of verb forms and time words. Write up about ten sentences and ask students to identify the correct ones, and correct those that are wrong.

d Rearrange students so they are working in pairs from different groups. Students share the information they found out in exercise 3c and find out if they have anything in common.

ADDITIONAL PRACTICE

Resource bank: Activity 4B *How long have you had it?* (Present perfect simple and Present perfect continuous)

Study, practice & remember: Practice 2

Workbook: Language focus 2: *Present perfect simple and Present perfect continuous*, pages 26–27

Vocabulary (PAGE 42)

Personal qualities

See *Teaching tips: Working with lexis*, page 21.

WARM UP

Tell students that you are going to do a personality test. Ask students to write down three adjectives of personality – the first three that they can think of. Elicit the adjectives they wrote first, then explain that this is how they think of themselves. Elicit the second adjective, then explain that this is how other people see them. Elicit the third, then explain that this is how they truly are. Find out if they agree.

1 If you have access to dictionaries, distribute them to students so they can check the meanings. Students work in pairs before checking answers with the class. Check the pronunciation of *courageous* /kəˈreɪdʒəs/, *determined* /dɪˈtɜːmɪnd/, *egotistical* /iːgəʊˈtɪstɪkəl/ and *inspiring* /ɪnˈspaɪrɪŋ/, paying particular attention to word stress.

ANSWERS:

Positive: charming, courageous, creative, dedicated, determined, inspiring, original, self-confident, talented, He/She's got strong principles, He/She's a strong leader, He/She cares a lot about other people, He/She inspires respect.

Negative: egotistical, obsessive, ruthless, He/She doesn't care about other people, He/She likes publicity.

2a Elicit one or two examples from students. Students work individually, then compare answers in pairs.

b Encourage students to use the words and phrases from exercise 1. When they are ready, they compare and explain their answers in groups. In feedback, nominate students from each group to share their ideas with the class.

3 Give students time to complete the sentences individually. When they have finished, arrange them in groups to compare their answers.

ADDITIONAL PRACTICE

Resource bank: Activity 4C *What sort of person are you?* (Vocabulary extension: personal qualities)

Workbook: Vocabulary: *Personal qualities*, page 27

Task (PAGES 42–43)

Nominate someone for an award

See *Teaching tips: Making tasks work*, page 23.

Preparation (PAGE 42)

Listening

1 Check the meaning of *remarkable*, *outstanding* and *against the odds*. Students read the information, then answer the question in pairs.

ANSWER:

someone who has inspired others, helped others, provided a role model or achieved something very difficult

2 Focus attention on the photos and elicit students' ideas.

3a 🎧 **4.8–4.12** Give students a minute to choose three people and then do a tally on the board to find out who wants to listen to their nominations. If not all the people are mentioned, you won't need to play all of the recordings. Play the recordings, pausing for students to make notes before comparing their ideas. Play the recording again if necessary before checking answers with the class.

ANSWER:

1 Emma Watson: She hasn't let fame and money change her.
2 Lionel Messi: He's an excellent role model for boys and young men because he shows that you don't have to be selfish and egotistical to be successful. **3** Mark Zuckerberg: He's changed the way we live and how we communicate./He's an excellent role model for young people because he wanted to change the world and he succeeded.
4 Aung San Suu Kyi: She has led and inspired people for more than 20 years. **5** Jamie Foxx: He is incredibly talented.

b Focus students' attention on the Useful language box and go through the phrases. Students listen and tick the phrases they hear. Check answers with the class, then drill the phrases in the Useful language box.

ANSWERS:

1 He/She became famous (playing the role of ...); He/She has (won gold medals/written some amazing songs, etc.).; He/She's exceptionally talented/determined.; I really admire him/her because ...
2 My nomination for the Inspiration Award is ... ; He/She has done a lot for (sick children).; He/She's an excellent role model for (young people).
3 He has done a lot for (sick children).; He/She cares (a lot) about other people.; He/She's an excellent role model for (young people).
4 My nomination for the Inspiration Award is ... ; What is amazing about him/her is ...; I think she deserves to win because ...
5 What is amazing about him/her is ... ; I think he deserves to win because ...

Task (PAGE 43)

Speaking

1 Give students time to choose a person they want to nominate. Emphasise that it doesn't need to be someone famous.

2 Go through the headings with the class, then encourage students to make notes on the person they chose in exercise 1. Circulate, answering vocabulary questions.

3 Remind students to look back at the phrases in the Useful language box, sections a–d, then plan what they are going to say. Circulate and help where necessary.

4a Students take turns to give their nomination speeches to the class. If possible, select a clip from a video-sharing website which shows music/applause at an awards ceremony to play before and after each speech to add atmosphere. Encourage students to take notes as they listen, as they will need these for the next stage.

b Give students time to choose the winner, runner-up and third place, then hold a class vote, writing the results on the board.

ADDITIONAL PRACTICE

Resource bank: Activity 4D *Wordspot:* take (Collocations with *take*)

Follow up (PAGE 43)

Writing

1 This can be done either in class or as homework. Display the students' finished work on the classroom wall.

Share your task

Some additional ideas could include:

- Students film themselves giving each nomination speech, then compile them as a documentary.
- Students could show their recordings to another class, who choose the winner.
- Students imagine they are the person who received the award and film/record themselves giving an acceptance speech.

World culture (PAGES 44–45)

Charles Dickens: Writer and campaigner

Culture notes

Charles Dickens was an English writer, journalist and social campaigner who lived from 1812–1870. He is considered to be the greatest English writer of the Victorian era and his works often provided a social commentary of the time, criticising attitudes that were common among the middle classes at the time. His works often aimed to shock with their descriptions of poverty and crime, perhaps most notably in his novel *Oliver Twist*. Other famous works include *David Copperfield*, *Great Expectations*, *A Tale of Two Cities*, *The Pickwick Papers*, *Bleak House*, *The Old Curiosity Shop* and *Little Dorrit*.

His novels were often published in weekly or monthly parts and he was the first writer to serialise his novels in this way.

One of his most famous stories, *A Christmas Carol*, is considered to be one of the most influential works ever written and remains popular today, with numerous film adaptations.

Find out first (PAGE 44)

1 Focus attention on the pictures and elicit what students can see (a Victorian workhouse for the poor and Charles Dickens). Discuss the questions as a class and write students' ideas on the board. Don't feed in any information from the Culture notes yet.

2a Students discuss the questions in pairs. Don't check answers with the class yet. Students may know the titles of other famous novels in their own language, but not in English. If this is the case, then ask them to try and translate before giving them the titles in English.

b If you have access to the internet, students can research the answers individually, then check in pairs, using the search terms to help them. In feedback, check answers with the class and feed in any additional information from the Culture notes.

ANSWERS:

1 1812–70 **2** *Oliver Twist, David Copperfield* **3** *A Christmas Carol, Bleak House, Great Expectations, The Old Curiosity Shop, The Pickwick Papers, A Tale of Two Cities, Little Dorrit*
4 He was a journalist and social campaigner.

View (PAGE 44)

See *Teaching tips: Using the video material in the classroom*, page 24.

3a Give students time to read the definitions in the glossary, then be ready to answer any questions students have with further examples/explanations if necessary. Check the pronunciation of *debt*: /det/.

View, exercise 3a: Alternative suggestion

With stronger classes, ask students to close their books and write the words on the board. Students use dictionaries or search online to find out what they mean, then check in pairs. Ask students to open their books and compare their definitions with those in the book before checking understanding with the class.

b Go through each sentence with the class and ask students to predict each answer, writing their ideas on the board. Play the DVD for students to watch and check their answers. Students check answers in pairs before checking with the class. As you go through the answers, tick any predictions on the board that students made correctly.

ANSWERS:

1 W **2** W **3** C **4** F **5** C/F **6** C **7** W **8** W

4 Give students time to read the reasons and check understanding before playing the DVD again. Students check answers in pairs before checking with the class.

ANSWERS:

He seems very human and real.
He really wanted to make the world a better place.
He was very passionate about what he believed in.
What he wrote about is still relevant today.

World view (PAGE 45)

5 Go through the questions with the class and check students understand what to watch for. Play the DVD for students to make notes.

ANSWERS:

1 George Orwell **2** Frederico Garcia Lorca **3** Tom Hanks
4 Desmond Tutu

6 Students compare their notes in small groups before checking answers with the class.

ANSWERS:

George Orwell: to ask why he wrote the books, admires his work; Frederico Garcia Lorca: he was a man of the people, admires him taking theatre to rural Spain; Tom Hanks: he's inspirational, admires the diverse roles he's played, the awards he's won and the fact he does a lot for charity; Desmond Tutu: a great leader and political figure, admires his energy and the fact he takes issues personally

7 Students discuss the question in small groups.

World view: Additional activity

After students have compared and checked their notes in exercise 6, ask them to stay in the same groups and discuss the questions from exercise 5 about people from their country/-ies. In feedback, nominate a student from each group to share their information with the class.

Find out more (PAGE 45)

8a Books closed. Write the names of the three people on the board and elicit what students know about them. Students then work in pairs to complete the table with as much information as they can. Emphasise that they shouldn't worry if they don't know much, as they'll have a chance to research the people afterwards.

ANSWERS:

	Mother Teresa	Florence Nightingale	Desmond Tutu
Where/ when born	26 August 1910, Albania	12 May 1820, Florence, Italy	7 October 1931, South Africa
Family background, etc.	father involved in Albanian politics; left home at 18 to become a missionary and never saw her mother or sister again	from a rich, upper-class, well-connected British family	father a teacher, mother a cleaner and cook
Job/role	Catholic nun	nurse	archbishop
What they campaigned for/ achieved	ministered to the poor, sick, orphaned and dying; received the 1979 Nobel Peace Prize	helped to found professional nursing with the establishment, in 1860, of her nursing school at St Thomas' Hospital in London	human rights

b Students go online to research the three people and complete the table. Focus on the search terms given to help them. Circulate while they are online and help with any vocabulary where necessary. When they are ready, students compare what they found out in small groups.

Write up your research

9 Go through the prompts with the class and elicit ways to finish each one as examples. Students write their paragraphs individually, using their notes from exercise 8b. Circulate and help where necessary and write any new words/phrases on the board. When they have finished, put students in pairs to check and correct each other's work.

Write up your research, exercise 9: Alternative suggestion

Ask students to write their paragraphs on a piece of paper, and to use *X* instead of *he* or *she*. When they have finished, collect the paragraphs and display them around the class. Students walk around, read the paragraphs and guess which person each one is describing.

Students can now do Unit test 2 on the Teacher's Resource Disc.

Study, practice & remember

(PAGES 141–143)

See *Teaching tips: Using the Study, practice & remember sections*, page 25.

Practice 1

ANSWERS:

1

1 achieved, achieved **2** built, built **3** brought, brought **4** chose, chosen **5** designed, designed **6** heard, heard **7** inspired, inspired **8** produced, produced **9** read, read **10** taught, taught **11** thought, thought **12** won, won

3

1 wrote, have been **2** died, has had, produced **3** has had, has worked, has received, has won, won, received **4** is, has made, appeared, won, came, won, has made

Practice 2

ANSWERS:

1

for: five minutes, ages and ages, months, 30 years, ten seconds, three weeks **since:** 6 o'clock, 2009, I was born, last summer

2

1 finished, emailed (The actions are both complete.)
2 has been staying (The action is not complete.)
3 been working (We want to emphasise the action is long.)
4 written (The focus is on the result.)
5 been driving (We want to emphasise the action is long.)
6 had (a state verb)
7 been going (The action is repeated.)
8 made (The focus is on the result.)

Remember these words

ANSWERS:

1

1 e **2** k **3** a **4** i **5** l **6** o **7** j **8** g **9** n **10** c **11** b **12** h **13** f **14** d **15** m

2

to admire, admiration, admiring
to inspire, inspiration, inspirational
to respect, respect, respectable/respectful
charm courage determination dedication
self-confidence talent

3

1 admire **2** deserved **3** won **4** chase **5** does a lot **6** get

Study tips

1 Before students read the tips, ask them how they usually read grammar summaries in books. Students read the tips and tick the ones they follow.

2 Students compare their answers in pairs. In feedback, go through the sentences and elicit the benefits of each one. Allow the discussion to develop naturally and write any other tips the students have on the board.

OVERVIEW

PAGES 46–47

Reading: Getting ahead in the 21st century

Vocabulary: Word families

Pronunciation: Word stress

Common European Framework: Students can read straightforward factual texts on subjects related to their field of interest; can express themselves on topics such as work.

PAGES 48–49

Grammar: Future forms

Vocabulary: Work

Common European Framework: Students can express their thoughts about abstract or cultural topics such as the future; can express themselves on topics such as work.

PAGES 50–51

Grammar: Future clauses with *if, when, unless*, etc.

Listening and speaking: Career crossroads

Common European Framework: Students can communicate with accuracy in familiar contexts; can understand the main points on familiar matters encountered in work.

PAGES 52–53

Task: Choose who to hire or fire!

Common European Framework: Students can exchange, check and confirm accumulated factual information on familiar matters with confidence.

PAGES 54–55

Writing: A CV

Speaking: Making a formal telephone call

Common European Framework: Students can write connected texts on familiar subjects within their field of interest; can find out and pass on factual information.

Reading (PAGES 46–47)

WARM UP

Write *the four 'C's* on the board, and explain that these relate to '21st century skills'. Elicit what they are and write them on the board (*communication, collaboration, critical thinking* and *creativity*). Ask students to think about how they use these skills in their jobs or studies and share ideas in pairs.

1 Go over the examples with the class, then students work in small groups. In feedback, elicit students' ideas and write them on the board.

2 Check the meaning of *graduates, make a fortune* and *avoid distractions*. Encourage students to read the text quickly, just looking for the ideas they came up with in exercise 1. Check answers with the class and tick any of the ideas on the board that were mentioned in the article.

3 Give students time to read the sentences first and decide if they are true or false. Students work individually to read the text again, then check answers in pairs. Check answers with the class and ask students to tell you which part of the text helped them decide.

4 Ask students which advice they found the most useful.

ANSWERS:

1 T 2 F (He suggests spending ten percent of your time on personal improvement.) 3 F (He tried at least 6,000 different materials for his light bulb before finding one that worked.) 4 T 5 F (She believes we should tackle our most important projects first.) 6 F (Her boss fired her after reading what she wrote in her online profile.) 7 F (Your contacts are important as well as talent, imagination and hard work.) 8 T

Find out more ⓢ

This can be done in class or set for homework if you are short of time. Students choose one of the people in the article and search individually online to find out as much information as they can. When they are ready, arrange students in pairs and ask them to interview each other, imagining they are the people they found out about. Nominate students to share any interesting information with the class.

Vocabulary (PAGE 47)

Word families

See *Teaching tips: Working with lexis*, page 21.

1 Students work in pairs to complete the table before checking answers with the whole class.

ANSWERS:

1 experience 2 failure 3 imagination 4 improvement
5 knowledge 6 productive 7 success

PRONUNCIATION

See *Teaching tips: Helping students with pronunciation*, page 20.

1 🎧 5.1 Students mark the stress, saying the words aloud to their partner to help them decide where the stress falls. Play the recording as many times as necessary, pausing after each word for students to decide where the stress is.

ANSWERS:

ex<u>pe</u>rience, <u>fail</u>, i<u>ma</u>gine, im<u>prove</u>, <u>know</u>, pro<u>duce</u>, suc<u>ceed</u>

2 🎧 5.2 Play the recording once for students to decide if the stress is the same or different. Check answers, then play the recording again, pausing after each group of words for students to mark the stress.

ANSWERS:

dis<u>tract</u>, dis<u>trac</u>tion, dis<u>trac</u>ting ex<u>pe</u>rience, ex<u>pe</u>rience, ex<u>pe</u>rienced <u>fail</u>, <u>fail</u>ure i<u>ma</u>gine, ima<u>gi</u>nation, i<u>ma</u>ginative im<u>prove</u>, im<u>prove</u>ment <u>know</u>, <u>know</u>ledge, <u>know</u>ledgeable pro<u>duce</u>, pro<u>duc</u>tion, pro<u>duc</u>tive <u>pro</u>fit, <u>pro</u>fit, <u>pro</u>fitable suc<u>ceed</u>, suc<u>cess</u>, suc<u>cess</u>ful

Highlight that:

- in nouns which end with *-tion* or *-sion*, the stress is always on the preceding syllable.
- the letter *-e* in the first syllable of a word, when it is unstressed, shortens to /ɪ/.
- *succeed* is pronounced /sək'si:d/, not /su:k'si:d/.

3 Drill the words before students practise saying them aloud with a partner.

2a Students work in pairs to complete the quotes, then check their answers on page 126.

ANSWERS:

1 Imagination **2** sucess, failure
3 Knowledge **4** profit

b Students discuss the questions in pairs. In feedback, nominate students to share their ideas with the class and find out if other students agree.

ADDITIONAL PRACTICE

Workbook: Vocabulary: *Word families*, page 28

Language focus 1 (PAGES 48–49)

Future forms

See *Teaching tips: Using a discovery approach to grammar*, page 20.

WARM UP

Before class, cut up some blank strips of paper, one for each student. Write on the board: *Next year, I hope ...* and ask students to finish the sentence in a way that is true for them on their strips of paper. Circulate and help with vocabulary where necessary. Collect the strips of paper and redistribute them so that each student has a different one. Students walk around and find the person who wrote that sentence by asking: *Do you hope to ... next year?*, then ask that person questions to find out more information. In feedback, nominate students to share their ideas with the class.

1a Check students' understanding of *enrol, get a promotion, deal with (a problem)* and *maternity leave*. Students do the quiz individually.

b Students check their score on page 127 and read the interpretation. Ask students if they agree with the results.

2 Students compare their results in pairs. In feedback, nominate a few students and ask if they agree with the description of their partner, giving reasons.

3a Do an example with the first question and answers to demonstrate. Students work individually, then check answers in pairs before checking with the class.

ANSWERS:

***going to* + verb:** you're going to do it, you're not going to show it, I'm only going to work hard if, I'm going to do my best
***will* + verb:** will be useful, he'll do a great job, your family will be upset, I'll achieve what I want, I'll find a job
Present continuous: your local college is running a course, you're doing a lot, you're not going

b With weaker classes, point out *intend to* in answer 2a as an example. Students work individually before checking answers with the class.

ANSWERS:

you're (just) about to, you intend to, one of your colleagues is due to, you hope to, you're planning to, you're thinking of

GRAMMAR

Future forms

Notes on the approach to future forms

Will versus *going to*: we have chosen not to contrast *will* for spontaneous decisions with *going to* for plans for several reasons. Research suggests that *will* is the most common way of talking about the future and that the most common use of *will* is the one described here. *Will* for spontaneous decisions is less frequent. When it does occur, it is often in the communicative context of 'offers' or 'on the spot' responses. This is dealt with separately in Unit 8, within the context of polite requests.

1 Students choose the correct alternative, then find examples in the quiz for each of the three forms. Explain or translate the following: *to predict, an intention*. Students work in pairs to try to complete the rules. All three forms should be familiar, but it may be useful to remind students briefly of the following points:

- the contraction of *will* (*'ll*) and *will not* (*won't*)
- the difference in form between the Present continuous and *going to* (with *going to,* the main verb is in the infinitive)

ANSWERS:

1 the Present continuous **2** going to **3** will

2 Students find the examples in the quiz, then discuss with the whole class. Check the meaning of the verbs and phrases, especially *about to* and *due to*. Point out, by using examples, which constructions are followed by a gerund and which are followed by an infinitive. Highlight the following:

- the use of prepositions with these verbs/phrases
- that *due* can be used either with an infinitive (as in the example given) or without (*You're due at a meeting*).

ANSWERS:

You intend to find out why, I intend to be successful
You're planning to speak to your boss
Secretly, you hope to keep the job
You're thinking of asking your boss about it
you're just about to enter the world of work, You are about to leave work
One of your colleagues is due to go on maternity leave

Potential problem with *going to* and the Present continuous

Students may find the difference between these two forms difficult to see. This is partly because there is a genuine overlap: *going to* can almost always be used instead of the Present continuous. However, the Present continuous cannot be used where there is just a vague intention; there must be some kind of arrangement, involving more than one person. A simplified way of showing the difference is by asking: *What's the minimum number of people an intention can involve?* (1) *What's the minimum number of people an arrangement can involve?* (2).

You may want to ask students to read Study 1 on page 144 for a more detailed explanation of future forms.

PRACTICE

If you think students need more controlled practice before doing these exercises, they could do Practice 1 on pages 144–145 first.

1 Students work in pairs before checking answers with the class. Emphasise that form is important.

ANSWERS:

1 My best friend is due to join the army next month.
2 My boss is about to go on maternity leave.
3 I hope to get a pay rise soon.
4 My dad is going to retire next month.
5 Ally doesn't intend to work here for long.
6 I'm thinking of applying for a master's degree next year.

2 Look at the examples with students. Emphasise that they should make sentences with a future meaning and that they don't need to use all the prompts. Circulate as students work individually, checking the accuracy of their work. Check answers as a whole class.

3a Put students into pairs and refer them to page 127. Do an example with the class by choosing three numbers yourself and asking a student to read out the three instructions to you. As students write complete sentences, circulate and help with any extra vocabulary they need. Note down any errors with the use of future forms for correction later on.

b Students compare their answers.

ADDITIONAL PRACTICE

Resource bank: Activity 5A *Back to the future* (Future forms)

Study, practice & remember: Practice 1

Workbook: Language focus 1: *Future forms*, pages 28–29

Vocabulary (PAGE 49)

Work

See *Teaching tips: Working with lexis*, page 21.

1 Check the meaning of *wouldn't mind doing*. Emphasise that students should keep their notes secret until later.

2a Students work individually or in pairs, using a dictionary. At the feedback stage, check the meaning and pronunciation of *physically* /'fɪzɪkli:/, *qualifications* /kwɒlɪfɪ'keɪʃənz/, *secure* /sɪ'kjʊə/, *competitive* /kəm'petɪtɪv/, *challenging* /'ʧæləndʒɪŋ/, *responsibility* /rɪspɒnsɪ'bɪlɪti/ and *opportunities* /ɒpə'tju:nɪtɪz/.

Potential problem with the vocabulary

Students may have difficulty distinguishing between *training*, *qualifications* and *skills*.

Training is education aimed at providing you with the skills to do a job (*training to be a doctor, teacher-training, etc.*).

Qualifications are exams/certificates you get, especially those which enable you to do a particular job.

Skills are the abilities you have in a particular area; you get them from training courses or experience, or you have them naturally. This word is often used in the plural – *people skills, management skills*, etc.

b Put students into pairs to discuss their opinions.

3 Students decide which jobs they think would interest their partner before working in pairs. Do some class feedback to find out if anybody's suggested jobs matched what their partner had written.

ADDITIONAL PRACTICE

Workbook: Vocabulary: *Work*, pages 30–31

Language focus 2 (PAGES 50–51)

Future clauses with *if*, *when*, *unless*, etc.

See *Teaching tips: Using a discovery approach to grammar*, page 20.

1 Focus students' attention on the photos and check the meaning of *crossroads* in this context. Students read the text, then discuss the question in pairs.

2 Emphasise that some of the sentences can refer to more than one choice. Students work individually, then check answers in pairs before checking with the class.

ANSWERS:

1 travel/get married **2** work as a lawyer **3** travel
4 travel/get married **5** get married **6** retrain

GRAMMAR

Future clauses with *if*, *when*, *unless*, etc.

1 Do the first example with the class and then get students to do the other examples before checking answers together.

ANSWERS:

1 settle down **2** fail **3** feel **4** get back
5 make up my mind **6** have

2 Discuss the questions with the whole class.

ANSWERS:

We use the Present simple after the conjunction. Future forms are used in the other clause.

3 Students compare the sentences in pairs before checking with the whole class.

ANSWERS:

1 'If I leave my job' = It is a possibility I will leave;
'When I leave my job' = It is certain that I will leave.
2 The two sentences have similar meanings.

You may want to ask students to read Study 2 on page 145 for a more detailed explanation of future clauses with *if, when, unless*, etc.

PRACTICE

1 Students work individually or in pairs before checking answers with the class.

ANSWERS:

1 If, goes, 'll still need **2** won't be, unless, listens **3** will love, as soon as, walks **4** If, becomes, won't earn **5** won't get, until, gets **6** When, makes, 'll feel **7** will be, if, goes **8** will need, before, makes

2a Students complete the sentences individually. Circulate and help with ideas and vocabulary.

b Students compare their answers in pairs.

3 Look at the examples with the class. Students work in small groups. As students work, circulate and note down any errors in the use of future clauses with *if, when*, etc. to focus on in feedback.

ADDITIONAL PRACTICE

Resource bank: 5B *The great diamond robbery* (Future clauses with *if, when, unless*, etc.)

Study, practice & remember: Practice 2

Workbook: Language focus 2: *Future clauses with if, when, unless, etc.*, page 31

Listening and speaking (PAGE 51)

Career crossroads

1 Discuss the questions with the whole class and encourage everyone to contribute.

2 5.3 Focus students' attention on the photos and ask what they think their chosen careers are. Check the meaning of *promote yourself, a catch 22 situation, CV* and *volunteer*. Play the recording for students to answer the questions and then check in pairs. If necessary, play the recording again before going through the answers with the class.

ANSWERS:

1 Gavin: advertising, Molly: (graphic) design, Delmar: he doesn't know yet **2** Gavin: no, Molly: yes, Delmar: no

3a Students work in pairs to allocate the questions before listening again. Check answers with the class.

ANSWERS:

1 D **2** G **3** M **4** M, D **5** D **6** M **7** G **8** D **9** G **10** D

b Students work in pairs to see how much they can remember. If necessary, play the recording again before checking answers with the class.

ANSWERS:

1 Delmar worked in banking for five years until his job was cut after a merger. **2** Gavin mainly uses the internet to promote himself, but he also checks job websites every day. **3** Molly found that you can't get a job without experience and you can't get experience without a job. **4** Molly offered to work for free for a few months to get experience and she is now doing that part-time. Delmar is working as a volunteer for a wildlife conservation project. **5** Delmar got a nasty shock when he was told that his job didn't exist anymore. **6** Molly is optimistic that the company she is working for will offer her a permanent job soon because they seem to like her and what she's doing. **7** Gavin is advertising his skills online by setting up a website with examples of what he can do and he also has a blog. **8** Delmar is working for a wildlife conservation charity in Africa. **9** Gavin is using social networking sites like Twitter to tell his online contacts that he's looking for work. **10** Delmar is fulfilling his dream to spend time in the African wilderness.

4 Students discuss the questions in groups while you circulate and supply any vocabulary needed.

Task (PAGES 52–53)

Choose who to hire or fire!

See *Teaching tips: Making tasks work*, page 23.

Preparation (PAGE 53)

Reading and listening

1 Focus students' attention on the photos and explain that they show contestants in a reality TV show called *The Executive*. Ask the class what they think the programme is about. Students read the text and then answer the questions in pairs. Go through the answers with the class.

ANSWERS:

1 a $75,000-a-year position as an executive in one of Sir Darren Sweet's companies **2** work in teams on business-related tasks **3** Sir Darren Sweet and his board **4** Sir Darren is a 'self-made man' – he left school at 15 with no qualifications and started working on a market stall. However, he now owns several companies and is a multi-millionaire. **5** three

2a 5.4 Go through the list of qualities with the class and check understanding. Students listen and tick the ones Sir Darren mentions, then check answers in pairs.

ANSWERS:

He mentions all of them.

b Students listen again and answer the question in pairs. Check answers with the class.

ANSWERS:

good business sense and the ability to achieve things

Preparation: Reading and listening: Alternative suggestion

If you are short of time, briefly introduce the TV show yourself, summarising the skills and qualities needed and omitting exercises 1 and 2 completely.

Task (PAGE 53)

Speaking and listening

1a Check the meaning of *wealthy/poor background* and *supermarket checkout*. Give students three minutes to read the profiles and memorise as much information as they can.

b Students close their books and see how much they can remember in groups. When they have finished, ask them to look at the profiles again and see if they missed anything.

2 5.5 Play the recording, pausing after each candidate is discussed for students to compare their notes.

3 Arrange students in groups of four and ask them to choose one candidate each. If you don't have the right number of students, you could have a group of five, where two students discuss the same candidate, or a group of three, where one student describes two candidates. Circulate and help where necessary.

ANSWERS:

Mark: Strengths: everyone likes him, works well in a team, has leadership skills, takes responsibility for things, achieves things, very hard-working and motivated
Weaknesses: doesn't always make good decisions, not a natural businessman, doesn't have great business sense, not always clear what he's trying to say
Melody: Strengths: funny and honest, good at motivating people, a leader, makes decisions and gets things done
Weaknesses: gets into lots of arguments, not very good in a team,
Freddie: Strengths: fluent, charming, intelligent, talented, has potential
Weaknesses: all talk and doesn't like making decisions, lets other people do the hard work
Nikita: Strengths: gets things done in a quiet way, proved she's a businesswoman by raising money for charity, focused and determined, takes responsibility and makes decisions, can be a leader
Weaknesses: may not inspire other people, not a great communicator

4 Give students time to work individually and decide what they are going to say. Refer them to the Useful language box, sections a–c. When they are ready, students discuss their choices in the same groups as exercise 3 and agree on three candidates to go through.

5a Give students time to plan how they are going to present their choices and refer them to the Useful language box, section d. When they are ready, groups take it in turns to present their choices to the class.

b **5.6** Play the recording for students to compare their choices with Sir Darren's.

ANSWERS:

4th: Freddie, 3rd: Mark, 2nd: Nikita, 1st: Melody

ADDITIONAL PRACTICE

Resource bank: 5C *Vocabulary extension* (Talking about work and training)

Task: Speaking and listening: Alternative suggestion

Using the feedback/correction stage of the task for revision purposes
This task brings together much of the language that students have studied in the first five units of this book. While performing the task, students will almost certainly need to use present tenses, past tenses, the Present perfect simple and continuous, comparatives, superlatives and future time clauses. Collect errors in these five categories as a lead-in to a revision session. Copy these onto the board and give them to students to correct in pairs. Refer students to the appropriate rules and Study, practice & remember sections for revision where necessary.

Share your task

Some additional ideas could include:

- Students film/record themselves giving their summaries, then the class watches/listens and chooses the best three.
- Students take on the roles of the candidates and Sir Darren in groups and film themselves informing the candidates of their choices in the style of a reality TV show.
- Students each choose a candidate and record themselves explaining why they should go through. The class then listens and chooses the best one.
- Students imagine they are candidates on the TV show, but describe themselves. They then record themselves explaining why they should go through for the class to listen and choose.

Language live (PAGES 54–55)

Writing

A CV

WARM UP

Write the following jobs on the board: *fitness instructor, computer programmer, teacher, secretary, scientist, fashion designer*. Remind students of the vocabulary in exercise 2a on page 49 and ask them to discuss which skills are needed for each job in pairs.

1 Check the meaning of *charity, elderly, disadvantaged* and *domestic appliances*. Students read the job adverts, then discuss the questions in pairs.

2a Introduce the idea of a CV (Curriculum Vitae) and ask if it's common in the students' countries. Students read Sean's CV, then answer the question in pairs. In feedback, nominate students to share their ideas with the class.

b Students work individually, then check answers in pairs. Check answers with the class. Check pronunciation of *interpersonal* /ɪntə'pɜːsənəl/, *placement* /'pleɪsmənt/, *tongue* /tʌŋ/ and *combined* /kəm'baɪnd/.

ANSWERS:

1 strong interpersonal skills **2** work placement **3** graduate
4 mother tongue **5** the ability to work in a team
6 non-smoker **7** combined with

3a Discuss the question as a class.

ANSWER:

computer trainer

b Students work individually, then check answers in pairs before checking with the whole class.

ANSWERS:

Profile: excellent computer skills, experience of one-to-one training, strong interpersonal skills, the ability to work in a team
Experience: learning how good IT trainers work, helping to train people in basic computer skills, volunteer: working with disadvantaged teenagers and helping them to learn new computer skills
Excellent computer skills and *strong interpersonal skills* come directly from the advert.

4 Go through the example with the class and explain that it's important (in Britain) to keep a CV concise. Student find more examples in pairs before checking with the class.

ANSWERS:

I am a final year student in Information Technology at the Leeds Metropolitan University.
I have excellent computer skills combined with experience of one-to-one training.
I have strong interpersonal skills and the ability to work in a team.
I did a two-month work placement with an IT training company.
I worked as a volunteer for a local charity.
I'm doing/studying for a BA degree in Information Technology at the Leeds Metropolitan University and I'm due to graduate in July.
I'm a high school graduate. I studied at Thomas Manly Secondary School in Leeds.
I have a full clean driving licence.
I'm a non-smoker.
I speak English and Hindi to mother tongue level, I speak fluent Urdu and I have conversational Spanish.
My interests include sport, reading and photography.
References are available on request.

5a Allow plenty of time for students to make notes and go round answering their questions about vocabulary. Refer students back to *Vocabulary* on page 49 if necessary.

b Give students time to write their CVs individually. Circulate and help where necessary. When they have finished, go through the checklist with the class, then give students time to check their writing.

6 Students swap CVs with a partner, then read and decide if they would get an interview.

Writing, exercise 6: Alternative suggestions

a When students have written their CVs, brainstorm common interview questions with the class and write them on the board. Students swap CVs in pairs and interview each other for the job.

b Arrange students in groups of three and swap their CVs with another group. Students imagine they are board members and decide whether to give each CV an interview.

Speaking

Making a formal telephone call

See *Teaching tips: Using the video material in the classroom*, page 24.

1a Check understanding of the questions, then play the DVD for students to answer them. Students compare answers in pairs before checking with the class.

ANSWERS:

Sean is calling about a job application and a job advert.
The first receptionist is more polite.

b Students complete the phrases in pairs before watching the DVD again to check their answers. Go through the answers with the class.

ANSWERS:

1 speak **2** available **3** calling **4** concerning **5** message **6** back
7 take **8** urgent **9** let **10** speak **11** about **12** speaking

PRONUNCIATION

See *Teaching tips: Helping students with pronunciation*, page 22.

1 Play the DVD, pausing after each question for students to copy the intonation. Use gestures to show the direction of the intonation when students are repeating.

2 Students write their answers individually before checking in pairs. Go through the answers with the class and drill the phrases, paying attention to intonation.

ANSWERS:

Can I ask who's calling?
Could I ask what the call is concerning?
OK, could you hold the line while I try to put you through?

3 Refer students to the correct pages (As: page 128; Bs: page 130) and give them time to think about what they are going to say. Students practise the conversations in pairs. If you have time, ask students to swap roles and practise again. When they have finished, ask one or two pairs to perform their conversations to the class.

ADDITIONAL PRACTICE

Workbook: Writing: *A letter of reference*, page 33
Language live: *Making a formal telephone call*, page 33

Study, practice & remember

(PAGES 144–146)

See *Teaching tips: Using the Study, practice & remember sections, page 25.*

Practice 1

ANSWERS:

1

1 a **2** b **3** b **4** c **5** a **6** b **7** b

2

1 I'm meeting **2** I'm going to have **3** you'll like it
4 we're not going to have **5** they'll get married one day

3

1 to start **2** planning **3** going **4** to start **5** to buy

4

1 I am planning to study engineering.
2 My sister is thinking of joining the army.
3 I am due to take my driving test next week.
4 Alex says he is not going to apply to university.
5 I know I won't get the job.
6 My boss is about to retire.
7 I probably won't see you before next week.

Practice 2

ANSWERS:

1

1 if **2** before **3** As soon as **4** unless **5** until

2

1 if **2** when **3** before **4** unless **5** after **6** until **7** when
8 as soon as **9** If **10** after

3

1 I will get home **2** I don't live at home **3** you will leave
4 unless it will rain **5** they move house **6** I will find another one

4

1 'll ask, gets **2** arrives **3** 'll pass, remember **4** Will you visit, are

Remember these words

ANSWERS:

1

1 a/h **2** e **3** b **4** h/a **5** f **6** g **7** c **8** d

2

1 sucess, successful **2** talent, talented **3** focus, focused
4 determination, determined

3

1 distracting **2** produce **3** stressful **4** experienced
5 determined **6** responsibility **7** ambitious **8** imaginative
9 failure **10** knowledgeable

Study tips

1 Before students read the tips, elicit their answers to the question and write their ideas on the board. Students read the sentences quickly to see if any of their ideas are mentioned. Students then read the tips again and tick the ones they follow.

2 Students compare their answers in pairs. In feedback, go through the sentences and elicit the benefits of each one. Allow the discussion to develop naturally and write any other tips the students have on the board.

3 Students work individually, then compare their ideas in pairs.

OVERVIEW

PAGES 56–57

Grammar: Past perfect

Pronunciation: Past simple and Past perfect

Common European Framework: Students can describe past activities; can understand the information content of audio material delivered in clear speech.

PAGES 58–59

Grammar: Reported speech

Vocabulary: *say* and *tell*

Common European Framework: Students can synthesise and report information and arguments from a number of sources.

PAGES 60–61

Reading and speaking: It really happened to me!

Vocabulary: Adverbs for telling stories

Common European Framework: Students can read factual texts on subjects related to their interest; can express themselves on topics pertinent to their interests.

PAGES 62–63

Task: Retell a story

Common European Framework: Students can narrate a story.

PAGES 64–65

World culture: A story that rocked the world

Common European Framework: Students can understand most TV news and current affairs programmes; can describe experiences and events.

Language focus 1 (PAGES 56–57)

Past perfect

See *Teaching tips: Using a discovery approach to grammar*, page 20.

WARM UP

Tell the class about a book or film that you have enjoyed recently and encourage them to ask you follow-up questions to find out more information. Students work in groups to tell each other about a book or film they have enjoyed recently. In feedback, nominate a student from each group to share their ideas with the class.

1a Go through the types of story with the class and check understanding. Students think of examples in groups. Emphasise that they can think of examples from real life (e.g. the news) as well as books and films.

b Students work individually, then compare answers in the same groups as exercise 1a. Check answers with the class.

ANSWERS:

crime stories / mysteries F romantic stories F anecdotes T
science fiction / fantasy F ghost stories F adventure stories B
'human interest' stories T biographies T

c Tell the class which stories you like first, as an example. Students discuss the question in groups, giving examples.

2a Focus attention on the photo and the title and elicit students' ideas.

ANSWER:

It's a 'human interest' story.

b Check the meaning of *mannerisms*. Students work individually, then check answers in pairs before checking with the class.

ANSWERS:

1 at a local McDonald's restaurant
2 because they looked so alike
3 Justin Lattore, a friend of Adriana's, saw Tamara at her birthday party.
4 Possible answers: appearance, height, love of hip-hop, the way they walked and talked, mannerisms, interests, school grades
5 They feel like sisters, but the relationship is more like friends.

3 🎧 **6.1** Students work individually, then check answers in pairs. Play the recording for students to check their answers.

ANSWERS:

1 c **2** d **3** a **4** e **5** b

4 Students discuss the questions in pairs. In feedback, elicit students' ideas and feed in the ideas below if they are having difficulty.

SUGGESTED ANSWER:

The article is called 'A twist of fate' because it describes an unexpected situation which involved a lot of coincidences, such as the girls growing up in the same area and both knowing Justin Lattore.

5 The idea of this exercise is to lead into Grammar. Students answer the questions in pairs before checking answers with the class.

ANSWER:

All of the actions in exercise 3 happened before the twins met.

GRAMMAR

Past perfect

1 Give students a few minutes to identify the different verb forms, then check answers with the class.

ANSWERS:

met = Past simple, *had died* = Past perfect
form of Past perfect: *had* + past participle
The action in the Past perfect (*their adoptive fathers had died*) happened before the action in the Past simple (*they met*).

Check the form of the Past perfect on the board, highlighting:

- the form (*had* + past participle for all persons)
- the question and negative forms
- the contractions *'d* and *hadn't*.

2 Give students a few minutes to identify the incorrect explanation, then check answers with the class.

ANSWER:

Explanation 1 is incorrect.

For many students, the concept of the Past perfect will cause few problems since it will be similar in their own language. The incorrect rule highlights a common misconception about the Past perfect. Point out that the Past perfect is only used in reaction to a Past simple action to show that it came first. If you are talking about a single action in the past, however long ago, you use the Past simple (e.g. *Dinosaurs died out millions of years ago*). The relationship between two past events means the Past perfect is commonly found in the following constructions:

- after verbs like *knew* (*When she saw Peter's face, Fiona knew that she had made a mistake.*), *thought* (*He thought I'd told everyone.*) and *remembered* (*He remembered that he hadn't locked the door.*).
- with time words like *when* (*When she got home, she'd spent all her money.*), *after* (*After he'd spoken to her, John realised it was Janet's birthday.*) and *before* (*Before he was a doctor, Fred had been an artist.*).

Potential problem with the Past perfect

Students may confuse the Past perfect with the Present perfect. If this is the case, then explain that the Present perfect always relates a past action to the present; the Past perfect relates a past action to one further in the past (it describes the 'time before the past').

Make sure that students are clear about the difference between the way the Present perfect and Past perfect are formed. Point out that many of the same words are used with both (for example, *already*). You may want to ask students to read Study 1 on page 147 for a more detailed explanation of the Past perfect.

PRACTICE

1a Give students three minutes to read the text, ignoring the gaps, to find the similarities mentioned in the text, then check answers with the class. Students work individually to complete the text, then check answers in pairs before checking with the class.

ANSWERS:

1 met **2** soon found **3** had **4** had both chosen **5** owned **6** had competed **7** had even tried/even tried **8** met **9** discovered **10** had/had had **11** had been born **12** met **13** had given **14** soon discovered **15** had divorced **16** had remarried **17** had **18** died

b Students discuss the question in groups. In feedback, nominate students to share their ideas with the class and allow the discussion to develop naturally.

PRONUNCIATION

See Teaching tips: Helping students with pronunciation, page 22.

1 **6.2** Point out that students will need to listen very carefully. Pause the recording after each sentence to allow students time to discuss their answers. Students may find this challenging as the contraction (*'d*) is difficult to hear, being unstressed. Play the recording again if necessary, rather than giving the answers.

ANSWERS:

1 PS **2** PP **3** PS **4** PS **5** PP **6** PP **7** PP **8** PS

2 Check the difference in meaning, if necessary, between *I'd left my umbrella at home* and *I left my umbrella at home* to show students how important this practice is. Students work in pairs to practise.

2a Go through the example with the class, then give students time to write their introduction.

b Students work in pairs. In feedback, nominate students to read their introductions for the class to guess the story type.

ADDITIONAL PRACTICE

Resource bank: Activity 6A *Ralph and the guitar case* (Past perfect, Past simple and Past continuous)

Study, practice & remember: Practice 1

Workbook: Language focus 1: *Past perfect*, page 34; Pronunciation: *Past perfect and Past simple in connected speech*, page 35

Language focus 2 (PAGES 58–59)

Reported speech

See *Teaching tips: Using a discovery approach to grammar*, page 20.

1a Check understanding of *Halley's Comet* and the meaning of *gap year*. Give students time to read the stories and think of endings. When they are ready, students compare their ideas in pairs. Ask two or three students to share their ideas with the class.

b **6.3** Play the recording for students to check their ideas. Ask if anyone guessed correctly.

ANSWERS:

Josh Lewis: When he got home, there was a voicemail from his girlfriend saying she didn't want to see him anymore.
Maria Lopez: Mark Twain died in 1910, the day after the comet reappeared.
Hui Zhong: Jung Xiu had just had a dream about her and had found her email address online. They've since met up a couple of times.
Liam Bentley: The person who was hired to help had gone to the same school as Liam and his friend.

c Students discuss the questions in pairs. In feedback, ask if anyone has experienced similar coincidences.

2a Go through the example with the class and point out that students should identify people from the stories, not just the speakers. Students work individually, then check answers in pairs before checking with the class.

ANSWERS:

1 Jung Xiu **2** Josh's girlfriend **3** Mark Twain **4** Liam's manager **5** Jung Xiu

b The idea of this exercise is to gauge how much students already know about reported speech. Go through the example with the class, then refer students to the audio script on page 171 to find the sentences. Circulate and check how much students know. This will give you an idea of how much detail to go into in Grammar.

ANSWERS:

1 He always said that we would get married one day.
2 She said that she didn't want to see me anymore.
3 Twain said that he had come in with the comet and he expected to go out with it.
4 One day the manager said he was hiring another worker to help us.
5 He said he'd just had a dream about me ...

GRAMMAR

Tenses in reported speech

1 Give students a few minutes to compare the sentences in exercise 2 individually before checking answers with the class.

ANSWERS:
1 will get married → would get married
2 don't want to see → didn't want to see
3 came in → had come in, expect to go out → expected to go out **4** am hiring → was hiring **5** have had → had had
In reported speech, the tense often moves back into the past.

Time words in reported speech have to reflect the past time frame (for example, *the next day* rather than *tomorrow*). This is logical and should not cause problems if students are using reported speech in a natural context.

2 Go through the example with the class. Students work individually, then check answers in pairs. Write the answers on the board as you go through them with the class.

ANSWERS:

Direct speech	Reported speech
Present simple: I don't want to see you anymore.	**Past simple:** She said (that) she didn't want to see me anymore.
Present continuous: I'm hiring another worker to help you.	**Past continuous:** The manager said (that) he was hiring another worker to help us.
Present perfect: I've just had a dream about you.	**Past perfect:** He said (that) he'd just had a dream about me.
Past simple: I came in with the comet and I expect to go out with it.	**Past perfect:** Twain said (that) that he had come in with the comet and he expected to go out with it.
will: We'll get married one day.	***would:*** He always said (that) we would get married one day.

Potential problem with tenses in reported speech
Sometimes the tense doesn't change when we report speech if the time frame is still true. For example:
'*I hate being stuck in traffic.*' (always true)
She told me that she hates being stuck in traffic.
It's best to avoid this explanation at this stage unless students ask.

Reported questions

3 Students discuss the questions in pairs. Check answers with the class.

ANSWERS:
He asked me if I was still living in Beijing. (Are you still living in Beijing?)
We asked him where he was from. (Where are you from?)
Then we asked him which school he'd gone to. (Which school did you go to?)
The verb ask introduces the reported questions.

4 Discuss the question as a class.

ANSWER:
The word order in reported questions is the same as in statements (there is no inversion of subject and verb).

5 Discuss the question as a class. There is no difference in meaning between *if* and *whether*.

ANSWER:
We use *if* and *whether* in *yes/no* reported questions.

You may want to ask students to read Study 2 on page 148 for a more detailed explanation of reported speech.

PRACTICE

If you think students need more controlled practice before these exercises, they could do Practice 2 on page 148 first.

1 Give students time to read the start of the story, then ask them how they think it ends. Students work individually, then check answers in pairs before checking with the class.

ANSWERS:
1 Feifer told Hopkins that he didn't have a copy of the book anymore.
2 Hopkins asked him what had happened to his copies.
3 Feifer said that he had lent his last one to a friend and she had lost it.
4 Hopkins asked where she had lost it.
5 Feifer said that she had left it on a bench in London.
6 Hopkins asked if that book was Feifer's/if that was Feifer's book and said that he had found it on a bench in London.
7 Feifer said that it was his and that it was incredible.
8 Hopkins said that he would give it back to him when filming was finished.

2a Give students time to choose the four people and answer the questions. Early finishers can answer all of the questions.

b Go through the example with the class. Make sure that students don't write anything here, as the aim is to give them practice in producing the sentences orally. When they have finished, nominate students to share their answers with the class.

ADDITIONAL PRACTICE

Resource bank: Activity 6B *Jungle survivors* (Reported speech)
Study, practice & remember: Practice 2
Workbook: Language focus 2: *Reported speech*, pages 35–37

Vocabulary (PAGE 59)

say and tell

See *Teaching tips: Working with lexis*, page 21.

1a Check the meaning of *lies, prayer* and *joke*. Students work individually, then check answers in pairs.

b 6.4 Play the recording for students to check their answers, then drill the phrases with the class.

ANSWERS:
1 tell, tell **2** tell **3** say **4** tell **5** tell **6** say **7** tell **8** say **9** tell **10** say **11** tell **12** say

2 Do the first two examples together, then get students to underline the phrases and complete the diagram.

ANSWERS:
say: say hello/goodbye/thank you, say a prayer, say sorry, say something to someone, say yes/no
tell: tell jokes, tell someone what to do, tell the truth, tell someone something, tell someone off, tell the difference between ... and ... , tell lies

3 Demonstrate a question with a student. Students work in pairs. Round off with brief feedback, asking students about the most interesting/unusual answers they heard.

ADDITIONAL PRACTICE

Resource bank: Activity 6C *Vocabulary extension* (Verbs to use instead of *say*)

Workbook: Vocabulary: *Say and tell*, page 37

Reading and speaking (PAGES 60–61)

1 Focus attention on the poster and find out if students have seen the film. Students discuss the question in pairs.

Reading and speaking, exercise 1: Alternative suggestion
Instead of using the film poster, find the trailer for the film on the internet and show it to the class. Students watch the trailer, then discuss the question in pairs.

2a Students discuss the questions in pairs. In feedback, write students' ideas on the board.

b Check the meaning of *gasp, brace for impact, grab, sink, waist* and *ferry*. Students read the text, then compare their ideas in pairs. Go through the ideas you wrote on the board in exercise 2a and tick any that are mentioned.

ANSWERS:

1 As the plane was going down, Josh thought about his wife, Tesa, and their two children.
2 When he was safe, he went to the men's room (toilet) and cried.

3 Students work individually, then check answers in pairs before checking with the class.

ANSWERS:

1 f 2 i 3 d 4 c 5 a 6 g 7 b 8 j 9 h 10 e

4 Students discuss the questions in pairs.

ANSWERS:

He thought about one small step at a time: get the door open, throw the door out, etc.

5a Check understanding of the words, then ask students to work in pairs to categorise them. In feedback, draw two columns on the board (*shipwreck* and *shark attack*) and ask students to tell you where to write the words.

ANSWERS:

(These are the correct answers from the texts, although students may offer other acceptable answers in discussion.)
to bite = SA the crew of a boat = SW a rubber dinghy = SW
a flare = SW to feel numb = SA to hold on = SW/SA
to let go = SA a life belt = SW to paddle = SA
a searchlight = SW a surfboard = SA

b Arrange students in two large groups (A and B) to read the stories. Students work individually, then check answers in pairs. When they have finished, check answers with each group in turn.

ANSWERS:

Shipwrecked
1 on a boat tour of the Galapagos Islands
2 when the boat began rocking violently
3 that he had to find his wife
4 by holding on to a life belt and then getting into a rubber dinghy
5 by using flares to attract the attention of another ship
6 like it didn't really happen to him, but also has a feeling of good fortune

Attacked by a shark
1 off the coast of Cape St Francis in South Africa
2 twice (assumes that when the shark let go and then took another bite, this is part of the first attack)
3 when the shark went under the water and Dunstan couldn't see where it was
4 two men on the beach
5 a week
6 He appreciates that he's been given a second chance; he's more careful; he gets a strange feeling when the water is the same colour as that day and he is no longer the first person to go into the water.

6a Arrange students in pairs, with a member from each of the groups in exercise 5b. Students use the questions in their books to find out about their partner's story.

b Students read their partner's texts individually. Go back to the columns on the board from exercise 5 and check answers.

7 Students discuss the questions in the same pairs from exercise 6.

Find out more

Put students in pairs to search online for information about *Josh Peltz* and *US Airways Flight 1549*. Students find as much information as they can, then use this to do a roleplay between Josh Peltz and one of the other passengers or crew in pairs, which they then perform for the class. Alternatively, ask students to search online for other experiences, which they then share in groups.

Vocabulary (PAGE 61)

Adverbs for telling stories

See *Teaching tips: Working with lexis*, page 21.

1 Check the meaning of *to search, to lose touch* and *evidence*. Students work individually or in pairs before checking answers with the class.

ANSWERS:

1 e 2 a 3 h 4 f 5 d 6 b 7 i 8 g 9 c

2 Go though the example with the class, making it clear that students must continue the sentences logically, according to the meaning of the adverbs. Students work in pairs. Do this as a spoken exercise initially, then get students to write sentences. Circulate, noting down any problems with the use of adverbs to focus on later.

ADDITIONAL PRACTICE

Workbook: Vocabulary: *Adverbs for telling stories*, page 39

Task (PAGES 62–63)

Retell a story

See *Teaching tips: Making tasks work*, page 23.

Preparation (PAGE 62)

Listening and vocabulary

1 Focus attention on the picture and biodata, and ask if students have read any of Saki's stories. Students answer the questions in pairs before checking answers with the class.

ANSWERS:

1 short stories
2 The story is set in the early 20th century (the Edwardian period covered the years 1901–1910).
3 Frampton Nuttel is standing on the right of the picture. Mrs Sappleton is seated in the foreground. Vera is standing next to the window.
4 a man and two teenage boys with a dog

2 If you have access to dictionaries, distribute them for students to check the meaning of the key phrases. Otherwise, check the meanings with the class.

ANSWERS:

to find a body: to find the body of a dead person
a great tragedy: a very sad event (when something will be wasted, lost or harmed)
to go shooting: to take part in the sport of shooting animals and birds with guns
to sink in a bog: to go down below the surface of water, mud, etc., in this case, an area of low wet muddy ground, known, as a bog
to chase someone: to quickly follow someone in order to catch them
snarling dogs: if an animal snarls, it makes low angry sounds and shows its teeth
to see a ghost: to think that you see the image of a dead person
a letter of introduction: an important part of polite social interaction in the 18th and 19th centuries. A person would not interact socially with others unless they had been properly introduced, in person or by letter. A person of lower social status would request a patron of higher social status to write a letter of introduction to a third party.
French windows: a pair of doors made mostly of glass, usually opening onto a garden
to go insane with grief: to become mentally ill because of the extreme sadness you feel after someone you love has died
a cure for bad nerves: A cure is something (often a medicine) that solves a problem or illness. If someone has bad nerves, they are easily worried and frightened.
to have a nervous breakdown: to experience a mental illness in which someone becomes extremely anxious and cannot deal with the things they usually would
to knock someone off their bicycle: to cause someone to fall off their bicycle by getting in their way or hitting them with a vehicle you are driving

3a **6.5** Go through the questions with the class, then play the recording for students to answer the questions and check answers in pairs.

b Play the recording again before checking answers with the class.

ANSWERS:

1 to try to cure his bad nerves by resting
2 because he had been given a letter of introduction to Mrs Sappleton by his sister (Note: this is implied, it is not said specifically.)
3 Mrs Sappleton's niece, Vera
4 the disappearance/death of Mrs Sappleton's husband and two brothers
5 that they will come back some day
6 'I hope Vera has been amusing you?'

Task (PAGE 63)

Speaking and listening

1 Go through the phrases in the Useful language box, sections a and b, and drill them with the class. Students practise retelling the story so far in pairs.

2a Demonstrate with the phrase *to chase someone* from exercise 2 on page 62, by asking *Who do you think chased who?* Give students time to think about what happened next individually, making notes if they want.

b Students compare their ideas in groups. In feedback, nominate a student from each group to share their best idea with the class.

3a **6.6** Students listen to the ending, then answer the questions in pairs before checking answers with the class.

ANSWERS:

1 No, she was focused on the garden and looking for her husband and brothers.
2 three figures walking across the garden, carrying guns, one with a white coat over his shoulders accompanied by a tired brown dog
3 because he thought he was seeing the ghosts of Mrs Sappleton's husband and brothers
4 that he was a very strange man who only talked about his illnesses and looked as if he had seen a ghost before running off without saying goodbye
5 by saying that he was frightened of dogs because he was once chased by wild dogs in India
6 telling stories at short notice: the story about her aunt's husband and brothers dying on a shooting trip; the story about Frampton Nuttel being chased by dogs in India

b Discuss the question as a class.

4 Refer students to the phrases in the Useful language box, sections a–c. Students practise retelling the story together in groups, with each student retelling a different part. When they are ready, groups tell their stories to the class.

5 Students listen to the story again, then discuss the questions in groups before sharing their ideas with the class.

Follow up (PAGE 63)

Writing

1 This can be done either in class or as homework. Display the students' finished work on the classroom wall.

Task: Alternative suggestions

If you have a creative group, they may prefer to tell their own frightening stories right from the beginning. However, it would still be useful to provide a model. Tell a story yourself about a mysterious/frightening event. As a task, you could write a list of key words from your story on the board, then tell students to listen and order them or explain their significance in the story.

The next stage is to get students to tell their own stories. It is simplest if each student works individually. The following framework should help:

- Give them time to think of a story, suggesting possible sources (films, personal experiences, etc.). The story does not have to have a supernatural element – it could be frightening, for example, because they were in danger.
- Give students 15–20 minutes to plan their stories.
- If you think they need additional practice, get them to tell their stories in pairs before telling them to the class.

If you have a large class, instead of listening to everyone's story as a class, get students to tell their stories in groups. Alternatively, you could spread the story-telling over the next few lessons.

Share your task

Some additional ideas could include:

- Students film themselves performing the story, with different students playing the parts of the characters in the story.
- Students record themselves retelling the story, but add background music to add atmosphere.

ADDITIONAL PRACTICE

Workbook: Writing: *Checking for mistakes*, page 39

World culture (PAGES 64–65)

A story that rocked the world

Culture notes

Chile: The Republic of Chile is a long, thin country on the west coast of South America. It is the 'longest' country in the world in terms of its length–width ratio and as such has a diverse climate, from the world's driest desert, to alpine tundra, to glaciers in the south.

Northern and central Chile was home to the Inca civilisation until the 16th century, when it came under Spanish rule, before declaring independence in 1818. From 1973 to 1990, the country was ruled by a military dictatorship which left more than 3,000 people dead or missing.

The capital of Chile is Santiago, situated in the north, and the country is famous for exporting copper and wine. It is one of only two countries in South America which doesn't have a border with Brazil (the other is Ecuador).

2010 Copiapo mining accident: On 5th August 2010, the 121-year-old San José copper-gold mine collapsed, trapping 33 miners 700 m underground and about 5 km from the mine's entrance.

Because the mine had a history of safety violations and previous geological instability, it was not expected that the men would survive.

17 days after the incident, when a drill was pulled to the surface, it had a note attached which was written by the miners, saying they were alive. The men, who became known as 'Los 33', attracted global media attention as efforts were made to rescue them.

Finally, on 13th October 2010, all 33 men were brought safely to the ground. The rescue was watched by an estimated 1 billion people on live TV around the world.

Find out first (PAGE 64)

1a Focus attention on the photos and elicit what students know about Chile. Students work in pairs to choose the correct answers in the fact file. Emphasise that they shouldn't worry if they don't know all the information as they'll have a chance to research it afterwards.

b Go over the search terms to help students as they go online. Ask them to also note down any other interesting information they discover while researching. Students research the answers individually, then compare information in small groups. In feedback, check answers with the class and feed in any additional information from the Culture notes.

ANSWERS:

Population: 17 **Neighbours:** Peru **Capital:** Santiago **Life expectancy:** 78 **Biggest export:** copper **Extraordinary fact:** driest

View (PAGE 64)

See *Teaching tips: Using the video material in the classroom*, page 24.

2 Ask students if they can remember any big news stories from Chile in recent years. Write *The 2010 Copiapo mining accident* on the board and ask students what they can remember about it. Students read the newspaper extract to check ideas, then discuss what they think the numbers mean in pairs. Don't give any answers yet.

3a Play the first part of the DVD for students to check their answers. Students check answers in pairs before checking with the class.

SUGGESTED ANSWER:

In October 2010, 33 miners spent 69 days trapped underground when the mine in Chile collapsed. A 700,000-tonne block of rock trapped them almost 700 metres below ground.

b Students discuss the questions in pairs.

c Play the second part of the DVD for students to check their answers before checking answers with the class.

ANSWERS:

They rationed food and got water from the machines' radiators.
It caused strange behaviour and emotional problems.

4 Students read the sentences, then choose which two are correct in pairs. Play the DVD again for students to check answers before checking with the class.

ANSWERS:

1 It was a copper and gold mine.
2 Angelique was waiting at home for her boyfriend to finish his shift.
3 Correct: The news made her feel sick.
4 A drill found the miners.
5 Correct: Edison cut himself off from the other miners.
6 Angelique needs to show Edison more love.

World view (PAGE 65)

5 Focus attention on the table and check students understand what they need to watch for. Play the DVD for students to complete the table. Students compare answers in pairs, then watch the DVD again if necessary. Check answers with the class.

ANSWERS:

	Luis	Eben	Kirsten
What was the event?	Spain winning the World Cup	Obama elected US President	2012 Olympic Games
When was it?		7th November 2008	2012
What happened and what made it memorable/ important?	Spain had also won the European Cup and this had never been done before.	Obama walked out to the crowds to make his acceptance speech and like Obama, Eben had lived in Chicago.	People from around the world were united and helped each other.

World view, exercise 5: Alternative suggestion

Put students in three groups and allocate one speaker to each group. Ask each group to complete the table for their speaker only (though they can watch the other speakers, too). After watching, students compare their notes and complete as much information as possible. Rearrange students into groups of three, with one member from each of the previous groups. Students share their information and complete the remaining sections of the table. Play the DVD a second time for students to check the information in their tables.

6a If you have a multi-nationality class, try to arrange students in groups of the same nationality to discuss the questions. Otherwise, encourage groups to think of/discuss different events. Circulate and help with vocabulary, writing any new words/phrases on the board.

b Nominate a student from each group to summarise the main points of their discussion for the rest of the class.

Find out more (PAGE 65)

7a Students discuss the events in pairs. In feedback, elicit their ideas and write any information on the board as notes. Avoid giving any information here.

ANSWERS:

the Three Mile Island accident: Pennsylvania, United States, on 28th March1979
Apollo 13: blew up halfway to moon, in 1970
US Airways Flight 1549: aircraft flying this route, an Airbus A320-214, landed in Hudson River, on 15th January 2009
asteroid 2012 BX34: came close to Earth, on 28th January 2012

b Either ask students to choose two of the incidents to research, or allocate them to students if you feel this would work better. Encourage students to use the search terms provided and make notes under the questions. Monitor and help with vocabulary where necessary.

Write up your research

8 Students write their paragraphs individually, using the prompts to help them. Encourage students to add any additional information they found online. When they have finished, ask students to swap paragraphs with someone who wrote about a different incident. In feedback, ask students what information they found most interesting.

Students can now do Unit test 3 and the Mid-course test on the Teacher's Resource Disc.

Study, practice & remember

(PAGES 147–149)

Practice 1

ANSWERS:

1

1 f: She spoke French well because she had lived in Paris as a child.
2 h: I had left my umbrella at home, so I got really wet.
3 g: My uncle didn't want to move because he'd lived in the same house for 40 years.
4 d: There was no food in the house because I had forgotten to go to the supermarket.
5 b: My grandparents had never flown before, so they were nervous when they got on the plane.
6 c: When I got home my father was angry because I had not phoned him.
7 a: They had already sold all the tickets, so we didn't get into the concert.
8 e: We didn't have to queue in the restaurant because my uncle had reserved a table.

2

1 had gone **2** had ever spent **3** had done **4** had seen **5** had threatened **6** had not flown **7** had started **8** had been

3

1 had met, was **2** had read, had forgotten **3** had gone, was **4** didn't know, had started **5** was, didn't come **6** walked, had forgotten

Practice 2

ANSWERS:

1

1, 4, 6, 7

2

1 The teacher asked me why I was late.
2 He asked us if we were going home.
3 They asked her where she was going.
4 My brother wanted to know where I was./I wanted to know where my brother was.
5 I didn't ask him how he was.

Remember these words

ANSWERS:

1

1 a ghost story **2** science fiction **3** a crime story **4** an adventure story **5** a romantic story

2

1 b **2** f **3** a **4** d **5** e **6** c

3

1 tell **2** say **3** tell **4** tell **5** tell **6** say **7** say **8** tell

Study tips

If you do these exercises in class, then it would be useful to do them just before handing back corrected written work.

1 Emphasise that students should be honest when selecting their answer. Students compare their answers in pairs and give reasons.

2 If you are going to hand back corrected written work, then give it back now so that students can refer to it when doing the exercise. Go over the sentences with the class, then give students time to think about their answers and tick the things they find difficult before comparing answers in pairs.

3 Elicit the first mistake as an example. Students work individually, then compare answers in pairs. Check answers with the class and ask which of the problems in exercise 2 each mistake is an example of.

ANSWERS:

1 I'm just writing to say thank you *(full stops and commas)* for the lovely pullover you ~~send~~ *sent (verb tenses)* me for my birthday. It ~~fit~~ *fits (the 's' on the third person)* perfectly *(full stops and commas)* and the colour *is (missing out words)* great.

2 Sorry I ~~couldn't~~ *can't (verb tenses)* come to the ~~ristorant~~ *restaurant (spelling)* tomorrow, but I have to ~~make~~ *do (using the wrong word)* my homework and study for *an (articles)* exam. I'm very ~~worrying~~ *worried (using the wrong word)*!

3 I ~~am~~ *(putting in words you don't need)* agree – ~~peoples~~ *people (using the wrong word)* should ~~no~~ *not (using the wrong word)* ~~smoking~~ *smoke (using the wrong word)* in public ~~place~~ *places (using the wrong word)*.

07 MUST SEE!

OVERVIEW

PAGES 66–67

Vocabulary and speaking: Entertainment and television

Grammar: *-ed/-ing* adjectives

Common European Framework: Students can express and respond to feelings; can express opinions and attitudes.

PAGES 68–69

Speaking: Film quiz

Grammar: The passive

Common European Framework: Students can communicate with accuracy in familiar contexts; can narrate the plot of a film and describe their reactions.

PAGES 70–71

Reading: News stories

Vocabulary: Extreme adjectives

Common European Framework: Students can read factual texts on subjects related to their interests; can use a range of language to be able to give clear descriptions.

PAGES 72–73

Task: Talk about a show you love or hate

Common European Framework: Students can give clear, systematically developed descriptions and presentations.

PAGES 74–75

Writing: A review

Speaking: Making a social arrangement

Common European Framework: Students can write clear, detailed descriptions of real or imaginary events and experiences; can exchange, check and confirm information.

Vocabulary and speaking (PAGE 66)

Entertainment and television

See *Teaching tips: Working with lexis*, page 21.

WARM UP

Tell students about a TV or radio programme you have watched/listened to in the last week. Include as much detail as possible about the format, actors/presenters, etc. and how popular it is in general. If possible, play the class a short clip from the programme and answer any questions students have. Students then tell each other about a programme they have watched/listened to recently in pairs.

1a Put students into small groups to discuss the question.

b With stronger classes, get them to brainstorm types of TV and radio programmes in groups first, then elicit their answers and write them on the board. Students then compare with the types of programme in the box. Otherwise, check the meaning and pronunciation of *documentary* /dɒkjuː'mentəri/, *reality show* /rɪ'jælɪtiː'ʃəʊ/, *sitcom* /'sɪtkɒm/ (= situation comedy), *soap opera* /'səʊpɒprə/, *weather forecast* /'weθə'fɔːkɑːst/ and *murder mystery* /'mɜːdə'mɪstəri/. Students work individually before comparing answers in groups. Emphasise that they can use their dictionaries to check meaning.

c Students work in pairs or small groups. If your students come from different countries, ensure that there is a mix of nationalities in each group. If all your students come from the same country, ask them to think of one or two examples for each type of TV and radio programme.

Vocabulary and speaking: Additional activity

Before class, write the words in exercise 1b on cards and make one set of cards for each group of three or four students in your class. Ask students to sit in a circle and place one set of cards face-down in the middle of the group. Students take turns to take a card and describe the TV or radio programme for others to guess. The student who says the word first keeps the card. The student with the most cards at the end is the winner.

2 Students work individually to read the three statements and think about their answers before comparing answers in pairs.

3 Go through the example with the class. Students discuss the question in small groups.

Vocabulary and speaking, exercise 3: Alternative suggestion

If you have time, this activity could be extended into a mini-task. Students work in pairs to think of five recommendations they would make to change TV and/or radio in their countries. Circulate and help with vocabulary where necessary. When they are ready, arrange the pairs into groups of four in order to share their ideas, then agree on four recommendations for the group. Nominate students from each group to read out their recommendations and ask if other groups agree.

ADDITIONAL PRACTICE

Workbook: Vocabulary: *Entertainment and television*, page 40; Vocabulary: *Entertainment and television*, page 43

Language focus 1 (PAGE 67)

-ed/-ing adjectives

See *Teaching tips: Using a discovery approach to grammar*, page 20.

1 Focus attention on the pictures and discuss the question with the class. You could ask students to discuss the question in pairs first.

ANSWERS:

a sports programme a horror film

2 Students work in pairs, matching the descriptions in A with the adjectives in B.

ANSWERS:

1 c 2 d 3 a 4 b

GRAMMAR

***-ed/-ing* adjectives**

> **Language focus 1: notes on the approach to *-ed/-ing* adjectives**
>
> These adjectives have been put before the passive in this unit in the hope that this will help students understand the passive better, since the *-ed* adjectives are, in origin, passive forms. You could point out that these adjectives are all formed from verbs: *I am disappointed* means something disappoints me. Do not mention the passive explicitly at this point unless students ask.

1 Students choose the correct answers individually, then check answers in pairs before checking with the class. Refer back to the pictures in exercise 1 when checking answers. Point out that *-ed* adjectives describe a feeling and *-ing* adjectives describe something/someone that makes us feel like this. Explain that *-ed* adjectives are, in fact, past participles – adjectives like *upset* are not exceptions, but are simply formed from irregular verbs.

ANSWERS:

1 *-ed*:
The women are very excited.
The children are terrified.

2 *-ing*:
The tennis match is very exciting.
The film is terrifying.

2 Students work alone, then check answers in pairs. In feedback, write students' answers on the board. You may want to ask students to read Study 1 on page 150 for a more detailed explanation of *-ed/-ing* adjectives.

PRACTICE

1 Check the meaning of the adjectives by describing typical situations in which you might feel *disappointed, embarrassed, frustrated*, etc. Students work individually or in pairs before checking answers with the class.

ANSWERS:

1 shocking **2** pleased **3** confusing, frustrated **4** annoyed **5** embarrassing **6** amazing **7** disappointed **8** inspiring

2 Focus on the example and the suggested responses, highlighting the following:

- *I'd* (*I would*) is used because you are imagining this situation; it is hypothetical.
- *-ing* adjectives are very often used in the construction *I find … boring/annoying*, etc.

Students discuss their responses in groups, then do brief feedback as a class.

ADDITIONAL PRACTICE

Study, practice & remember: Practice 1

Workbook: Language focus 1: *-ing/-ed adjectives*, pages 40–41

Speaking and listening (PAGE 68)

1 Students discuss the questions in pairs. Nominate students to share their answers with the class and find out if anyone has the same views.

2 Introduce the idea of a quiz and check the meaning of *to be produced* and *to play the role of*. This quiz can be done in pairs, individually or as a team game.

3 **7.1** Play the recording for students to check their answers.

ANSWERS:

1 c **2** a **3** c **4** c **5** c **6** b **7** a

Language focus 2 (PAGES 68–69)

The passive

See *Teaching tips: Using a discovery approach to grammar*, page 20.

1a Do the first item as an example with the class. Students work individually or in pairs before checking answers with the class. Some students may ask about the passive at this point. This is fully dealt with in Grammar.

ANSWERS:

1 P **2** A **3** A **4** P **5** A **6** P **7** P **8** P **9** P

b Discuss the question with the class.

ANSWERS:

Sentence 1: We don't know who chose Daniel.
Sentence 2: We know that JK Rowling chose Daniel.

GRAMMAR

The passive

Note: we have used the term 'doer' in preference to 'agent' because it seems more transparent, but if your students know 'agent' already, make it clear that this is what is meant.

1 Students work individually before checking answers with the class.

ANSWERS:

1 Examples are sentences 2, 3, and 5.
2 Examples are: 1, 4, 6, 7, 8 and 9.

> **Potential problem with the passive**
>
> If students have problems understanding the concept of the 'doer' in passive sentences, check (by translation if necessary) that they understand what the subject of a verb is. Write out the first two sentences, underlining the subject and verb in each. The 'doer' (agent) of the verb can be shown with arrows, like this:
>
> *The author, JK Rowling, chose Daniel herself.*
>
> → (*subject*) → (*verb*) → (*object*)
>
> *Daniel* (*subject*) *was chosen* (*verb*) *to play Harry Potter when he was 11.*
>
> In the second sentence, the subject is not the 'doer'. If students have problems with this concept, go through more of the sentences, identifying the subject and the 'doer'.

2 Remind students of the basic form of the passive verb, then ask them to identify the tenses one by one, contrasting them with a similar active sentence, for example:

However, he is better known as Jackie Chan./People know him better as Jackie Chan.

ANSWERS:

1 sentence 4 (is known) **2** sentence 1 (was chosen) and sentence 7 (was directed) **3** sentence 8 (is being filmed) **4** sentence 6 (have been made) **5** sentence 9 (will be made)

Point out also:

- the formation of the negative and question form in each case, particularly in the Present perfect, where students have two auxiliary verbs to manipulate.
- that contractions can be used with the passive as with other verb forms.
- that the *be* + past participle rule for forming the passive is completely regular.

You may want to ask students to read Study 2 on pages 150 and 151 for a more detailed explanation of the passive.

PRACTICE

1 Students work individually or in pairs before checking answers with the class. Remind them to think about the tense of the verb as well as whether it is passive or active.

ANSWERS:

1 are produced, are made, are released **2** was shown, has been lost **3** were made, was played **4** will be released, have already been made **5** is being filmed, is being shot

2 Students read the text quickly to see what it is about. Feed back briefly with the whole class before getting students to select the correct forms.

ANSWERS:

1 was released **2** won **3** has made **4** has been described **5** has been called **6** holds **7** has been nominated **8** cost **9** wrote **10** was removed **11** lost

3a Explain that students are going to make their own quizzes. Students work individually to make their lists.

b Put students into teams of three or four. Tell students that each question in the quiz must contain a passive phrase. Remind them of the passive phrases in the quiz they have just done and check the meaning and pronunciation of the words/phrases in the prompts.

c Go through the example with the class, then give students five to ten minutes to write their answers and background information. If you have access to the internet, let students search online for background information. Circulate and help with vocabulary where necessary.

4 Put students into groups of two teams each, or do the quizzes as a whole class, with each team taking turns to read out a question and answer. Allocate points for correct answers.

ADDITIONAL PRACTICE

Resource bank: Activity 7A *Passive dominoes* (The passive)

Study, practice & remember: Practice 2

Workbook: Language focus 2: *The passive*, pages 41–42

Reading (PAGES 70–71)

News stories

WARM UP

Bring/download three photos from recent stories which have been in the news. Students discuss what they think they show in pairs. Circulate and answer any questions they have, but be careful not to give away too much detail. When they are ready, elicit their ideas as a class, then explain the rest of the details of each story.

1a Focus on the question in the example, then go through the other prompts and elicit the questions for each one. With weaker classes, write the questions on the board. Otherwise, this can be done orally. Students mingle and ask and answer the questions with other students in the class. Ask them to note down when another student answers *yes* to a question.

ANSWERS:

Do you read a newspaper every day? Do you (ever) read newspapers? Do you watch 24-hour news channels? Do you often listen to the news on the radio? Do you usually check the news online? Are you (very) interested in the news?

b Put students in groups to compare results and answer the questions.

2 Tell students they are going to read some news items from English newspapers. Check the meaning of *to sue someone, the main feature, pirates* (= people who illegally copy films), *consecutive* and *to go down on one knee*. In groups, students predict what the articles are about. As they are doing this, copy the headlines onto the board. Write their suggestions under each headline on the board, without saying whether or not they are correct.

3 Students read the articles and match them with the headlines. Set a time limit of three minutes for this and explain that students will have a chance to read the texts again more carefully afterwards.

ANSWERS:

1 C **2** D **3** A **4** B

4 Students work individually before checking answers in pairs. Encourage them to find the places in each text where the answer is given.

ANSWERS:

1 she had to wait a long time to see the film **2** show pictures of the audience **3** towards, he was extremely tired **4** surprised, she didn't expect her boyfriend to propose

5 Elicit the first answer from a student as an example. Students work individually, then check answers in pairs before checking with the whole class. Check the pronunciation of *trailer* /'treɪlə/, *audience* /'ɔːdɪəns/, *broadcast* /'brɔːdkɑːst/ and *applaud* /ə'plɔːd/, and drill the words.

ANSWERS:

1 a trailer **2** a romantic comedy **3** the audience **4** a broadcast **5** the set **6** a graphic **7** to applaud

6a Give students time to read the questions and choose three they would like to discuss.

b Students discuss the questions in pairs.

ADDITIONAL PRACTICE

Resource bank: Activity 7B *Vocabulary extension* (Passive verbs often in the news)

Vocabulary (PAGE 71)

Extreme adjectives

See *Teaching tips: Working with lexis*, page 21.

1a Check that students understand *extreme*. Students do the exercise individually or in pairs. Check the pronunciation and stress of the extreme adjectives.

ANSWERS:
1 b 2 d 3 c 4 e 5 a

b Discuss the question as a class.

ANSWER:
Writers use extreme adjectives to make what they are writing more interesting and descriptive, and to avoid overusing the word 'very'.

2 Students write the definitions individually or in pairs. Check the pronunciation and stress of the extreme adjectives.

ANSWERS:
1 very funny **2** very good **3** very good **4** very bad
5 very cold **6** very hot

3 Point out that extreme adjectives are often used in headlines in English newspapers. Check the meaning of *performance*, *criticism* and *nomination*. Students work in pairs before checking answers with the class.

ANSWERS:
1 furious **2** terrible/awful **3** exhausted **4** Freezing
5 hilarious **6** terrified **7** astonished

Potential problem with extreme adjectives
If students want to use *very* with extreme adjectives, explain that we use *very* and *really* with ordinary adjectives. We can use *absolutely* with extreme adjectives to add emphasis. This is, in fact, logical, as something is either 'extreme' or not – it can't be graded. *Absolutely* is therefore only used for emphasis.

PRONUNCIATION

See *Teaching tips: Helping students with pronunciation*, page 22.

1 🎧 **7.2** Play the recording and pause after each word to allow students to compare their answers in pairs.

ANSWERS:

Oo	Ooo	oOoo	oOo
boiling freezing	excellent furious terrible	hilarious ridiculous	astonished delighted exhausted

2 Drill chorally and individually, using your hand to indicate when a syllable is stressed, like a conductor. If students are confident, put them into pairs to practise further.

ADDITIONAL PRACTICE

Resource bank: Activity 7C *Adjective snap* (Extreme adjectives)

Workbook: Vocabulary: *Extreme adjectives*, page 42; Pronunciation: *Word stress*, page 42

Task (PAGES 72–73)

Talk about a show you love or hate

See *Teaching tips: Making tasks work*, page 23.

Preparation (PAGE 72)

Vocabulary and listening

1a Focus attention on the photos and ask students to match them with the types of entertainment, individually or in pairs. Check as a class.

ANSWERS:
The Crying: rock concert The House of Elliot: TV drama
World dance festival: ballet Turandot: opera

b Explain that students are going to do a survey in groups to find out about what forms of entertainment are the most and least popular in the class. Check the meaning of *musical* and *ballet*. Students work individually to rank the activities.

c Focus attention on the example and encourage students to give reasons for their choices. Students compare their rankings in groups. Each group reports back to the class.

2 Students work individually before comparing answers in groups. Check the meaning of *costumes*, *the set*, *the cast* and *the plot*.

3a 🎧 **7.3** Explain that students will hear four people talking. Emphasise that they should make notes as they listen. Pause the recording after each person, to allow students to compare answers in pairs. If necessary, play the recording more than once.

ANSWERS:
Speaker 1: 1 the film *Lord of the Rings* **2** doesn't say **3** She loved it. **4** She liked the cinematography, the performances and casting, and the fact that it was filmed in New Zealand.
Speaker 2: 1 the TV show (drama) *Modern Family* **2** All we know is that it's a show he's watching at the moment. **3** He really likes it. **4** He thinks the show is funny and likes the fact that the characters say and do things you would like to do but can't in real life.
Speaker 3: 1 the TV show *The X Factor* **2** She saw it last Saturday night. **3** She disliked it. **4** She didn't like the fact that people were being judged on their appearance and image rather than for their singing.
Speaker 4: 1 the ballet *Alice in Wonderland* **2** She saw it at the Royal Opera House in Covent Garden, London, on her friend's birthday. **3** She adored it. **4** She liked the set/the design of the stage, the Queen of Hearts character and the fact that it was a comedy as well as a ballet.

b Focus attention on the the Useful language box on page 73. Students listen again and tick the phrases they hear, then check answers in pairs before checking with the class. Drill the phrases from the box with the class.

ANSWERS:
Speaker 1: It's based on … ; The performances were (great/terrible).; I loved the fact that … ; I've never seen a better (movie).
Speaker 2: A (TV show) that I really like at the moment is … ; It's about …
Speaker 4: I want to tell you about (the first time I went to a ballet).; It's based on … ; I thought it was (really amazing/disappointing).; I'd recommend it to anybody!

Task (PAGE 73)

Speaking

1a Students make notes individually. Make it clear that they do not need to write out a script, but should make notes based on the questions. Circulate, supplying any vocabulary and writing any new words/phrases on the board.

b Refer students to the Useful language box, sections a and b, and give them time to prepare what they are going to say. Circulate, supplying vocabulary and making a note of any errors or useful phrases to analyse later.

2 Put students into pairs to rehearse their talks. At this point you can feed in some of your corrections/alternative suggestions if appropriate.

3 Tell students that they are going to give their talks to the class and listen to the other students. Ask students to make a note of what they would like to see most and any questions they would like to ask. As they give their talks, make a note of further errors for analysis and correction.

Share your task

Students could make their own 'review' radio/TV programme, following this procedure. Make it clear that you will be recording/filming students later to make a class radio/TV programme so they understand what they are preparing for. Appoint a presenter to introduce and link together the items. This could be yourself or a strong student, with plenty of initiative. The following tips might be useful:

- Get the presenter to circulate among the rest of the class and make a list of what items to include and in what order.
- Give him/her the following useful phrases: *Hello and welcome to … , Later in the programme we have … , First of all on today's programme we have … , And next we have … , And now for something different … , And finally … .*
- Make sure that he/she has an opportunity to rehearse, as with the other students.
- If you want to film the programme, nominate one student to plan any visual aids or props which might be used, for example, a desk for the presenter.
- Include items other than reviews, too, according to the interests of your students.
- Feed in useful language as necessary.
- Before recording the programme, give students ample opportunity to rehearse what they are going to say. They are bound to be more nervous when recording formally. Either record the whole programme in front of the class or send students (including the presenter) to a different room to record their sections in private.

Use the finished programme for correction and further language input. The first time students listen or watch, they may be preoccupied – it may be more appropriate to listen/watch a second time for correction work.

Language live (PAGES 74–75)

WARM UP

Separate the board into three columns: *concert, play* and *film*. Put students in two large groups and give a board pen to each. Each turn, call out one of the words from exercise 2 on page 72 of the Students' Book. Students run to the board and write the word in the correct column(s). The first team to do so correctly wins a point. If the word can go in more than one column, then accept the first correct answer. Make sure a different student comes to the board each time.

Writing (PAGE 74)

A review

1 Focus attention on the poster and elicit what type of show it is and what students think it's about. Students read the description individually, then answer the questions in pairs.

ANSWERS:

1 We know the musical is successful because it has been running for eight years at the same theatre, it has been seen by 20 million people and voted 'Best Musical of the Decade' by an entertainment magazine.

2 Ask students if they ever read or write online reviews, and what for. Emphasise that students shouldn't worry about new vocabulary for now, but just read the reviews to put them in order. Students work individually, then check answers in pairs before checking with the class.

ANSWERS:

1 = most positive, 4 = least positive:

1 Alejandro **2** Miu **3** Selma **4** Jozef

(It could also be argued that Selma's review should be number 2.)

3a Students answer the questions individually before checking answers in pairs.

ANSWERS:

a 3 **b** 4 **c** 1 **d** 2

b Read the example with the class. Students work in pairs before checking answers with the class.

ANSWERS:

Paragraph 1: It's based on the film *The Wizard of Oz* and the novel *Wicked* by Gregory Maguire.

Paragraph 2: It's set in the imaginary land of Oz. The main characters are two girls studying to be witches: Elphaba becomes the Wicked Witch of the West and Glinda becomes the Good Witch of the North. The story focuses on their relationship and how they deal with the evil Wizard.

Paragraph 3: There are catchy songs, spectacular special effects and lighting, but British actors put on American accents.

Paragraph 4: Selma would recommend the musical.

4 Do one or two examples with the class first. Students work individually, then check answers in pairs. In feedback, elicit students' answers and check the meaning of the words.

ANSWERS:

Positive: epic, catchy, really spectacular, absolutely fantastic, eleven out of ten, a triumph, I was hooked

Negative: didn't quite sound real, a bit disappointing, I wasn't moved, hard to follow

Neutral: imaginary

Language live, Writing: Additional activity

Bring/download some authentic reviews of films, musicals and concerts to class, or ask students to find some online. After doing the vocabulary work in exercise 4, ask students to look through the reviews and see if they can find any of the vocabulary they've just studied, as well as any other useful language for reviews. Ask students to share their ideas with the class and write any new/useful vocabulary on the board.

5a Students work individually to make notes. Circulate and help with vocabulary, writing any new words/phrases on the board.

b Students write their reviews. Emphasise that they should write between 120–150 words. When they have finished, go through the checklist and give them time to check/correct their work. Circulate and help where necessary. Collect the finished reviews and display them round the class. Ask students to walk around, read the reviews and choose one they would like to see.

Speaking (PAGE 75)

Making a social arrangement

See *Teaching tips: Using the video material in the classroom*, page 24.

1 Discuss the question as a class.

2 Go through the questions first and check students understand what information they are watching for. Students watch the DVD, then answer the questions in pairs. Check answers with the class.

ANSWERS:

1 because he said he was busy and couldn't go
2 The librarian can't go because he's going to his mum's.
3 Josh

3a Students work individually to complete the gaps from memory, then check answers in pairs. When they are ready, play the DVD again for students to check their answers before checking with the class.

ANSWERS:

1 it's, phoning to ask **2** give me, call? **3** Would, like to
4 Oh, sorry, I can't. **5** another time, maybe? **6** How about
7 I'd love to **8** Shall we **9** I'll see

b Read the example with the class. Students work in pairs to find the phrases, then check answers with the class.

ANSWERS:

1 I'm phoning to ask if you'd like to … ; Would you like to come?
2 Oh, sorry, I can't. (refusing); Yeah, I'd love to. Thanks. (accepting)
3 How about next week instead? Shall we meet at 8 o'clock?

PRONUNCIATION

1 Play the DVD, pausing after each phrase for students to practise saying the sentences.

4 Students turn to page 128 and read the instructions. Put them in pairs to act out their conversations. When they are ready, nominate one or two pairs to perform their conversations to the class.

ADDITIONAL PRACTICE

Resource bank: Activity 7D *What time shall we meet?* (Making a social arrangement)

Workbook: Language live: *Making a social arrangement*, page 45; Writing: *Email invitations*, page 45

Study, practice & remember

(PAGES 150–152)

See *Teaching tips: Using the Study, practice & remember sections*, page 25.

Practice 1

ANSWERS:

1

1 interesting **2** surprising **3** embarrassed **4** annoying
5 boring **6** pleased **7** worrying **8** confused

2

1 disappointed **2** confusing **3** depressed **4** amazed
5 annoying **6** frustrating

Practice 2

ANSWERS:

1

1 are injured **2** have been found **3** is being built **4** was stolen
5 will be completed

2

1 Over 30 demonstrators were arrested.
2 A number of buildings have been damaged.
3 Thousands of trees are destroyed every year.
4 The man will be sentenced tomorrow.
5 My computer had been stolen.
6 Are you being looked after?
7 Sarah was presented with a gold watch./A gold watch was presented to Sarah.
8 The museum was built in 1874.

3

a **1** was given **2** landed **3** became **4** was given
5 has been known

b **1** had been **2** was murdered **3** then decided **4** was elected
5 died

c **1** became **2** was launched **3** be brought **4** died
5 was named

Remember these words

ANSWERS:

1 (suggested answers)

1 travel news: The rest tell a story.
2 a character: The rest are types of show.
3 a drama series: The rest involve the general public.
4 the cast: The rest aren't people.
5 an advert: The rest are programmes that give information.
6 a comedy show: The rest involve music.

2

1 excellent **2** terrible **3** delighted **4** furious **5** ridiculous
6 hilarious **7** freezing **8** boiling

3

1 h **2** c **3** g **4** a **5** i **6** d **7** b **8** j **9** e **10** f

Study tips

1 Give students time to read the tips individually and tick the things they've done.

2 Students compare their answers in pairs, then choose two things they would like to try. In feedback, ask students to share their ideas with the class and suggest any other ways they can use English outside the classroom.

OVERVIEW

PAGES 76–77

Reading and vocabulary: My big night out!

Common European Framework: Students can scan longer texts in order to locate desired information and gather information from different parts of a text in order to fulfil a specific task.

PAGES 78–79

Grammar: Polite requests; *will* and *shall* for instant responses

Common European Framework: Students can express themselves confidently, clearly and politely in a formal or informal register, appropriate to the situation and person(s) concerned.

PAGES 80–81

Vocabulary and listening: Social behaviour

Vocabulary: Talking about norms and customs

Common European Framework: Students can express their thoughts about abstract or cultural topics; can use a good range of vocabulary for most general topics.

PAGES 82–83

Task: Give tips on how to behave

Common European Framework: Students can understand and exchange advice on familiar matters.

PAGES 84–85

World culture: Addicted to games

Common European Framework: Students can understand documentaries in standard dialect; can exchange, check and confirm factual information.

Reading and vocabulary

(PAGES 76–77)

WARM UP

Write the following prompts on the board: *friends, family, stay in, go out, exercise, TV* and *food*. Tell the class what you did last weekend, working through each of the categories (e.g. *On Friday night I went out with some friends after work. On Saturday I went to my mother's for lunch*, etc.). Students then tell each other what they did last weekend in pairs. In feedback, nominate students to describe their partner's weekend to the class and find out who had the most interesting weekend.

1a Check that everyone understands what is meant by *go out* and ask one or two students to tell the class what they did when they went out recently. Check the meaning of *karaoke, live music, clubbing* and *grab a snack*. Students work individually.

b Students work in small groups to discuss the questions before reporting back to the class.

2 Students discuss the questions in the same groups as before. Encourage them to use the phrases from exercise 1a.

3 Focus attention on the photos and quotes. Discuss the questions as a class and write students' ideas for question 2 on the board.

ANSWERS:

1 Jiao Wu lives in Beijing, China. Hassan Kashani lives in Tehran, Iran. Ewen Anderson lives on the Isle of Eigg, Scotland.

4a Check understanding of *unwind* (/ʌnˈwaɪnd/) and *hang out*. Students read the text, then discuss what the expressions mean in pairs before checking answers with the class.

ANSWERS:

Jiao Wu: BPT (Beijing Party Time) is the 'time zone' of Beijing's night life. Jiao goes out at midnight, when most people are going to bed. Bling is the name of a nightclub that Jiao and his friends go to. (In informal English, *bling* means expensive objects such as jewellery that people wear in order to be noticed.) At Bling, the DJ sits in a Bentley car in the middle of the dance floor. A Bentley is a very expensive luxury car. Ghost Street is a road where the restaurants stay open all night. Jiao and his friends go there at around 4.00 a.m.

Hasson: On Saturday nights Hassan and his friends go driving in the fashionable centre of Tehran. They write their mobile phone numbers on pieces of paper, which they throw into girls' cars. Girls only read the phone numbers of men who drive smart cars (a smart car is one which is new and fashionable).

Ewen: Only 70 people live on the Isle of Eigg, so Ewen doesn't have much choice about where to go out. The community hall is a building used for public events and it is where people go on Saturday nights. Ewen and his friends go at about 9 o'clock. One unusual thing about life on the island is that young and old people socialise together, so people of all ages go to the community hall. A folk band from the mainland performs at the community hall on Saturday nights and people dance.

b Students answer the questions in pairs before checking answers with the class.

ANSWERS:

1 There's a lot more choice than in the past and people go to nightclubs much more. Before, people usually went out for dinner and then to a karaoke bar.
2 Because one of the men who threw a phone number into the car she was in was her boyfriend.
3 Young and old people go to the community hall, but the young people stay out much later.

Reading and vocabulary, exercise 4: Alternative suggestion

Put students in groups of three and allocate one of the texts to each student. Students read their text and make notes, then tell the other students in the group what they found out. When they have finished, give students a few minutes to quickly read the other two texts before checking answers with the class.

5 Using the first expression (*we* ***hit*** *the bars in ...*, line 05), do an example with the whole class, following this procedure:

- Students find the word in the text and underline it.
- They decide what type of word it is (verb, noun, adjective, etc.).
- They try to guess its meaning. If they are unsure, they try to guess something about the word, for example, if it is positive or negative.

Note: guessing the meaning of unknown vocabulary from context (before looking it up in a dictionary) is a very important reading skill. It helps students to increase their vocabulary and also makes them more independent learners.

Students check the meanings in dictionaries before checking answers with the class. In feedback, ask students how close their guesses were.

ANSWERS:

1 we hit the bars in ... : (informal) go to bars
2 to be outrageous: to be extremely unusual, shocking and slightly amusing
3 to make excuses: to invent reasons for your actions (which often hide your real intentions)
4 what he's up to: (informal) if you are 'up to something', you are doing something secret or something you should not be doing
5 we all head down to ... : if you 'head' somewhere, you go or travel towards it
6 a foe: an enemy
7 it's our way: it's a custom/normal behaviour in our culture
8 the mainland: the main/large area of land that forms a country, compared to the islands near it which are part of the same country

6a Students discuss the questions in groups. Circulate, supplying any vocabulary they need. Nominate students from each group to share their answers with the class.

b Give students a few minutes to read the facts, then discuss in pairs which they found most interesting. Ask the class if they know any similar facts about their own country/-ies.

ADDITIONAL PRACTICE

Resource bank: Activity 8A *Vocabulary extension* (Informal words and phrases)

Language focus 1 (PAGES 78–79)

Polite requests

See *Teaching tips: Using a discovery approach to grammar*, page 20.

WARM UP

Dictate the following requests:

1 Give me the bill. 2 Do you mind if I sit here? 3 Excuse me, can I get past, please? 4 Lend me your pen. 5 I want a coffee.

Students decide in pairs which requests are polite (requests 2 and 3), then discuss how they could make the other requests sound more polite. Elicit their ideas and write them on the board.

1 **8.1** Focus attention on the pictures and elicit what's happening in each one. Pause the recording after each request for students to look at the pictures and decide who is talking, then compare their ideas in pairs. If they do not hear the first time, replay the request rather than repeating it yourself.

ANSWERS:

Picture A

1 *Can I have the bill, please?* the businessman sitting at the table alone
2 *Excuse me, can I get past please?* the waiter carrying a tray of drinks
3 *Could you pass me the water, please?* the girl at a table with two friends

Picture B

4 *Is it alright if I sit here?* the man standing next to the empty bar stool
5 *Do you mind if I leave a bit early today?* the barman talking to his boss
6 *Would you mind watching my bag while I go to the toilet?* the woman with the shopping bags

2a **8.2** Students listen to the complete conversations and answer the questions before comparing their answers in pairs.

ANSWERS:

The other person only says *no* in conversation 5. The boss says she needs the barman at work at the moment.

b With stronger classes, ask students to complete the questions and answers from memory before listening to check their answers. Otherwise, play the recording, pausing after each question and answer for students to write the missing words.

ANSWERS:

1 A: **Can I** have the bill, **please**? B: Certainly, sir.
2 A: **Excuse me**, can I get past please? B: **Sure**.
3 A: **Could you** pass me the water, please? B: Here you are.
4 A: **Is it** alright **if I** sit here? B: Sure, **go** ahead.
5 A: **Do you mind if I** leave a bit early today?
B: I'm afraid I need you here at the moment.
6 A: **Would you mind watching** my bag while I go to the toilet?
B: **Of course** not.

GRAMMAR

Polite requests

Check that students understand the difference between asking if you can do something (a request for permission) and asking someone else to do something (a request). Students work in pairs, underlining the different types of phrases in the audio script before checking answers with the whole class. If you did the Warm up activity, go back to the polite forms you wrote on the board and tick any that appear in the audio script.

ANSWERS:

1 Can I ... , Is it all right if I ... , Do you mind if I ...
2 Could you ... , Would you mind ...
3 Certainly. Sure. Sure, go ahead.
(Notes: *Here you are* is only used when you give/pass something to someone.
Of course not is used in response to the questions *Would you mind ... ?* and *Do you mind ... ?*)
4 I'm afraid ...

Point out the following:

- *Will/Would* are only used to ask other people to do things. *Can/Could* can be used with both types of request.
- The modal verbs here are followed by an infinitive without *to*, but *Do you mind ... ?/Would you mind ... ?* are followed by either a gerund or an *if* clause.
- Strictly speaking, with *Do you mind ... ?/Would you mind ... ?*, if you want to grant a request (say *yes*), the answer is *No* or *Of course not*.
- Other common phrases are: *Will you ... ? Would you ... ? Could/Can I possibly ... ?* More polite phrases are: *Do you think you could possibly ... ? Would you be so kind as to ... ?* These are not used very often, however, and students may sound sarcastic or ridiculous to native speakers if they use them inappropriately.

You may want to ask students to read Study 1 on page 153 for a more detailed explanation of polite requests.

PRONUNCIATION

See *Teaching tips: Helping students with pronunciation*, page 22.

Potential problem with polite requests

Students often equate being *formal* with being *polite* and, as a result, may use formal phrases, but actually sound impolite. To demonstrate the difference, go through the following example situation:

You want to get past someone in a shop and say, 'Excuse me.' The person ignores you, so you say (in a slightly agitated voice), 'Excuse me, please.' The person still ignores you, so you say (angrily, almost shouting), 'Would you possibly mind moving?!'

The aim here is to show that when being polite, *how* you say something is much more important than *what* you say.

8.3 Point out that how you say these polite requests is just as important as the words you choose. Play the recording and point out the intonation patterns. Get students to copy them. Exaggerate or hum the pattern to help them hear it better if necessary. Students practise the requests, saying them first to themselves and then, when they are more confident, to a partner.

PRACTICE

If you think students need more controlled practice before these exercises, they could do Practice 1 on page 153 first.

1 Write the example on the board, without the handwritten additions, and ask students what is wrong with it. Ask for their suggestions about how to make it more polite and compare what they say with the corrections in the book. Check the meaning of *to lend someone something, a flat battery, to give someone a lift, to tell someone the way* and *to pick something up from somewhere*. Students work in pairs before checking answers with the class. Focus on appropriate levels of formality and remind students that an overly polite phrase for a simple request can sound sarcastic. Get students to practise the dialogues in pairs, paying attention to intonation.

SUGGESTED ANSWERS:

1 A: Could I use your pen? **B:** Yes, of course.
2 A: Could you pass me my coat, please? **B:** Sure, here you are.
3 A: Could you possibly* lend me €10 till tomorrow?
B: I'm afraid I haven't got any money.
4 A: Could you bring me another coffee? **B:** Certainly.
5 A: Can you lend me your phone? **B:** Sorry, but the battery is flat.
6 A: If you're going into town, would you mind giving me a lift?
B: Of course not.
7 A: Could you tell me the way to the bus station?
B: I'm sorry, but I don't know this area.
8 A: Can you pick up my suit from the dry cleaner's?
B: I'm afraid I won't be able to. I'll have too much to carry.
*Asking for money is potentially embarrassing even between friends, so this very polite language is appropriate.

2a Give one or two examples of the kinds of requests students could make. Give them a few minutes to think of the requests, circulating to supply any vocabulary they need.

b Look at the example with the class, then put students into pairs to do the activity. Insist that if students say *no*, they give a reason why.

ADDITIONAL PRACTICE

Study, practice & remember: Practice 1

Workbook: Language focus 1: *Polite requests*, pages 46–47; Pronunciation: *Polite intonation in requests*, page 47

Language focus 2 (PAGE 79)

will and *shall* for instant responses

See *Teaching tips: Using a discovery approach to grammar*, page 20.

1 **8.4** Focus students' attention on the pictures and get them to guess as a class what the person wants to do in each case. Play the recording for students to check their answers.

ANSWERS:

A: The woman wants to go on the rollercoaster, but the man doesn't. The woman gets what she wants.
B: The woman on the left wants to go for a coffee, but the woman on the right doesn't. The woman on the right gets what she wants.

2 Students choose the correct answers individually, then check in pairs. Play the recording again for students to check their answers.

ANSWERS:

1 Shall we **2** I'll **3** Shall I **4** I'll **5** Shall we **6** I'm going to **7** I'm going to **8** Shall I

GRAMMAR

will **and** ***shall*** **for instant responses**

Language focus 2: Language notes

- No distinction is made here between 'spontaneous decisions' and 'offers', as we feel that this distinction is artificial as far as *will* is concerned.
- The distinction between *will* and *going to* is described further in Study 2 on page 154.

1a Elicit the first example, then get students to work individually to find the other examples.

ANSWERS:

1 Shall I help you? Shall I take you to the supermarket?
2 Shall we go on the roller coaster? Shall we have a quick coffee?

b Disucss the question as a class.

ANSWERS:

We use *Shall I ...* ? for offers and *Shall we ...* ? for suggestions.

2a Students discuss the questions in pairs before checking answers with the class.

ANSWERS:

1 sentences 6 and 7 **2** sentences 2 and 4

b Discuss the question as a class.

ANSWER:

1 We use *going to* if the speaker has already decided what to do and *will* if he/she is deciding as they speak.

Highlight that:

- *shall* is used in the question form here.
- in this meaning, we don't use *will* in the question form.

You may want to ask students to read Study 2 on page 154 for a more detailed explanation of *will* and *shall* for instant responses.

PRACTICE

If you think students need more controlled practice before these exercises, they could do Practice 2 on page 154 first.

1 Check understanding of *a get-well card* and *to be stuck* (*with homework*). Students turn to page 127 and discuss which responses they'd give and why. Nominate students to share their answer with the class.

2 Give students one minute to read the conversation and decide which situation it comes from. Students complete the conversation individually, then check answers in pairs before checking with the class.

ANSWERS:
The conversation is based on situation 1.
1 Shall we **2** I'm going to **3** I'll **4** I'll **5** I'm going to **6** I'll

3 Students prepare their conversations in pairs. Weaker classes might like to write the conversations in full. Otherwise, students can take notes or practise orally. Circulate and check students are using *will* and *shall* correctly, and note any common errors for analysis later. When they are ready, students act out their conversations for the class. Ask other students to listen to the conversations and guess which situation from exercise 1 each one comes from.

Language focus 1 and 2: Additional activity

Among the language studied in this unit are many 'fixed' or 'semi-fixed' polite phrases which will be useful in a wide range of social situations. It might be useful to make a wall poster or a series of posters to remind students of these phrases. Possible sections are:

in a restaurant: *Could you bring me the bill? Could I have a light?/ Could you bring me the menu?*

at someone's house: *Could you pass me the salt?/Would you like me to open the wine?/Could I use your phone?/I'll do the washing-up.*

in the street/on the train, etc.: *Can you tell me the time?/Could you tell me the way to … ?/Could I get past, please?/Is it alright if I open the window?*

helping people: *I'll do that for you if you like./I'll lend you … if you like./I'll help you with that./I'll give you a lift.*

ADDITIONAL PRACTICE

Resource bank: Activity 8B *Willing!* (*will* and *shall* for instant responses)

Study, practice & remember: Practice 2

Workbook: Language focus 2: Will *and* shall *for instant responses*, pages 47–48

Vocabulary and listening

(PAGES 80–81)

Social behaviour

See *Teaching tips: Working with lexis*, page 21.

1a Check that students understand *good manners* and *bad manners*. Go through the examples with the class and ask if they agree. Students work in pairs to add three more ideas to each column.

b If you have a multilingual class, try to organise students in pairs from the same countries. Ask each pair to read out their ideas to the class and ask if other students agree.

2a Students match the verbs and expressions individually, using a dictionary, then check answers in pairs. Check answers with the class and check understanding of each phrase. Drill the expressions and check the pronunciation of *share* /ʃeə/, *shake* /ʃeɪk/, *hug* /hʌg/ and *refuse* /rɪ'fjuːz/.

ANSWERS:
1 c **2** f **3** k **4** e **5** a **6** g **7** b **8** d **9** h **10** i **11** j

Vocabulary and listening, exercise 2a: Alternative suggestion

With stronger classes, write the verbs in A on the board and ask students to close their books. Students work in pairs to suggest ways to finish the phrases. When they have finished, elicit their ideas and write them on the board, next to each verb, in a different colour.

After exercise 2a, go back to the list on the board and compare students' ideas with those in the Students' Book.

b Students find the phrases in the quiz and underline them. Check answers with the class and ask students if they were correct.

ANSWERS:
1 *offer to pay* is in 5b **2** *share the bill* is in 5c **3** *shake hands* is in 1a **4** *go out on a date* is in question 5 **5** *kiss someone on both cheeks* is in 1c **6** *take someone home* is in 6c **7** *hug each other* is in 1d **8** *insist on paying* is in 5b **9** *refuse an invitation* is in 7a
10 *invite someone to your house* is in question 3
11 *pick someone up* is in 6a

3 Students do the quiz in pairs, asking and answering the questions and explaining their answers. Nominate students to share their ideas with the class.

4a **8.5** Focus students' attention on the questions and check they understand what to listen for. Students listen to the recording, then answer the questions in pairs before checking answers with the class.

ANSWERS:
1 Florence is a young woman (late teens /twenties). Ruth is much older (seventies). Ruth is Florence's grandmother.
2 A 3 **B** 1 **C** 5 **D** 2 **E** 8

b Play the recording again, pausing after each answer for students to answer the questions in pairs. Check answers with the class.

ANSWERS:
A Ruth: a; Florence: c
B Florence: d, but c (kiss on cheeks) for close female friends; Ruth: b, or a (shake hands) for someone you haven't seen for a long time
C Florence: a on a first date, but the woman should offer to pay (b). After that, c if they have the same amount of money, or d if one has more than the other; Ruth: a
D Ruth: c; Florence: b
E Ruth: d; Florence: c

5 Students discuss the questions in pairs. Encourage them to give reasons and examples.

ADDITIONAL PRACTICE

Workbook: Vocabulary: *Social behaviour*, page 49

Vocabulary (PAGE 81)

Talking about norms and customs

See *Teaching tips: Working with lexis*, page 21.

1 Check understanding of *be in someone's way, jump queues, take turns* and *be offended*. Students read the tips and tick or cross each one individually. When they are ready, nominate a different student for each tip to share their answer with the class and find out if other students agree.

2 Point out the generalisation which has been taken from the tips in exercise 1. Students work individually or in pairs to find three more in the text. As you check answers, highlight:

- the impersonal construction *It is … (for someone) to do something*.
- some other adjectives often used in this construction, for example, *common, OK, sensible*.
- the use of adjective + infinitive to talk about general situations, and adjective + *for* to talk about people.

ANSWERS:

(Note: *It's perfectly normal to …* can go in two categories.)

Phrases for making generalisations: *It isn't usual to … , tend to/ don't tend to … , It's perfectly normal to …*

Phrases for saying what is good manners/acceptable: *It's good manners to … , It's OK to … , It's important to … , It's perfectly normal to …*

Phrases for saying what is bad manners/unacceptable: *It's considered rude to … , It's unacceptable to …*

3a Go through the example with the class. Students rewrite the sentences individually before comparing in pairs or groups. There will obviously be differences in multi-nationality groups, but even in mono-nationality groups there will probably be differences of opinion for students to discuss/explain.

b Point out the example with the class. Students write their sentences individually before comparing answers in pairs or groups. Encourage them to use the phrases in exercise 2.

ADDITIONAL PRACTICE

Resource bank: 8C *Doonbogs!* Vocabulary extension (Talking about norms and customs)

Workbook: Vocabulary: *Talking about norms and customs*, page 51

Task (PAGES 82–83)

Give tips on how to behave

See *Teaching tips: Making tasks work*, page 23.

Preparation (PAGE 82)

Listening

1 **8.6** Explain that students will hear the seven people in the order in which they are listed on the page. Give students time to read the topics. Students listen and match. Emphasise that in some cases there may be more than one possible answer. Warn students that the extracts are quite short and that they should listen for gist by finding clues as to the topic(s) being talked about by each person. Emphasise that they only need to listen for the topic and that they will listen again to find further information. You could pause the recording after each speaker to give students time to think and compare answers. Check answers with the class.

ANSWERS:

1 a 2 c/e 3 b 4 c/e 5 a 6 b 7 d

2 Students discuss what they can remember in pairs. Play the recording again, pausing after each person to give students time to make a few notes and compare their answers in pairs. Check answers with the class.

ANSWERS:

1 People usually shake hands every time they greet each other.
2 Act cool when you start going out with someone. Don't reply to texts immediately and if a man doesn't reply to your text after two days, it means he isn't interested.
3 When you go out, you are expected to dress smartly and women should wear nice make-up and jewellery.
4 When you start seeing someone, don't become friends on Facebook immediately.
5 In Peru, it's normal to arrive about an hour late when you visit friends. If you really want people to arrive on time, you have to specify 'English time'.
6 In Madrid it is normal to go out late – about 11 p.m. – and stay out all night.
7 Young people tend to eat with their families. You can only go on a date with someone if you're engaged. After dinner, Khalid drives around with his friends or goes to a shopping mall to hang out.

3 Focus students' attention on the Useful language box on page 83. Students listen and tick the phrases they hear, then check answers with the class. Drill the phrases with the class.

ANSWERS:

Aleksander: It's normal to …
Mei: You should always …
Lee Kuan: It's important to … ; People expect you to …
Simone: You should definitely …
Rosa: You should never … ; It's perfectly OK to …
Ramon: It's perfectly normal to …
Khalid: Generally speaking, (people) …

Task (PAGE 83)

Speaking

1 Put students in groups and ask them to choose one of the topics from exercise 1 on page 82 together.

2a Students work individually to make lists of tips. Circulate and help with any vocabulary and feed in phrases from the Useful language box, sections a and b, where appropriate.

b Students share their lists in groups and choose the best tips to compile a list.

3 When they are ready, nominate a student from each group to read out their tips to the class. Ask other students to add ideas or if they disagree with any of them.

Task: Alternative suggestion

a If you do not have enough time to cover the whole task in one lesson, do Preparation: Listening and get students to make a list of tips/points in one class (Task: Speaking, exercise 1) and present them in the next class (Task: Speaking, exercise 2).

b If you have a young mono-nationality class who have difficulty in seeing their own culture from an outside perspective, try the following:

- Get students to think of a specific culture or person to focus their advice on. It could be a famous British/American person they identify with (a film star, footballer, etc.).
- Get students to think about British/American films and any differences in social behaviour they have noticed, before imagining what British/American people would find strange in their culture.
- Tell students about some of the things you found different when you first arrived in their country.

Follow up (PAGE 83)

Writing

1 Students use their notes from exercise 2 to write a list of tips. If you have time and think students could use the practice, ask them to choose another topic from the one they spoke about.

Share your task

Some additional ideas could include:

- Students film/record short scenes which show someone committing a 'faux pas', i.e. not following the advice on social behaviour they spoke about during the task. They then play it to the class, who guess what the mistake was.
- Students film/record themselves giving their advice from the task for a culture programme.
- Students film/record themselves giving advice, with one erroneous piece of advice. They then play it to the class, who must guess which piece of advice is wrong.

ADDITIONAL PRACTICE

Resource bank: Activity 8D *Wordspot:* go (collocations with *go*)

World culture (PAGES 84–85)

Addicted to games

Culture notes

The earliest known video game was produced in 1947 and was called *Cathode Ray Tube Amusement Device*. Video games continued to be developed throughout the 1950s and 1960s, but it wasn't until the 1970s that they became popular, with the release of *The Magnavox Odyssey* in 1972, which was the first home console. Later, in 1977, a simple tennis-style game called *Pong* was created, which became so popular that a surge in clone devices appeared. The 1980s are often referred to as 'the golden age' of video games, when numerous new companies appeared in new markets, producing a range of different games.

Nowadays, the video game industry is worth US$10.5 billion and the three largest markets are North America (USA and Canada), the UK and Japan, though China and India are growing markets. Traditionally, video games have been played on either consoles, a home computer or a handheld device, though the distinction is now becoming blurred, and a platform may include a social networking site, whether it is accessed on a computer, a smart phone or a smart TV.

There are many different genres of video games, including casual games such as hidden object, simulation or tower defence games, action games such as first person shooters or massively multiplayer online role-playing games (MMORPGs), adventure games and educational games such as flight simulators.

The average gamer is aged between 25–40 and has been playing for 12 years. It is estimated that there are now more female gamers than boys under 17, and the average gamer spends eight hours a week playing games. The most popular game ever sold was *Super Mario Bros 3*.

WARM UP

Write the following prompts on the board: *name, where/when it's set, main characters, how to play, best thing about it, worst thing about it*. Tell students about a video game you like playing, or have enjoyed in the past, using the prompts on the board. If possible, show students part of the game itself. Students describe a favourite video game in small groups. In feedback, nominate students to share their ideas with the class and find out what the most popular games are.

Find out first (PAGE 84)

1a Go through the categories in the fact file and check understanding. Students work in pairs to complete the fact file.

b Students research the answers individually, then check in pairs, using the search terms to help them. In feedback, check answers with the class and feed in any additional information from the Culture notes.

SUGGESTED ANSWERS:

(These are likely to vary.)
Total revenue: $10.5 billion **Average age:** 34 years old
Female gamers: 40%
Average number of hours playing: 8 per week
Most popular game ever: Super Mario Bros 3

View (PAGE 84)

See *Teaching tips: Using the video material in the classroom*, page 24.

2a Students discuss the questions in pairs. In feedback, nominate students to share their ideas with the class and ask students what they think are the signs that someone is addicted to gaming (e.g. they prefer gaming to going out with friends, they feel anxious if they can't play, etc.)

b Give students plenty of time to read the sentences and check understanding. Play the DVD for students to complete the sentences, then check answers in pairs. Check answers with the class.

ANSWERS:

1 c 2 a 3 b 4 c

View, exercise 2b: Alternative suggestion

With stronger classes, write the four sentence starters on the board and ask students to close their books. Play the DVD for students to complete the sentences with their own ideas before checking answers in pairs.

Students open their books and use their notes to choose the correct answers. Check answers with the class.

3a Go through the numbers with the class and elicit students' ideas. Play the DVD again for students to check their answers before checking in pairs. Check answers with the class.

ANSWERS:

five years: British government wants everyone to have broadband internet access in five years' time; gaming has become more popular in last five years **three billion:** amount spent a year on gaming
20 hours a day: Chris played *World of Warcraft* up to 20 hours a day
85 percent: percentage of people in Korea who have fast broadband
ten hours: Korean boy in video sometimes spent ten hours gaming
two percent: percentage of Korean children seriously addicted

b Students discuss the questions in pairs.

World view (PAGE 85)

4a Go through the questions with the class and check students understand what to watch for. Play the DVD for students to watch and decide which question each speaker is answering. Students check answers in pairs before checking with the class.

ANSWERS:

Imogen: questions 1 and 4 **Steve:** questions 1, 2 and 3
Carol: questions 2, 3 and 4

b Students work in pairs. Play the DVD again for students to make notes, then check answers with the class.

ANSWERS:

	Imogen	Steve	Carol
1	variety is important	moderation is important	
2		depends on who they are intended for	a lot of games are too violent; worried about her son seeing too much violence and how this will affect him
3		children not supposed to watch violent games	research shows that video games with guns affects children's behaviour
4	parents should encourage a variety of interests		parents should allow children a certain amount of time to play video games

c Put students in small groups and ask them to discuss and try to agree on a group answer to each question. Circulate and help with vocabulary, writing any new words/phrases on the board.

Find out more (PAGE 85)

5a Check understanding of the things in the box by eliciting examples of each one. Students discuss the questions in pairs.

b Go through the questions with the class and elicit possible answers. Students choose one of the possible addictions and research it online, using the search terms provided and making notes. Circulate and help with vocabulary where necessary.

Write up your research

6 Go through the prompts with the class and elicit ways to finish each one as an example. Students write their paragraphs individually, using their notes from exercise 5b. When they have finished, put students in pairs to check and correct each other's work. In feedback, ask students to share any interesting information they found out.

Students can now do Unit test 4 on the Teacher's Resource Disc.

Study, practice & remember

(PAGES 153–155)

See *Teaching tips: Using the Study, practice and remember sections*, page 25.

Practice 1

ANSWERS:

1

1 Would you mind passing my bag? **2** Could you possibly take me into town? **3** Do you think you could cook dinner this evening? **4** Do you think I could borrow $10 until tomorrow? **5** Is it alright if I use your phone? **6** Could I have a window seat? **7** Will you turn the light off? **8** Do you mind if I take the car tonight? **9** Would you tell Jenny about the part? **10** Could I possibly leave early on Friday?

2

1 Would you mind ... , No, not at all. **2** Do you think you could give ... , Yes, of course. **3** Is it alright if ... , ... someone is sitting there **4** Could I possibly ... , Here you are.

3

1 turning down your music **2** to read/if I read your magazine **3** you fetch my glasses **4** if I call you tomorrow **5** you translate **6** you make (me) **7** you could take a photo **8** you change **9** having a look at **10** I could go home early

Practice 2

ANSWERS:

1

1 c **2** e **3** a **4** f **5** b **6** d

2

1 1, 2, 4, 5 **2** 3, 6

3

1 c **2** a **3** a **4** b

4

1 I'll close **2** I'll check **3** I'm going to have **4** I'll look after **5** I'll help **6** I'm going to sit **7** I'll lend you **8** I'm going to lose

Remember these words

ANSWERS:

1

1 d **2** f **3** e **4** c **5** b **6** a

2

1 for people to shake hands when they meet. **2** rude to blow your nose in public. **3** manners to ask another person's age. **4** to share the bill.

3

1 to refuse an invitation **2** to stay out late **3** to borrow **4** the host **5** bad manners **6** uncool

4

1 to pay **2** on both cheeks **3** On the whole **4** insisted on **5** have dinner **6** take her home **7** to vibrate

Study tips

1 Introduce the topic by referring back to any times students have recorded/filmed themselves after doing the tasks in the Students' Book and find out how useful they were. Students work individually to tick the ideas, then compare in pairs.

2 Students choose which ideas would suit them best. Elicit answers from the class and discuss any other ideas students have.

09 STUFF!

OVERVIEW

PAGES 86–87

Reading and speaking: Consumer crazy

Common European Framework: Students can understand articles and reports concerned with contemporary problems; can pass on detailed information reliably.

PAGES 88–89

Grammar: Defining relative clauses

Vocabulary: How gadgets work

Common European Framework: Students can define the features of something; can understand straightforward instructions for a piece of equipment.

PAGES 90–91

Grammar: Quantifiers

Vocabulary: Describing everyday objects

Common European Framework: Students can explain why something is a problem, discuss what to do next, compare and contrast alternatives; can understand simple technical information, such as operating instructions for everyday equipment.

PAGES 92–93

Task: Talk about things you couldn't live without

Common European Framework: Students can give clear, detailed descriptions, expanding and supporting ideas with subsidiary points and relevant examples.

PAGES 94–95

Speaking: Buying things

Writing: A short thank-you message

Common European Framework: Students can cope with routine situations in shops; can write personal letters describing experiences, feelings and events in some detail.

Reading and speaking (PAGES 86–87)

WARM UP

Tell students that you are going to dictate a short story to them and they need to listen and take notes in order to rewrite the story afterwards. Emphasise that they shouldn't try to write every word, but just take notes. Read out the following story at a normal speed. Repeat it as many times as students want, but don't slow down at any stage.

A woman was in the supermarket with a small child. As they passed the cookie section, the little girl asked for cookies. When the woman said she couldn't have any, the girl began to cry. The woman kept repeating softly: 'Don't cry, Monica, don't scream, Monica, don't be upset, Monica, keep calm, Monica. 'A woman standing next to her said: 'Wow, you're really patient with little Monica!' The mother replied: 'I'm Monica!'

When they are ready, students rewrite the story in pairs. In feedback, ask students to read out the stories they wrote and compare with the original.

1a Check understanding and pronunciation of *gadgets* /ˈgædʒɪts/. Give students one or two minutes to complete the sentences and emphasise that they can use the ideas in the box or their own ideas. When they are ready, students compare their ideas in pairs.

b Students discuss the questions in pairs.

2 Focus attention on the photos and title. Students read the introduction, then check answers in pairs before checking with the class.

SUGGESTED ANSWER:

The article is about consumerism, where people are encouraged to buy goods in ever-greater amounts, and how two people respond to this.

3a Check understanding of *matching* (e.g. *matching shoes*), *to blame*, *technology mogul* (/ˈməʊgəl/), *entrepreneur* (/ɒntrəprəˈnɜː/) and *bills*. Put students in pairs and go through the questions. Students read their texts and make notes to answer the questions.

b Students share their answers from the texts they read. Check answers with the class.

SUGGESTED ANSWERS:

Louise:

1 lives in a flat, 31 years old, single, no children, highly paid job, doesn't smoke or drink
2 She has lots of clothes, shoes, handbags and make-up because she goes shopping every Saturday.
3 Louise works hard all week and likes to reward herself by going shopping. She doesn't spend her money on smoking or drinking and she sees shopping as her main hobby.
4 There are more and more women like Louise who are addicted to shopping. They often have busy careers and this can mean other parts of their lives are not satisfactory. Shopping is an easy way to feel good about themselves.
5 The lifestyle of modern women is to blame.

Andrew:

1 technology mogul and successful entrepreneur, voluntarily homeless, travels between New York and Silicon Valley (California) with his work
2 Andrew has only 15 possessions because he sold everything else.
3 He wants freedom from the responsibility of possessions.
4 There are other people like Andrew, who have given up their apartments and possessions and now rely on technology.
5 In the 21st century, digital technology can replace physical possessions.

4 Give students a few minutes to read the other text quickly. When they are ready, students discuss the meanings of the words and phrases in pairs. Check answers with the class, giving further explanations/examples where necessary.

ANSWERS:

1 a reward: something that you get because you have done something good or helpful or have worked hard
2 a purchase: something you buy
3 to deserve: to have earned something by good actions or behaviour
4 time-poor: not having much free time because of work commitments
5 a quick-fix solution: a solution to a problem that is quick, but not good or permanent
6 homeless: without a home
7 to seek: to try to get something
8 lack of choice: not having too many things to choose between

5 Put students in groups of four or five. Each student takes turns to choose a question for the group to discuss. In feedback, nominate a student from each group to share their ideas with the class.

Find out more

This could be done in class or set for homework if you are short of time. Divide the class in half and ask one half to find out about shopaholics and the other to find out about extreme minimalists. When they are ready, put students in pairs with one student from each group and ask them to make two lists of 'facts' about each type. Circulate and help with vocabulary where necessary. When they have finished, display their lists round the class and ask students to walk around and read them.

ADDITIONAL PRACTICE

Workbook: Listen and read: *eBay*, pages 52–53

Language focus 1 (PAGE 88)

Defining relative clauses

See *Teaching tips: Using a discovery approach to grammar*, page 20.

1 Write the examples on the board. Ask students to close their books and think of the five things in pairs. Circulate and help with vocabulary where necessary. When they have finished, elicit students' ideas and write them on the board.

2 Students compare their ideas with the words in the box in pairs. Tell them not to worry if they don't understand all the words in the box, as they'll look at the meanings afterwards. In feedback, elicit how many of their ideas were included. Students work individually, to do the matching task, then check in pairs before checking with the class.

ANSWERS:

1 an app store **2** sat-nav **3** password **4** guyliner **5** blogger
6 wi-fi hotspot **7** personal trainer **8** internet addict
9 Facebook wall **10** energy drink

GRAMMAR

Defining relative clauses

1 Focus students' attention on the example, showing the relative pronoun underlined. Students underline the relative pronouns in the quiz. Check answers with the whole class.

ANSWERS:

(Sentences 4 and 7 don't have relative pronouns.)
1 It's a virtual shop which sells applications for phones, etc.
2 It's a machine that gives you directions when you are driving.
3 It's a secret word which you use to access computers, bank accounts, etc.
5 It's a person who writes a kind of online diary for others to read.
6 It's a public area where people can connect their phones and computers to the internet.
8 It's a person whose life is dominated by the internet.
9 It's a section of your social networking profile where people can leave messages for you.
10 It's a drink which is designed to give you more energy.

2 Students work individually or in pairs before checking answers with the class. Emphasise that they should look at the examples to help them work out the rules.

ANSWERS:

1 Who **2** Which **3** Where **4** Whose

3 Students choose the correct options in pairs before checking answers with the class.

ANSWERS:

1 object **2** passive

Potential problem with defining relative clauses

The relative pronoun can be omitted in definition 4 because *make-up* is the object rather than the subject of the relative clause. If students have difficulty with this concept, write the following sentence on the board:

Men put make-up on their eyes.
(S) (V) (O)

In sentence 7, *who* can be left out for the same reason. Contrast this with sentence 1, by writing the following sentence on the board:

The virtual shop sells applications.
(S) (V) (O)

The virtual shop is the subject, and so cannot be omitted. We cannot omit relative pronouns when they are the subject of the sentence. Point out that *whose* and *where* can also not be omitted.

4 Discuss the question as a class.

ANSWER:

3

You may want to ask students to read Study 1 on page 156 for a more detailed explanation of defining relative clauses.

PRACTICE

If you think students need more controlled practice before these exercises, they could do Practice 1 on page 156 first.

1a Students work in pairs before checking answers with the class. Do not pre-teach the words, but offer help if necessary.

ANSWERS:

1 photocopier, that/which
2 bodyguard, that/who
3 launderette, where
4 plumber, whose
5 vacuum cleaner, that/which

b To focus students' attention on the example, write the prompts on the board. Elicit first the item and then the definition. Students work in pairs before checking answers with the class.

ANSWERS:

1 A cooker is a machine that/which cooks food.
2 A cleaner is a person that/who you pay to clean your house or office.
3 A dry cleaner's is a shop where they clean your clothes for you.
4 A decorator is a person whose job is to paint houses.
5 A stationer's is a shop where you buy office supplies.
6 A boiler is a machine that/which heats water for batchs, etc.

c Students work individually, then check answers in pairs before checking with the class.

ANSWERS:

1a 5 **1b** 2

2 Put students into pairs, A and B. Demonstrate the activity with a strong student. Circulate and note down any errors.

3 Put students into teams, A and B. Direct them to the appropriate pages and do one example together. Emphasise that they should not use the relative pronoun if it is not needed.

ADDITIONAL PRACTICE

Resource bank: Activity 9A *Relative clauses crossword* (Defining relative clauses)

Study, practice & remember: Practice 1

Workbook: Language focus 1: *Defining relative clauses*, pages 53–54

Vocabulary and listening (PAGE 89)

How gadgets work

See *Teaching tips: Working with lexis, page 21*.

1 Go through the gadgets and check understanding of any new words. Check the pronunciation of *vacuum* /ˈvækjuːm/, *dishwasher* /ˈdɪʃwɒʃə/ and *photocopier* /ˈfəʊtəʊkɒpɪə/. Students discuss the questions in pairs. When checking answers, write up any possible problems with the gadgets on the board.

2 **9.1** Before listening, emphasise that students only have to identify which machine is being discussed and any words or phrases which helped them to decide.

ANSWERS:

1
1 a laptop **2** a photocopier **3** a touch screen phone
4 a DVD player

2
1 crashes, screen freezes, restart, reinstalling the software
2 paper gets stuck, machine breaks down, open it, large number of copies
3 ringtone, touch the icons, scroll down the menu with your finger, recharge the battery
4 the film's in, press the 'OK' button, ready to watch it, pause it

3 Play the recording, pausing after each conversation for students to check their answers in pairs. When checking answers with the class, check understanding of any phrases students aren't sure about.

ANSWERS:

1 try reinstalling the software: 4 I have to restart it: 3 it crashes: 1 the screen freezes: 2
2 switch the machine off at the wall: 2 the machine breaks down: 1 hold down this button: 4 unplug it: 3
3 recharge the battery: 3 touch the icons: 1 scroll down the menu with your finger: 2
4 press this button: 3 it's switched on: 1 it doesn't work: 4 pause it: 2

Potential problem with phrasal verbs

Switch off and *hold down* are separable phrasal verbs, which means that the object can be placed before or after the preposition. However, if the object is a pronoun, it must be placed between the verb and preposition. Show this by writing the following sentences on the board and asking students which one is not possible (the last one.)

Switch the phone off. *Switch off the phone.*
Switch it off. *Switch off it.*

4a Refer students back to the gadgets in exercise 1. Demonstrate the activity with an example on the board. Students work individually. Circulate and check students are using the phrases correctly.

b Students work in pairs. In feedback, ask one or two students to read out their verbs for the class to guess.

5 If students have a gadget with them, ask them to take it out and show their partner as they explain how it works. Circulate and help with vocabulary where necessary.

PRONUNCIATION

See *Teaching tips: Helping students with pronunciation, page 22*.

1 Explain what a compound noun is (a noun consisting of two parts, noun + noun/gerund or adjective + noun), and give an example. Go through the two rules, writing the examples on the board and marking the stress. Repeat the examples yourself several times to make sure that students can hear the difference.

2 Give students time to work out where the stress should be, without giving the answers at this stage.

3 **9.2** Play the recording, stopping after each compound noun to allow students time to check/correct their answers. Drill the compound nouns.

ANSWERS:

recycling bin, energy drink, bodyguard, mobile phone, washing machine, personal trainer, instruction manual, digital camera, internet addict, personal computer

ADDITIONAL PRACTICE

Workbook: Vocabulary: *How gadgets work*, page 55; Pronunciation: *Stress patterns in compound nouns*, page 55

Language focus 2 (PAGES 90–91)

Quantifiers

See *Teaching tips: Using a discovery approach to grammar*, page 20.

WARM UP

Write three sentences about yourself, each using a different quantifier from the lesson, on the board. Two should be true and one should be false, e.g. *There are a few teachers in my family. I eat too much chocolate. I've drunk several cups of coffee today.* Invite students to ask you *yes/no* questions about each statement, then ask them to guess which one they think is false. Write up some of the other quantifiers from exercise 3 on page 90 of the Students' Book (choose ones that you think students already know). Students then write their own statements and repeat the activity in pairs or small groups.

1a Focus students' attention on the photos and check the meaning and pronunciation of *desert*. Students discuss the questions in small groups. Elicit students' answers and write them on the board.

b Students discuss the question in pairs. Elicit their answers and write the names of the objects on the board. Accept any reasonable answers the students can justify.

2a 9.3 Play the recording, pausing after each speaker for students to write their answers, then check in pairs.

b Students listen again and compare their answers from exercise 1b to the recording. Check answers with the class.

ANSWERS:
In the desert: wet wipes, water, swimming gear, several plastic bags, hat, sunscreen, warm clothes
Climbing: warm clothes, insect repellent, high-energy food (e.g. raisins and peanuts, chocolate), GPS navigator, map and compass, plastic bag
At a music festival: tent, sleeping bag, torch, spare batteries, wellies, money

3 Students work individually to complete the sentences from memory. Play the recording again, then students discuss the question in pairs. Check answers with the class and ask students to give reasons.

ANSWERS:
Fadil
1 We tell people to bring **a couple of** packs of wet wipes.
2 We bring **plenty of** water with us.
3 It's good to bring **several** plastic bags.
4 **A lot of** people forget that the desert is freezing cold at night, so you need to bring some warm clothes.

Abigail
5 They haven't packed **enough** warm clothes to deal with a change in the weather.
6 I always advise people to take **some** insect repellent and **a bit of** food.
7 **Too many** people these days rely on a handheld GPS navigator ... but they can break.

Joel
8 You need a torch with **a few** spare batteries.
9 Often people bring **too much** food with them and they always regret it, because they spend **a lot of** time carrying it around and, actually, there are **plenty of** places to buy food.
10 So really ... all you need is **enough** money!

GRAMMAR

Quantifiers

1 Check that students know the difference between countable and uncountable nouns. Elicit further examples from the classroom and its surroundings (for example, *chair*, *noise*).

ANSWERS:
Countable: people, bag, battery
Uncountable: water, food, money

2 Do some examples with the class, using the sentences from exercise 3. Students do the rest in pairs. Check answers with the class and feed in any other quantifiers students know (for example, *many*, *loads of*).

ANSWERS:
1 a couple of, several, too many, a few 2 a bit of, too much
3 plenty of, enough, some, a lot of

3 Students discuss the question in pairs before checking answers with the class. Ask students to give reasons why the pairs of sentences are different.

ANSWERS:
1 different: *too much* has a negative meaning; *a lot of* does not have a negative meaning
2 different: *enough* means you have as much as you need; *plenty of* means 'more than enough'

Highlight the following:

Too much/a lot of: *too much* often carries negative meaning. For example, *I've eaten too much*. However, *a lot of* does not have any negative implication.

Potential problem with *too much/many*

Many languages don't have an equivalent of *too much/many*, and students may use it interchangeably with *a lot of*. If this is the case with your students, demonstrate the difference by asking the following questions:
If there are three people in a room, are there a lot of people? (no)
If they want to sit down and there is only one chair, are there too many people? (yes)

Enough/plenty: enough means that you have as much as you need. For example, *I've got enough money to buy a new car. Plenty* means 'more than enough'. For example, *I've got plenty of money if I buy this car. I can afford to go on holiday as well.*

Any: any is only negative when accompanied by a negative verb. For example, *I haven't got any money*. A common mistake is: *I've got any money* instead of *I've got no money*; on the other hand, *I didn't have no money* is wrong because it is a double negative.

Loads of: loads of is informal and is usually spoken, not written.

You may want to ask students to read Study 2 on page 157 for a more detailed explanation of quantifiers.

PRACTICE

1 Do the first item as an example, eliciting possibilities and making clear that students should make the sentences true in their opinion. This is best done by asking them to explain their answers. Do this as a spoken exercise initially, but get students to write their sentences afterwards for consolidation.

SUGGESTED ANSWERS:
On camping trips ...
1 there are a lot of insects.
2 there isn't a lot of space in your tent.
3 you need some equipment.
On trips to big cities ...
4 you can find a few cheap places to eat.
5 there are too many people.
6 there are usually plenty of interesting places to visit.
7 there are usually a couple of museums and art galleries.
At the beach ...
8 there is plenty of sand.
9 it's better if there is a bit of sun.
10 there are usually a lot of things to do.

2a Students work in pairs to choose three of the trips and decide what to take. You could ask them if they've been on any of these trips and what they took if so.

b Pairs take it in turns to read out their lists from exercise 2a for the class to guess the trip. If any students have been on these trips, ask them if they agree.

ADDITIONAL PRACTICE

Resource bank: Activity 9B *Camping holiday* (Quantifiers: *a few*, *a lot of*, etc.)
Study, practice & remember: Practice 2
Workbook: Language focus 2: *Quantifiers*, pages 55–56

Vocabulary (PAGE 91)

Describing everyday objects

See *Teaching tips: Working with lexis*, page 21.

1 Ask students to close their books. Give them two minutes to write down the objects they can remember. Elicit answers from the class and write them on the board. Students open their books again and compare the objects on the board with the list in exercise 1b on page 90.

Vocabulary, exercise 1: Alternative suggestion

Bring some everyday objects to class and try to include some of the objects from exercise 1b on page 90. You'll also need to bring a tablecloth or similar material. Arrange the objects on a table at the front of the class and cover them with the tablecloth. Put students in small groups and lift the tablecloth to reveal the objects. Let students look at the objects for 30 seconds and try to memorise them, then cover them again. Students then try to make a list of all the objects in their groups. Elicit the objects they can remember, then lift the tablecloth again for them to check.

2a Students work in pairs to match a description with each object.

ANSWERS:

1 compass **2** sleeping bag **3** wet wipes **4** torch **5** sunscreen **6** insect repellent

b Students work individually, then compare in pairs.

ANSWERS:

1 It's round and it's used for finding your way.
2 It's rectangular and it's made of fabric.
3 They're used for cleaning.
4 It's got batteries inside and it's made of metal.
5 It's used for protecting your skin.
6 It's used for keeping insects away.

3 Students work individually, then compare answers in pairs. When checking answers, highlight the following:
it's + adjective; *it's made of* + material; *it's got* + component; *it's used for* + *-ing*.

ANSWERS:

It's: round, rectangular
It's made of: rubber, fabric, metal
It's got: batteries inside
It's used for: keeping your feet dry, finding your way, cleaning, protecting your skin, keeping insects away

4 Emphasise that students can choose any everyday object and ask any questions they want, as long as the answer is *yes* or *no*. Look at the example questions with them. Circulate, supplying vocabulary.

ADDITIONAL PRACTICE

Resource bank: Activity 9C *Give us a clue* (Describing everyday objects)

Workbook: Vocabulary: *Describing everyday objects*, page 56

Task (PAGES 92–93)

Talk about things you couldn't live without

See *Teaching tips: Making tasks work*, page 23.

Preparation (PAGE 92)

Reading

1 Check understanding of: *insomnia, writer's block* and *a lock*. Students read the texts, then compare answers in pairs before checking with the class.

ANSWERS:

1
Jewellery: It makes her feel good on a grey morning.
Lemsip: She uses it for dealing with all sorts of problems.
Horror films: He loves movies and feeling scared.
Bicycle: It's the fastest way to get around London.
Spikes: They are very comfortable.
Pavoni coffee machine: He's addicted to coffee.
My cats: He's had his two cats for a long time and they are very special to him.

2a Go through the examples in the first text with the class. Students work individually, then check answers in pairs before checking with the class.

ANSWERS:

Jewellery: I just couldn't do without
Lemsip: I use it for dealing with everything
Horror films: I love
Bicycle: I completely rely on
Spikes: I can't do without
Pavoni coffee machine: I'm addicted to; I can't do without
My cats: I couldn't bear to live without

b Focus attention on the Useful language box. Students compare their phrases in pairs. In feedback, drill the phrases from the box.

ANSWERS:

Jewellery: I (just) can't/couldn't do without … ; It makes me feel (good) …
Lemsip: I use it for …
Bicycle: I (completely) rely on it.
Spikes: I can't do without … ; (These spikes are) incredibly comfortable.
Pavoni coffee machine: I am addicted to … ; I can't do without …
My cats: I couldn't bear to live without … ; I've had (these two) for a long time.

Task (PAGE 92)

Speaking

1a Students make their lists individually. Circulate and help with vocabulary where necessary.

b Give students time to plan what they are going to say and encourage them to use the phrases in the Useful language box, sections a–c.

2 Students work in groups of about four. Circulate, making notes about errors for correction later on.

3a Ask students from each group to share/compare answers with the class.

b Give the groups time to decide before sharing answers with the class.

Share your task

Some additional ideas could include:

- Ask students to bring in the objects they spoke about in the task and film themselves showing and talking about them.
- Students film/record themselves talking about their objects, but don't say what they are. They then play the recording to the class, who guess what the objects are.
- Students film themselves as presenters on a shopping channel, trying to 'sell' their objects to the class.

Language live (PAGES 94–95)

Speaking (PAGE 94)

Buying things

See *Teaching tips: Using the video material in the classroom*, page 24.

WARM UP

Bring in photos of different types of shops and display them round the classroom. Students walk around the class and name the shops (e.g. *chemist's, newsagent's*). Check answers and write the names of the shops on the board. Call out the names of different items and ask students to tell you where you can buy them (e.g. *toothpaste, magazines*).

1a Write the following question on the board: *Can I help you?* Ask: *Who usually asks this: a sales assistant or a customer?* (sales assistant). Students think of and write more questions in pairs. In feedback, elicit students' answers and write them on the board.

b Play the DVD for students to compare their questions. When checking answers, tick off any on the board that were used.

2 Go through the table and elicit what type of information students need to complete it. Pause the DVD after the first conversation to give students time to write. Check answers with the class.

ANSWERS:

	Conversation 1	Conversation 2
Product	jeans	colour cartridge for printer
Product code/ Brand name	Red Circle	Elmax/IL5939
Cost	£59.99	£25.99 each (£51.98)
Delivery cost		none
Address		76b Alton Road, NG16 7PP
Pay by ...	debit card	credit card
Other useful information	keep receipt for exchange/refund	free delivery for orders over £25

3a Students work in pairs to match sentences and responses. Check the pronunciation of *receipt* /rɪˈsiːt/ and *delivery* /dɪˈlɪvəri/ and check understanding of *VAT (= Value Added Tax)*. There is no need to check answers at this stage.

b Play the DVD, then check answers with the class. Drill chorally. Students practise in pairs.

ANSWERS:
1 f 2 b 3 i 4 d 5 a 6 e 7 g 8 h 9 c

4a Put students into pairs (a sales assistant and a customer) and explain that they will prepare and act out a similar conversation. Emphasise that they should use the phrases from exercise 3a and ask them to first decide if it's something you buy on the telephone or in a shop.

b Students act out their conversations.

Writing (PAGE 95)

A short thank-you message

1 Check that students understand *offended*. Students discuss the questions in pairs.

2a Explain that students will read four examples of written thanks. Emphasise that the first time they read, they only have to find out what each person is saying thank you for.

ANSWERS:
A hen party **B** a present (a new pair of jeans) **C** being given an interview **D** staying the weekend at a friend's house

b Students read again, putting a phrase in each gap before comparing ideas in pairs. Check answers with the whole class.

ANSWERS:
A Cheers **B** Thanks for **C** I wanted to thank you again for
D Thank you so much

c Students discuss the questions in pairs. Check answers with the whole class, asking students to justify their ideas.

SUGGESTED ANSWERS:
A 20s; friends **B** teenager; niece **C** 30s or older; interviewee
D middle-aged or older; friends

3a Students discuss the questions in pairs.

ANSWERS:
A is the least formal: Cheers girls, xx, fab, Speak soon
C is the most formal: Dear Mr Wallace, I wanted to thank you again for ..., I very much enjoyed, do not hesitate to get in touch, I look forward to hearing from you soon, Yours sincerely

b Students work individually, then check answersin pairs before checking with the class.

ANSWERS:
Informal: Cheers; I had a fab evening; They're so cool; Speak soon
Formal: I wanted to thank you (again) for ... ; I very much enjoyed ... ; I look forward to hearing from you soon; Yours sincerely

4 Emphasise that students have to write just a note or an email. Give them a few minutes to decide who they will write to and encourage them to use the phrases from exercise 3 to help them. Circulate, supplying vocabulary and noting useful language and corrections to focus on later.

Language live, Writing, exercise 4: Alternative suggestion

Write all of the students' names on pieces of paper and mix them in a bag, then give one name to each student. Students write their thank-you messages to the person on the piece of paper, thanking them for something they did in a recent lesson (e.g. helped them during a pairwork activity). Collect the messages when they have finished and redistribute them to the people they were intended for. Students then read their messages, find the person who wrote them and respond orally.

ADDITIONAL PRACTICE

Resource bank: Activity 9D *Wordspot:* make (Collocations with *make*)

Workbook: Language live: *Buying things*, page 57; Writing: *Formal and informal styles*, page 57

Study, practice & remember

(PAGES 156–158)

See *Teaching tips: Using the Study, practice & remember sections*, page 25.

Practice 1

ANSWERS:

1

1 which **2** who **3** that **4** where **5** whose **6** who **7** when **8** that **9** where **10** that **11** whose **12** which

2

1 – **2** that/which **3** when **4** that/who **5** where **6** – **7** whose **8** – **9** that/which **10** – **11** that/who **12** –

3

1 that's/who's a lot older than him **2** that/which her boyfriend gave her **3** whose children I look after **4** money that /which you lent me **5** that/who lives in South Africa **6** that/which everyone is talking about

Practice 2

ANSWERS:

1

1 several **2** a bit of **3** a few **4** too much **5** too many

2

1 much **2** any **3** no **4** lots/plenty **5** enough **6** lots/plenty **7** several **8** many **9** some **10** few **11** bit

Remember these words

ANSWERS:

1

1 e **2** d **3** a **4** b **5** c

2

1 a cleaner **2** a freezer **3** a plumber **4** a torch **5** a decorator **6** a dishwasher **7** a battery **8** to switch on **9** fabric **10** a digital camera

Study tips

If you do these exercises in class, you'll need to make sure students have access to monolingual dictionaries, either in book form or on the internet.

1. Students work individually, then compare answers in pairs. In feedback, ask students if any of these were new ideas and which they'd like to try.
2. Students work in pairs before checking answers with the class.
3. Students work individually, then check answers in pairs before checking with the class.

ANSWERS:

1 label **2** /ɪks'triːm/ **3** countable **4** a verb **5** unsatisfactory **6** irregular (*sought*) **7** for

Study tips, exercise 3: Alternative suggestion

Allocate different questions to different students. If you have more than seven students, allocate each question more than once. Students answer their question individually, then mingle with other students to share their answers until they have all seven answers. Check answers with the class.

10 SOCIETY AND CHANGE

OVERVIEW

PAGES 96–97

Reading: The future will surprise us

Vocabulary: Numbers and statistics

Common European Framework: Students can obtain information, ideas and opinions from highly specialised sources; can understand and exchange complex information.

PAGES 98–99

Grammar: Making predictions

Vocabulary and listening: Society and change

Common European Framework: Students can use a sufficient range of language to be able to express viewpoints, using some complex forms to do so.

PAGES 100–101

Grammar: Hypothetical possibilities with *if*

Pronunciation: contractions

Common European Framework: Students can describe events, real or imagined; can express their thoughts about abstract topics.

PAGES 102–103

Vocabulary: Society and social issues

Task: Balance the budget

Common European Framework: Students can outline an issue or a problem clearly, speculating about causes or consequences and weighing advantages and disadvantages of different approaches.

PAGES 104–105

World culture: In orbit

Common European Framework: Students can follow the essentials of lectures, talks and reports; can explain a viewpoint on a topical issue, giving the advantages and disadvantages of various options.

Reading (PAGES 96–97)

WARM UP

Before class, write the following predictions from the past on pieces of paper and display them round the classroom:

1 *'Everything that can be invented has been invented.'– Charles H. Duell, 1899.*

2 *'Democracy will be dead by 1950.'– John Langdon-Davies, 1936.*

3 *'And for the tourist who really wants to get away from it all, safaris in Vietnam.'–* Newsweek, *predicting popular holidays for the late 1960s.*

4 *'It will be years – not in my time – before a woman will become prime minister.'– Margaret Thatcher, 1969.*

5 *'Sensible and responsible women do not want to vote.' Grover Cleveland (US President), 1905.*

Students walk round and read the predictions, then discuss which they think was the worst/funniest in pairs. In feedback, ask students if they know of any other famous predictions which were wrong.

1 Check understanding of *life expectancy*. Students discuss the questions in pairs. In feedback, nominate students to share their ideas with the class.

2 Explain that students are going to read about three scientists' predictions for the future. Emphasise that they shouldn't worry about new vocabulary at this stage and that they will have a chance to read the text more carefully. Students check answers in pairs before checking with the class.

ANSWERS:

Dr Aubrey de Grey predicts we will be able to live to 1,000 years old in 20 years' time. Dr Michio Kaku predicts that 40,000 people will work in space by 2030. Ray Kurzweil predicts that robots and humans will merge before the end of the 2030s.

3 With weaker classes, do this in two stages. First ask them to check the meaning of the words in bold in pairs, then go through the answers with the class. When they are ready, demonstrate the activity by finding the information relating to sentence 1 in the text and eliciting the answer. Otherwise, students can check meanings and do the exercise at the same time. Give students a chance to check in pairs before checking answers with the class.

ANSWERS:

cure: to make an illness go away **diseases:** illnesses which affect people, animals or plants **damaged human cells:** living human matter that has been harmed **gravity:** the force that causes something to fall to the ground **space stations:** a large spacecraft that stays above the Earth and is a base for people travelling in space **implanted:** to put something into someone's body by performing a medical operation **brains:** the organ inside your head that controls how you think, feel and move **telepathic communication:** messages that are sent from one person to another using thoughts, not by talking or writing

1 D **2** S **3** S **4** D **5** S **6** S **7** D **8** D **9** S **10** S

4 Students discuss the questions in small groups before reporting back to the class.

Vocabulary (PAGE 97)

Numbers and statistics

See *Teaching tips: Working with lexis*, page 21.

1 **10.1** Get students to guess how the numbers are said before playing the recording. Drill any problem numbers.

2a Students try to guess in pairs. Emphasise that they should use the numbers in exercise 1.

b **10.2** Pause the recording if necessary to allow writing time. When checking, make sure students read out the full numbers correctly.

ANSWERS:

1 71% **2** -89°C **3** 2030 **4** 55,680,000 km **5** 8.2 billion **6** 300,000 km/sec **7** 127,000,000 **8** 892,000 m² **9** 17% **10** 199,859

3 Emphasise that the statistics don't need to refer to real things, but make sure students write a different type of number for each one. When they are ready, students practise saying their partner's numbers. Circulate and check they are pronouncing them correctly.

4a Put students into pairs and refer them to the appropriate page at the back of the book. Check that they understand the categories for the numbers given.

b Do the first item in each table as an example. When students have finished, discuss any surprising numbers as a class.

ADDITIONAL PRACTICE

Resource bank: Activity 10A *Hear, say!* (Making predictions), Activity 10B *Vocabulary extension* (Talking about numbers, amounts and ages without being exact)

Workbook: Vocabulary: *Numbers and statistics*, page 58

Language focus 1 (PAGES 98–99)

Making predictions

See *Teaching tips: Using a discovery approach to grammar*, page 20.

WARM UP

Write the following pairs of statistics on the board:

a 13%	*b 30%*
a 3,042 km	*b 3,402 km*
a -89°C	*b -85°C*
a 6.4 billion	*b 64 billion*
a 499,632	*b 499,623*
a 60 km/sec	*b 16 km/sec*

Put students into pairs to practise saying the statistics. One student reads out a figure and their partner says if it's a or b. Students take turns to test each other.

1 Check understanding of *by 2029* (= *some time before 2029*). Remind students of Ray Kurzweil from the text on page 97 and elicit what his prediction was (robots and humans will merge). Students read the predictions, then compare their ideas in pairs. In feedback, hold a class vote for each prediction as to whether students think it will happen.

2 **10.3** Go through the table with the class and make sure students know what to listen for. Play the recording, pausing after each extract for students to complete the table and compare answers in pairs. If necessary, play the recording again.

ANSWERS:

Prediction being discussed	Do you think it will happen? (yes/no/maybe)	Reasons
1 c	no	Machines can't listen or understand. They don't have feelings.
2 b	yes	The first mobile phones were huge – everything gets smaller and smaller.
3 d	no	Poverty probably won't disappear by 2099 – it is too big a problem.
4 a	yes	It makes sense to have computers in cars that stop you from speeding or driving dangerously.
5 e	no	Machines are not alive. They don't have wants.

Language focus 1, exercise 2: Alternative suggestion

With weaker classes, do the listening in two parts. The first time they listen to the recording, students only complete the first two columns (which prediction and if they think it will happen). Check answers with the class before playing the recording again for students to complete the last column. Pause after each extract for students to check answers in pairs. Play the whole recording again if necessary for students to check their answers.

3 Students attempt the exercise from memory first. When they are ready, play the recording again for them to check their answers, pausing at the relevant points if necessary. Students check answers in pairs before checking with the class.

ANSWERS:

1 may well **2** unlikely to **3** will almost certainly be
4 probably won't disappear **5** It's very likely

GRAMMAR

Making predictions

Go over the different phrases used for making predictions with the class and find out which ones the students already know and which are new to them.

1 Explain how the line works. Without explaining the meaning of the phrases, get students to work in pairs and try to work out where they should go. Discuss answers with the class. As you do, contextualise each phrase in an example sentence and point out the following:

- Adverbs like *probably*, *definitely* and *certainly* go after *will* but before *won't*. Refer students to the sentences they underlined in the reading text to highlight this.
- *May* and *might* can be used in the negative form here, but *could* cannot.
- We can say *may well*, *might well* and *could well* if we want to say that something probably will happen.

Drill the phrases both in isolation and in the context of a short sentence (*Crime almost certainly won't disappear.*).

ANSWERS:

1 will almost certainly **2** will probably **3** is/are likely to
4 could/may well **5** may/might not **6** is/are unlikely to
7 probably won't **8** almost certainly won't

Potential problems with making predictions

- *May not/might not*: students may ask which of these is more probable. Grammar books disagree on this – if there is any distinction, it is not significant. Intonation is more important in ascertaining how certain the person is.
- There is a large number of other ways of expressing degrees of possibility/certainty: *it is possible that*, *perhaps*, *maybe*, etc. At this stage it's best not to deal with these unless students specifically ask.

You may want to ask students to read Study 1 on page 159 for a more detailed explanation of making predictions.

PRACTICE

If you think students need more controlled practice before these exercises, they could do Practice 1 on page 159 first.

1a Go over the example and point out that students can change other parts of the sentences as well to reflect their opinions more accurately. This should be done as a spoken exercise in pairs initially, but the sentences can be written for further consolidation.

b Put students into groups to discuss their opinions.

2 To start students off, give a few personalised predictions of your own – stress that these can be either long- or short-term predictions.

ADDITIONAL PRACTICE

Resource bank: Activity 10C *Pigs will fly* (Making predictions)

Study, practice & remember: Practice 1

Workbook: Language focus 1: *Making predictions*, pages 58–59

Vocabulary and listening (PAGE 99)

Society and change

See *Teaching tips: Working with lexis*, page 21.

1a Put students in pairs to check understanding of the words/phrases in the topic column. In feedback, check understanding with the class and deal with any difficult words or phrases.

ANSWERS:

life expectancy: the length of time that a person or animal is expected to live
average income: the average amount of money that people earn
the amount of free time we have: how much time we have when we're not working
health care: the service that looks after people's health
education: the process of teaching and learning, usually at school or college
living standards: the level of comfort and amount of money that people have
our levels of happiness: how happy we are

b Students predict the answers in pairs. Elicit their answers as a class, but don't confirm them yet.

2a **10.4** Play the recording for students to check their answers, then check answers with the class.

ANSWERS:

1 a 2 a 3 a 4 a 5 a 6 b

b Students listen again, then answer the questions. Check answers with the class.

ANSWERS:

If our living standards have improved so much, why have our levels of happiness stayed the same? Why is our happiness not increasing with our income and our free time?

3 **10.5** Play the recording for students to compare their answers. Students check in pairs before checking with the class.

4 Emphasise that students need to change the tense here where necessary. Students work individually, then check in pairs before checking answers with the class.

ANSWERS:

1 decreasing/falling/going down **2** decreasing/falling
3 rising/getting worse

5 Give students a few minutes to go through the topics and think about their answers. When they are ready, discuss the topics as a class. Emphasise that students should give reasons for their opinions and remind them that we use the Present continuous to describe changing states.

Vocabulary, exercise 5: Alternative suggestion

If you have a multi-nationality group, put students in groups of the same nationality to discuss the questions. When they have finished, ask one or more students from each group to share their opinions with the class.

PRONUNCIATION

See *Teaching tips: Helping students with pronunciation*, page 22.

1 In pairs, students complete the table. Encourage them to guess words they are not sure of before using a dictionary.

ANSWERS:

Noun	Verb	Adjective
1 a decrease	to decrease	decreasing
2 the economy	-	economic
3 education	to educate	educational
4 equality	-	equal
5 an improvement	to improve	-
6 an increase	to increase	-

2 **10.6** Play the recording for students to check the forms of the words, and again to mark the stress patterns. Check answers with the class. Point out that the stressed syllable often changes in word families in English. Remind students that they can use their mini-dictionaries to check which syllables are stressed in a word.

3 Drill individual words that are difficult for your students, then put them into pairs to practise saying them.

ADDITIONAL PRACTICE

Workbook: Vocabulary: *Society and change, page 60*

Language focus 2 (PAGES 100–101)

Hypothetical possibilities with *if*

See *Teaching tips: Using a discovery approach to grammar*, page 20.

1 Introduce the topic by telling students what you would do. Students discuss the question in pairs.

2 Check understanding of *scientific breakthrough, to flirt, play a trick on someone, to run someone over* and *to bully someone*. Students read the texts, then compare with their own ideas in pairs. In feedback, ask students what they thought was the most interesting answer.

3 Check the meaning of *imaginary*. Give students time to read the comments again, then discuss the question as a class.

ANSWER:

The comments are all describing imaginary situations.

GRAMMAR

Hypothetical possibilites with *if*

1a Give students a moment to think about the answer before checking with the class.

ANSWERS:

1 an imaginary situation **2** a real situation

b Go through the examples again and elicit the verb forms used in each. Students work individually or in pairs before checking answers with the class.

ANSWERS:

1 would + verb **2** will + verb
1 I'd get on, I'd get back **2** I'd follow, I'd check, I'd also listen **3** I would definitely play, I'd rob **4** I'd follow round, I'd find out **5** I wouldn't cross the road **6** I'd take my revenge, I would stand next to her, I'd do something weird

Students should be familiar with both *will* and *would*, but it is worth contrasting them briefly. Highlight:

- the question forms
- the affirmative forms
- the negative forms
- the contracted forms

Do not at this stage go into the full 'second conditional' structure. Point out that *would* is very often used in sentences on its own. Particularly in speech, full conditional sentences are relatively uncommon – one 'half' of the conditional tends to be assumed.

2 Students work individually or in pairs before checking answers with the class.

ANSWERS:

If I was invisible, I'd follow my boyfriend around all day …
I would definitely play a few tricks on my friends if they couldn't see me … If I were invisible, someone might run me over!
If I were invisible for a day, I'd take revenge on a girl from school …

The past tense is used after *if*. It doesn't refer to past times; it refers to imaginary times.

Potential problems with the use of *was/were*

- This is the subjunctive in English – if students have a subjunctive in their own language or are already familiar with this grammatical term, point this out to them. Stress that the subjunctive is not very widely used in English – this use after *if* is the most important one.
- Because it is subjunctive, strictly speaking, *were* should be used rather than *was* in the first and third person. These days, though, many native speakers use *was*, so do not insist that students use *were*.

3 Students work individually before checking answers with the class.

ANSWERS:

The third sentence is incorrect.

Exercise 3 focuses on a common mistake – the use of *would* after *if*. The correct sentences illustrate the following points:

- the fact that either clause can begin the sentence
- the fact that *might* can be used instead of *would* if you are not sure what you would do.

You may want to ask students to read Study 2 on page 160 for a more detailed explanation of hypothetical possibilities with *if*.

PRACTICE

If you think students need more controlled practice before these exercises, they could do Practice 2 on page 160 first.

1a Students work individually or in pairs. Emphasise that they should use contractions where possible as this is more natural.

b **10.7** Play the recording for students to check their answers before checking with the class. Discuss the questions as a class as you go through each answer.

ANSWERS:

1 A: had, would you listen **B:** 'd be
2 A: Would you ever, could **B:** 'd never steal, knew, 'd feel
3 A: did, would you take **B:** 'd try A: was, might do
4 A: were, would you ever follow **B:** would be, thought, 'd ask
5 A: Would you ever travel **B:** wouldn't dare, caught, 'd feel

2a Check students understand the questions in *Never say never*, and the following phrases: *under what circumstances, to walk out of your job, to drop out of college, to give someone a lift*. Explain that students should think of all the possible circumstances in which they might do these things. Students work individually and make notes if they want to.

b Students work in small groups, comparing ideas. Circulate and make a note of any useful language and errors for analysis and correction later.

3a Go through the example with the class and discuss whether it is real or imaginary. Students work in pairs to complete the exercise before checking answers with the class. Stronger classes can do this exercise orally.

ANSWERS:

1 If you had the chance to travel in space, would you do it? IS
2 If you lived to be 1,000, how would your life be different? IS
3 If you live to be old, what will you do in your retirement? RP
4 If you bought a new computer, what type would you buy? IS (also accept: If you buy a new computer, what type will you buy? RP)
5 If you invented your own personal robot, what would it be able to do? IS
6 If you have more money next year, how will you spend it? RP
7 If you were a billionaire, what would you do with your life? IS
8 If you move house in the next few years, where will you move to? RP
9 If you could live anywhere in the world, where would you live? IS

b Give students a minute or two to choose their questions, then put them in pairs to discuss.

PRONUNCIATION

See *Teaching tips: Helping students with pronunciation*, page 22.

1 **10.8** Play the recording as many times as necessary. Students may find this difficult, as contractions are not usually stressed. However, it is important listening practice.

ANSWERS:

1 1 2 2 3 2 4 1 5 1 6 2 7 2 8 1

2 Get students to repeat the sentences individually and chorally, then in pairs.

Potential problem with the contraction of *will*

Students may have difficulty pronouncing *I'll*. If so, suggest they insert a small /j/ sound: /aɪjl/.

4 Students work individually to write their sentences. Circulate and check they are using *would* correctly. When they are ready, put students into groups to compare their ideas.

Practice, exercise 4: Alternative suggestion

Students choose four of the situations in exercise 2a and write one sentence for each. Circulate and check they are using *would* correctly. When they are ready, put students in small groups. Students take it in turns to read out a sentence for the group to guess the situation.

ADDITIONAL PRACTICE

Resource bank: Activity 10D *Election night special* (Hypothetical possibilities with *if* (second conditional))

Study, practice & remember: Practice 2

Workbook: Language focus 2: *Hypothetical possibilities with if*, pages 60–61; Pronunciation: *'ll or 'd in connected speech*, page 61

Vocabulary (PAGE 102)

Society and social issues

See *Teaching tips: Working with lexis*, page 21.

WARM UP

On the board, write the following ideas from Vocabulary and listening on page 99 of the Students' Book: *health care, average income, education, the amount of free time we have, life expectancy, living standards* and *our levels of happiness*. Students discuss which two are most important to improve in society and why. They then share their ideas with the class.

1 Students discuss the questions in small groups. Circulate and listen to see if they are using any of the vocabulary from exercise 2a at this stage.

2a Students work individually to categorise the words and phrases.

b Students check answers in pairs and work together to add more words to each category before checking with the class. In feedback, check understanding of the words. Drill the words with the class and check pronunciation of *wealthy* /ˈwelθi/, *health care* /helθ keə/, *racism* /ˈreɪsɪzm/, *homelessness* /ˈhəʊmləsnəs/, *government* /ˈɡʌvəmənt/ and *budget* /ˈbʌdʒɪt/.

ANSWERS:

Groups in society: the wealthy, tax payers, the opposition parties, the poor, the government, ordinary people
Social problems: corruption, racism, unemployment, homelessness, crime, pollution, poverty
Government responsibilities: education, health care, defence, transport, balancing the budget

3a Demonstrate the activity by giving one or two of your own answers first. Encourage students to use dictionaries where necessary to check understanding of the words and phrases. Students work individually to compare answers.

b Students compare ideas in pairs before reporting back to the class.

4 Discuss the question as a class.

ADDITIONAL PRACTICE

Resource bank: Activity 10E *How would your life be different?* (Hypothetical possibilities with *if* – second conditional)

Workbook: Vocabulary: *Society*, page 63

Task (PAGES 102–103)

Balance the budget

See *Teaching tips: Making tasks work*, page 23.

Preparation (PAGE 102)

Listening

1 Check understanding of *oil wells*. Students read the summary text, then answer the questions in pairs. Check answers with the class.

ANSWERS:

1 poverty and unemployment, businesses closing down, oil wells running dry, schools and hospitals becoming old, tourist numbers falling, the neighbouring island could attack

2a 🎧 **10.9** Go through the questions with the class and check students understand what they are listening for. Play the recording, pausing after each speaker for students to write their answers and check in pairs. Check answers with the class.

ANSWERS:

1 the economy of the island; spend more on promoting tourism to help businesses
2 the state of the schools; increase taxes on wealthy people to pay for the improvements to the schools
3 unemployment and defence; increase spending on defence in order to make the country more secure and give young people jobs as soldiers
4 cost of living; reduce taxes on ordinary people in order to have a better standard of living

b Focus attention on the Useful language box and check understanding of the phrases. Students listen again and tick the phrases they hear, then check answers in pairs before checking with the class. Drill the phrases with the class.

ANSWERS:

1 First we have to ... ; I'd suggest that we spend more on ...
2 To me, the biggest problem is ... ; I think the government should ... to pay for ...
3 This would help to ... ; The problem is ... ; I think the government should ...
4 The best option is to ...

Task (PAGE 103)

Speaking

1a Give students a few minutes to read through the options and ask you about any vocabulary they need to. Students work individually to choose four changes.

b Using one of the options, elicit possible results as an example. Refer students to the Useful language box, sections a–c, and give them plenty of time to make notes. Monitor and help with vocabulary where necessary and write any new words/phrases on the board.

2 Put students in groups to present and discuss their options. Circulate and note any common errors for later analysis.

3 Groups take turns to present their ideas to the class. When all groups have finished, discuss the questions as a class. Go over any common errors/examples of good language use that you noted during exercise 2.

Share your task

Some additional ideas could include:

- Students film/record a 'party political broadcast' for an upcoming general election in Peakoilia. First they think of a name for their party which reflects their budget choices, then plan and film/record a three-minute broadcast. When they have finished, watch/listen to the broadcasts with the whole class and hold a class election.
- Choose four or five students who will be politicians and allocate a budget measure to each. Ask them to plan reasons to support the measure, while the rest of the class will play the role of Peakoilia citizens and plan questions to ask the politicians. When they are ready, record/film a TV/radio debate, where each politician briefly outlines their budget decision and supporting reasons, then they take questions from the 'audience'.

World culture (PAGES 104–105)

In orbit

Culture notes

A satellite is an artificial object placed in orbit by humans. The first satellite, *Sputnik 1*, was launched in 1957 by the Soviet Union, though the idea of satellites can be traced back to 'Newton's Cannonball', when Isaac Newton conceived of the mathematical possibility of launching a satellite in 1728.

Since 1957, thousands of satellites have been launched and there are now around 3,500 satellites in orbit around the earth, as well as numerous artificial satellites in orbit around other planets in the solar system.

Satellites serve many different purposes, including military and civilian observation satellites, communications satellites, navigation, weather and research satellites, as well as space stations and human spacecraft.

The majority of satellites are in *low Earth orbit*, 200-2,000 km above the Earth's surface, though satellites can be as far away as over 40,000 km, in *high Earth orbit*. Satellites at this distance are in *geostationary orbit*, which means they move at the same speed as the Earth turns, while satellites in *low Earth orbit* can travel as fast as 30,000 km per hour.

Find out first (PAGE 104)

1a Focus attention on the photo and elicit what students can see (a satellite). Check understanding of *in orbit*. Students discuss what they know in pairs. In feedback, elicit students' ideas. Don't give any answers yet.

b Students can research the answers individually, then check in pairs, using the search terms to help them. In feedback, check answers with the class and feed in any additional information from the Culture notes. Ask students if they found out any other interesting information about satellites.

ANSWERS:

1957; 3,500; 200; 40,000; 30,000

View (PAGE 104)

See *Teaching tips: Using the video material in the classroom*, page 24.

2 Ask students how many satellites they think they have used before 9 a.m. today and write their answers on the board. Go through the questions and check students understand what to watch for. Play the DVD for students to check their answers, then check with the class.

ANSWERS:

1 She helps to make satellites. **2** wheat, milk, coffee, water
3 nearly 40

3a Go through the example with the class and check understanding. Students match the phrases individually, then check answers in pairs before checking with the class. Check understanding and give further explanations/examples where necessary.

ANSWERS:

1 c 2 d 3 e 4 f 5 h 6 g 7 a 8 b

b Play the DVD again for students to watch and tick the phrases they hear. Students check answers in pairs before checking with the class.

ANSWERS:

keep an eye on us from space deliver milk harvest the wheat
beam a signal to the TV forecast the weather

4 Discuss the question as a class.

World view (PAGE 105)

5a Ask students which items of technology they think have changed their lives and write them on the board. Focus attention on the items in the box and ask if any of their ideas are included. Play the DVD for students to watch and tick the items mentioned.

b Focus attention on the table and elicit what students can remember about what each person said. Play the DVD again for students to complete the table before checking answers in pairs. Check answers with the class.

ANSWERS:

Stephanie: smartphone; everything is on one phone (camera, music, etc.)
Sion: the internet, especially websites like Wikipedia; instantly find out information
Steve: Kindle; doesn't have to carry lots of books around
James: tablet computer; it will make things convenient and fun

6a Emphasise that students can either choose an item from exercise 5 or choose a different item of technology. Students work in pairs to make lists. Circulate and help with vocabulary and ideas where necessary.

World view, exercise 6a: Alternative suggestion

With weaker classes, write the following prompts on the board before they choose an item: *work, study, social life, free time, communication, family, friends*. Demonstrate the activity by telling the class about an item of technology that has changed your life, giving examples from the topics on the board. Students then work individually to make notes before discussing in pairs.

b Rearrange students into new pairs. When they have finished, nominate students to share their ideas with the class.

Find out more (PAGE 105)

7a Focus attention on the things in the list and elicit what students know about them. Discuss the questions as a class.

b Students research the issues individually, using the search terms provided. Monitor and help with vocabulary where necessary. When they are ready, students share their information in small groups.

Write up your research

8 Choose one of the issues, elicit positive and negative facts that students found online and write them on the board. Go through the prompts with the students and check understanding. Students write their paragraphs using the notes they made in exercise 7. When they have finished, students swap paragraphs with a student who wrote about a different issue. In feedback, ask students what they found out from their partner's paragraph.

Students can now do Unit test 5 on the Teacher's Resource Disc.

Study, practice & remember

(PAGES 159–161)

See *Teaching tips: Using the Study, practice & remember sections*, page 25.

Practice 1

ANSWERS:

1
1 Be careful or you could fall.
2 After Miran finishes school she will probably go to university.
3 Casabani definitely won't become president.
4 Dominic will almost certainly get promoted soon.
5 We probably won't arrive until about 10 o'clock.
6 It's likely to be very hot next week.
7 I might not see Lorenzo again.
8 Someone will definitely meet you at the airport.
9 It may well rain later this evening.
10 Nabil isn't likely to stay for very long.

2
1 'll probably go for a pizza
2 almost certainly won't be
3 may not come
4 's likely to hurt
5 will definitely be ready
6 could drop it
7 definitely won't win
8 may well rain
9 's unlikely to get married
10 probably won't remember it

3
1 may **2** could **3** may definitely **4** is likely **5** is definitely **6** may be

Practice 2

ANSWERS:

1
1 would you do **2** 'd pretend to be **3** lost **4** 'd never give **5** might not be **6** didn't pass **7** had **8** would lend **9** thought **10** were you

2
1 I would avoid paying taxes if I could.
2 I'd never drop litter in the street.
3 If a shop assistant gave me too much change, I'd tell him.
4 If I found $100 in the street, I wouldn't take it to the police.
5 I'd never drink and drive.
6 If everyone had good manners, life would be much easier.
7 I wouldn't like to be a celebrity.

3
1 c **2** e **3** b **4** f **5** a **6** d

4
1 had **2** will **3** were **4** would **5** might **6** could

Remember these words

ANSWERS:

1
1 a **2** b **3** a **4** c

2
1 D **2** S **3** D **4** D **5** S **6** D

3
1 c **2** a/d **3** e **4** d/a **5** b

4
1 unemployment **2** racism **3** homelessness **4** pollution **5** poverty **6** industry

5
increase, cure, damage, bully, rise, flirt, fall, waste

Study tips

1 Before starting this exercise, elicit the ways students use the internet to improve their English and write them on the board. Students then work individually to tick the things they do. In feedback, ask if any of their original ideas were mentioned.

2 Students discuss which of the things they would like to try in pairs.

Study tips: Additional activity

After exercise 2, ask students to try out one of the ideas they chose for a week. One week later, ask them to report back to the class. This could either be as a class discussion or you could ask each student to give a short presentation on what they did and any useful sites/apps they found.

OVERVIEW

PAGES 106–107

Listening: Annoying rules

Grammar: Obligation and permission in the present

Pronunciation: Word stress in phrases describing obligation and permission

Common European Framework: Can understand recordings in standard dialect and identify speaker viewpoints and attitudes, as well as the information content; can give brief comments on the views of others.

PAGES 108–109

Reading: Exclusive clubs

Vocabulary: Linking words

Common European Framework: Students can gather information from different texts in order to fulfil a specific task; can use a variety of linking words efficiently to mark clearly the relationships between ideas.

PAGES 110–111

Vocabulary: Crime and punishment

Grammar: Obligation and permission in the past

Common European Framework: Students can use a good range of vocabulary for most general topics; can communicate with reasonable accuracy in familiar contexts.

PAGES 112–113

Task: Discuss new laws

Common European Framework: Students can contribute, account for and sustain their opinions, evaluate alternative proposals and make and respond to hypotheses.

PAGES 114–115

Speaking: Expressing and responding to opinions

Writing: An opinion essay

Common European Framework: Students can account for and sustain their opinions in discussion by providing relevant explanations, arguments and comments; can write an essay that develops an argument systematically, with appropriate highlighting of significant points and relevant supporting detail.

Listening (PAGE 106)

WARM UP

Elicit rules of your school from the class and write them on the board, e.g. *You mustn't use your mobile phone in class for calls. You should do your homework.* Have a discussion on which rules students would like to change and ask them if there are any rules they'd like to introduce.

1 Check students understand the places in the box. Elicit an example before students work in pairs. You could allocate different places to each pair to get a wide range of sentences. Discuss ideas with the class. Do not focus explicitly on modals of obligation at this stage. Circulate and make notes on how well students are using them. In particular:

- are they only using *must* or are they using *have to* and *have got to* as well?
- do they seem to understand the difference between *must* and *should*?

Make a note of useful errors for correction after *Grammar*.

2 **11.1** Check understanding of *hanging around on street corners, speed cameras, to speed, terms and conditions* and *ID*. Students listen, then check answers in pairs. Check answers with the class.

ANSWERS:

1 parks and open spaces, D **2** motorways, A **3** websites, E
4 classrooms, B **5** nightclubs, C

3 Play the recording again, pausing after each speaker for students to write their answers. Check answers with the class.

ANSWERS:

1 Children should be able to play in public places to stop them getting into trouble.
2 Speed cameras and speeding fines on motorways are just a way for the government to make money.
3 There are too many terms and conditions to read and no one can understand them.
4 Mobile phones are part of everyone's life now and they are a means of getting information quickly from the internet.
5 The speaker doesn't like looking young for her age.
They don't agree with any of the rules.

4 Students discuss the questions in small groups before reporting back to the class.

Language focus 1 (PAGE 107)

Obligation and permission in the present

See *Teaching tips: Using a discovery to grammar*, page 20.

1 Look at the example and focus attention on the photos before getting students to do the task. Check answers with the class.

ANSWERS:

1 You can play ball games here.
2 You ought to use your phone in this lesson.
3 You have to drive at 120 kph on most motorways.
4 You shouldn't show ID to prove your age.

GRAMMAR

Obligation and permission in the present

Students categorise the verbs. Check answers with the class, highlighting the problems of form below. The phrases can be drilled, although pronunciation is dealt with later as part of the practice.

ANSWERS:

1 have (got) to; must **2** don't have to **3** can; are allowed to
4 are not allowed to; mustn't; can't **5** ought to **6** shouldn't

Potential problem with *must* and *have to*

Although *must* and *have to* have very similar meanings, *mustn't* and *don't have to* do not. *Mustn't* means the same as *can't* ('there is an obligation not to do something; there is no choice'). *Don't have to* means 'it isn't necessary to do this, but there is a choice – you can if you want to'.

You may want to ask students to read Study 1 on page 162 for a more detailed explanation of obligation and permission in the present.

PRACTICE

1 Emphasise that students have to complete the sentences to make them mean the same as the signs. Students work in pairs and write their answers before checking with the class.

ANSWERS:

1 sign F: aren't allowed
2 sign G: are allowed
3 sign G: don't have to, are allowed
4 sign C: have, should
5 sign H: ought
6 sign I: mustn't, should

PRONUNCIATION

See *Teaching tips: Helping students with pronunciation*, page 22.

1 **11.2** Pause the recording after each sentence and drill chorally and individually. Pay particular attention to the following:

- *can* is weak and unstressed, whereas *can't* is stressed.
- *to* is, in all cases where it is used before the infinitive, weak and unstressed.
- the 'v' in *have to* and the 's' in *has to* are pronounced /f/ and /z/ (in contrast to *have* used as a verb on its own).
- *mustn't*, *should*, etc. contain silent letters. You could also mention the pronunciation of *ought to* /ˈɔːtʊ/ here.

2 Encourage students to pay attention to stress and weak forms.

2 Check the meaning of: *a pedestrian crossing*, *a seat belt*, *a motorway*, *to pay a fine*. This can be done as a spoken or written exercise, with students working in pairs or groups. As you check answers, encourage students to give alternative suggestions as there is not necessarily one correct answer. For example, students might want to say any of the following:

- *Lorries are allowed to drive through the city centre.* (There's no law against this.)
- *Lorries shouldn't drive through the city centre.* (It's not a good thing – it causes pollution.)
- *Lorries don't have to drive through the city centre.* (There is a ring road they could use.)

The important thing is that students know why they are using the form they have chosen. Get them to explain their sentence when there is any doubt.

SUGGESTED ANSWERS:

In city centres ...
1 You **can** park in the city centre.
2 Lorries **mustn't** drive through the centre.
3 You **don't have to** pay to drive your car into the city.
4 Cars **should** stop at pedestrian crossings.

On roads ...
5 You **have to** wear a seat belt.
6 You **don't have to** pay to use the motorways.
7 You **are allowed to** drive at 180 kph.
8 You **can** take your driving test if you're 170 years old.

On trains ...
9 You **should** buy your ticket in advance.
10 You **aren't allowed to** buy your ticket on the train.
11 You **have to** pay a fine if you're caught without a ticket.
12 You **mustn't** smoke.

3a Students work individually to write rules. Allocate places to each student if you want a range of different places to be covered. Circulate as students work, noting down errors and useful language to focus on later.

b Emphasise that as students read out their rules, they should not say which place they are talking about.

ADDITIONAL PRACTICE

Resource bank: Activity 11A *Where am I?* (Obligation and permission in the present)

Study, practice & remember: Practice 1

Workbook: Language focus 1: *Obligation and permission in the present*, pages 64–65

Reading (PAGES 108–109)

1 Students discuss the questions in groups before reporting back to the class.

2 Emphasise that students only need to read the first few lines of each text to answer the questions. Set a time limit of three minutes to discourage students from reading further at this stage. Students check answers in pairs before checking with the class.

ANSWERS:

The Vidocq Society: crime specialists; solving 'cold cases'/murders that have never been solved
The French Foreign Legion: soldiers; fighting battles and wars
The Bullingdon Club: upper-class male students at Oxford

3 Students work in pairs before checking answers with the class.

ANSWERS:

The Vidocq Society: a murder case, to solve a crime
The French Foreign Legion: to surrender, a new recruit, a battle
The Bullingdon Club: to cause damage, to vandalise, an aristocrat, to smash

4 The reason for doing this as a race is that it will give students a real purpose to scan the text quickly for key information. Go through the sentences with the class so that students know what they are reading for. Students work in pairs to see who can find the information fastest. Check answers with the class.

ANSWERS:

1 the Bullingdon Club **2** the French Foreign Legion
3 the French Foreign Legion **4** the Bullingdon Club
5 the French Foreign Legion **6** the Vidocq Society
7 the Bullingdon Club **8** the French Foreign Legion
9 the French Foreign Legion

5a Students work individually before reporting back to the class. Allow the discussion to develop naturally here.

b Discuss the questions as a class.

Find out more

This can be done in class or set for homework if you are short of time. Students work in pairs to research each of the three groups and make notes. When they are ready, students use their notes to write some rules for each club. Monitor and help with vocabulary. Students read out their rules to the class, who guess which club each rule is for.

Vocabulary (PAGE 109)

Linking words

See *Teaching tips: Working with lexis*, page 21.

1 If necessary, do an example with the class. Students work individually, then check in pairs. Check answers with the class.

ANSWERS:

The Vidocq Society: However, the members of the society don't mind. They helped the family and as a result the suspect was quickly set free.

The French Foreign Legion: The Legionnaires are part of the French army, although most of them are not French. What is more, they are not allowed to surrender or lose their gun in battle.

The Bullingdon Club: However, after they have finished destroying things …

2 Do an example with the class. Students work in pairs before checking answers with the class.

ANSWERS:

1 also, besides, what is more **2** although, despite this, however
3 for that reason, as a result, therefore

If you think students need more controlled practice before this exercise, they could do Practice 2 on page 163 first.

3 Read the example with the class. Students work individually before checking in pairs. Circulate and check students are using the linkers correctly. Check answers with the class.

ANSWERS:

1 a For that reason,/Therefore **b** What's more,/Also,/Besides,
2 a What's more,/Also,/Besides, **b** As a result,/For that reason,/Therefore,
3 a Despite this,/However, **b** However,
4 a As a result,/For that reason,/Therefore **b** However,/Despite this,

ADDITIONAL PRACTICE

Resource bank: Activity 11B *The missing link* (Vocabulary extension: linking words)

Workbook: Vocabulary: *Linking words*, page 65

Vocabulary (PAGE 110)

Crime and punishment

See *Teaching tips: Working with lexis*, page 21.

WARM UP

Write the letters of the alphabet on the board, leaving a space next to each one. Put students in small groups and give them five minutes to write as many crimes as they can think of that begin with each letter of the alphabet. When they have finished, give a board pen to a member of each group and ask them to come and write them in the correct place on the board. Check spelling and understanding of the crimes with the class.

1 Focus attention on the pictures and elicit what students think they are about. Students discuss the questions in small groups before reporting back to the class.

2 Check understanding of *harsh*, *lenient* /ˈliːnɪənt/ and *hard labour*. Students read the text, then answer the questions in pairs. Check answers with the class.

ANSWERS:

1 murder, kidnapping, burglary, robbery, shoplifting, mugging
2 transportation to Australia

3a Go over the mind map and examples with the class. Students work individually or in pairs before checking answers with the class. Elicit any more words for each category that students thought of and write them on the board, but be careful not to let this go on too long.

ANSWERS:

Crimes: murder, kidnapping, burglary, robbery, shoplifting, mugging
Punishments: the death penalty, community service, hanging
Verbs: to be sent to prison, to commit a crime, to be arrested, to be punished, to be caught, to be sentenced, to be released
People: the judge, criminals, defendant, prisoners

b Read the example with the class. Students work individually or in pairs before checking answers with the class.

ANSWERS:

a murder, to murder, a murderer
a kidnapping, to kidnap, a kidnapper
a burglary, to burgle, a burglar
a robbery, to rob, a robber
shoplifting, to shoplift, a shoplifter
a mugging, to mug, a mugger

4a Check understanding of *carpenter*. Students complete the text individually, then check answers in pairs. As you check answers with the class, check comprehension of the story, too, by asking questions, e.g. *What was his first crime? Where did he usually steal from?*

ANSWERS:

1 committed, crime **2** shoplifting **3** was, arrested
4 burgling **5** got caught **6** robbed **7** was hanged **8** criminal

b Put students in pairs and ask them to cover the text in exercise 4a. Students take it in turns to retell the story. Circulate and check they are using the vocabulary from exercise 4a correctly.

5 Students discuss the questions in small groups.

ADDITIONAL PRACTICE

Workbook: Vocabulary: *Crime and punishment*, page 66

Language focus 2 (PAGE 111)

Obligation and permission in the past

See *Teaching tips: Using a discovery approach to grammar*, page 20.

1 Check understanding and pronunciation of *debts* /dets/ and *chains* /tʃeɪnz/. Students read the text then answer the questions in pairs before checking answers with the class.

ANSWERS:

1 If they had debts.
2 They didn't have money to pay off their debt or the cost of staying in prison.
3 Dickens' father was in prison.

2 The purpose of this exercise is for you to see how much students already know. While they are completing the text, circulate and note any common errors for correction during the *Grammar* stage.

ANSWERS:

1 had to **2** could/were allowed to **3** didn't have to
4 could/were allowed to **5** could/were allowed to
6 couldn't/weren't allowed to **7** had to **8** had to **9** had to

GRAMMAR

Obligation and permission in the past

1 Students work individually, working out the forms, before checking answers with the class. Check the pronunciation of *could* /kʊd/, *couldn't* /ˈkʊdənt/, *were allowed to* /wərəˈlaʊdtʊ/.

ANSWERS:

1 could **2** was/were allowed to **3** wasn't/weren't allowed to
4 couldn't **5** didn't have to **6** had to **7** no past form: had to
8 no past form: weren't allowed to/couldn't **9** had to

Highlight the following:

- *must* has no past form, so *had to* is used instead. In the negative form we use *couldn't* or *wasn't/weren't allowed to*. Students may find this confusing.
- *had got to/ hadn't got to* are not standard English; *had to/ didn't have to* are used in the past form instead.
- the past form of *should* is dealt with in Unit 12.

You may want to ask students to read Study 3 on page 163 for a more detailed explanation of the form of obligation and permission in the past.

PRACTICE

If you think students need more controlled practice before these exercises, they could do Practice 3 on page 163 first.

1 Check the meaning of *noblemen, flag, servant* and *vote*. Emphasise that there is sometimes more than one possibility. Students work alone, then check in pairs before checking answers with the class.

ANSWERS:

1 couldn't/weren't allowed to **2** had to **3** couldn't/weren't allowed to
4 had to **5** had to **6** didn't have to **7** couldn't/weren't allowed to
8 had to **9** couldn't/weren't allowed to **10** could/were allowed to

2 If you have a multilingual group, put students in groups of the same nationality to work together. Otherwise, students can work individually. Circulate and check students are using the past forms correctly. When they are ready, students compare their answers in pairs. If they worked in groups for exercise 1, rearrange them before putting in pairs. In feedback, nominate students to share their ideas with the class.

Practice, exercise 2: Alternative suggestion

If you have access to the internet, ask students to research 'strange laws' in pairs. When they have found two or three, ask them to share them with the class.

ADDITIONAL PRACTICE

Study, practice & remember: Practice 3

Workbook: Language focus 2: *Obligation and permission in the past*, page 66

Task (PAGES 112–113)

Discuss new laws

See *Teaching tips: Making tasks work*, page 23.

Preparation (PAGE 112)

Reading and listening

1 Give students plenty of time to read the suggestions and check they have understood them all. When they are ready, discuss the questions as a class.

ANSWERS:

1st photo: I would make a law ... same treatment themselves.; I think that hunting ... should be banned.
2nd photo: The long-term unemployed ... from the government.
3rd photo: I think speed limits ... should be abolished.
4th photo: I think everyone should have to ... allowed to vote.; I would change the law ... vote at 16.
5th photo: People who do dangerous ... hurt themselves.

2 **11.3** Play the recording, pausing after each speaker for students to write their answers and compare in pairs. With weaker classes, you may need to play it twice – once for them to identify the suggestion and a second time for them to note their reasons and examples. Check answers with the class.

ANSWERS:

1 'Drivers should have a trial driving licence for a couple of years before they are allowed to have a full licence. They should only get a full licence if they have shown that they are safe on the road.' Motorcycles have a trial licence and cars are more dangerous than motorcycles. People need a lot more practise before they're ready to go out on the roads. There should be an extra test to prove that someone is a competent driver.
2 'I think that hunting and harming animals for sport should be banned.' People shouldn't kill animals for the sake of it – in the past, people killed animals to eat the meat.
3 'I would make it the law that if you go and live in a foreign country, it should be compulsory to learn the language of that country.' This is important to integrate into society and make friends.
4 'The long-term unemployed should have to do voluntary work to get unemployment benefit from the government.' There are lots of projects that aren't being done because there isn't the money or people to do them. They could do something constructive to help society and their local community (e.g. fixing up local community centres, painting churches, working on local schools to make them better places for learning). It would also get them used to the routine of working, making it easier for them to get back into work when they eventually find a job.

3 Focus attention on the Useful language box and give students one or two minutes to read the phrases. Play the recording again for students to tick the phrases they hear. Check answers with the class and drill the phrases.

ANSWERS:

1 I think it should be compulsory to (have a trial licence).
2 I'm against hunting.; What I don't agree with is (hunting for sport).; To me, that doesn't make sense.; I don't think it should be banned.
3 It should be compulsory to ...
4 I think there should be a law that ...

Task (PAGE 112)

Speaking

1 Give students a few minutes to think of their suggestions. Point out the phrases in the Useful language box, section a, and elicit students' ideas, writing them on the board.

2a Give students a minute to choose two laws they would like to discuss. Emphasise that they can be from the list on the board or the website.

b Go over the phrases in the Useful language box, section b, and give students plenty of time to make notes. Circulate and help students with vocabulary where necessary.

3 Put students in groups to discuss their laws. Circulate and note any common errors for later analysis.

4 Before they present their ideas, give students time to plan how they are going to present them and point out the phrases in the Useful language box, section c. Groups take it in turns to present their laws to the group and find out if the class agrees. When they have finished, give students feedback on their use of language.

Task: Speaking: Alternative suggestions

a If you are short of time: adapt the task in one of the following ways:

- Set Preparation: Reading and listening for homework the previous lesson, then start with Task: Speaking.
- Do Preparation: Reading and listening in one lesson, then get students to prepare their opinions for homework, thinking about any vocabulary they need to express what they feel. In the next lesson, circulate and supply the vocabulary they need, before moving on to Task: Speaking.

b If you think students will find the discussion work difficult for any reason, adapt the task in one of the following ways:

- Replace some/all of the issues with ones you know are topical for your students. Present these in the form of provocative statements for students to agree/disagree with (like the controversial opinions in the task).
- Some students, particularly younger ones, may respond better to these issues if they are reformulated in more personal terms, for example: *I would be happy to have a trial driving licence for a couple of years before I'm allowed to have a full licence./would like to be able to vote at 16.*

Share your task

Some additional ideas could include:

- Students film/record a public information commercial to explain the introduction of one of their new laws, e.g. describing the harmful effects of passive smoking for a ban on smoking in public places.
- Students work in pairs. One of them is a politician introducing one of the new laws and the other is a journalist. Give them time to prepare their reasons and questions and help with vocabulary/ideas where necessary. When they are ready, students practise a TV/radio interview. When they are comfortable with it, they film/record it before showing it to the class.

ADDITIONAL PRACTICE

Resource bank: Activity 11C *In my opinion …* (Expressing and responding to opinions)

Language live (PAGES 114–115)

Speaking (PAGE 114)

Expressing and responding to opinions

WARM UP

Write *Punishments* in the middle of the board and draw a circle around it. Elicit types of punishments from the class and build a mind map on the board. Feed in the punishments from Vocabulary on page 110.

1 Check understanding of *till* and *to threaten (/ˈθretən/) someone.* Give students a few minutes to read the article and then think of a suitable punishment. Discuss the question as a class.

2a Play the DVD, pausing after each conversation for students to discuss the questions in pairs. Check answers with the class.

ANSWERS:

Conversation 1: husband and wife; The husband thinks 25 hours' community service is not enough and he should have been sent to prison. The wife thinks he perhaps needs to be helped, not punished.
Conversation 2: shopkeeper and his regular customer; The regular customer thinks it is terrible that he only got 25 hours' community service and that he should be sent to prison. The shopkeeper doesn't agree that he should have been sent to prison – He is only 16 and has had a difficult life.

b Play the DVD again for students to number the phrases and then check in pairs. Check answers with the class.

ANSWERS:

Conversation 1: c, e, f, b, d, a **Conversation 2:** b, d, c, a

3 Go through the examples with the class, then students work individually before checking in pairs. Check answers with the class and drill the phrases chorally and individually.

ANSWERS:

Expressing an opinion	Responding to an opinion
Terrible, isn't it? In my opinion … I don't know about you, but I don't think …	That may be so, but … But to be honest, I don't really agree. What do you mean? Really? Why do you say that? I don't know about that. You have to remember that … Well, I take your point.

PRONUNCIATION

See *Teaching tips: Helping students with pronunciation*, page 22.

Play the DVD and ask students to focus on the intonation. Play the DVD again, pausing after each phrase for students to repeat. Drill the phrases again if necessary.

4a Check understanding of the statements. Demonstrate the activity by taking the part of Student A and asking a stronger student to respond as Student B. Emphasise that Student B should give a reason for their response. Students work in pairs. When they have finished, ask them to swap roles and repeat the exercise.

b Give students a few minutes to think about their own opinions first. When they are ready, have a class discussion. Nominate quiet students to express their opinions, but don't force the issue if they don't want to.

Writing

An opinion essay

1a Students read the opinions individually, then check the meanings of the phrases and guess the topic in pairs. Check answers with the class.

ANSWERS:

Crime and punishment is being discussed.
life sentence: the longest prison sentence someone can receive; the length varies in different countries, but is usually around 15 years
good deterrent: something that makes someone unlikely to do something by making them realise it will have bad results
against: not agreeing with something
minor: not very serious
serious crimes: very bad crimes
effective: having the result that you want
community service: work to improve the community for other people
in favour of: support, approval or agreement for something
tougher punishments: harder punishments
leniently: not strict enough in the way you punish someone

b Check understanding of *tougher punishments*. Students discuss the questions in pairs.

ANSWERS:

The first and fourth statements support tougher punishments.
The second and third are against tougher punishments.

2 Introduce the text by asking if students have ever had to write essays like this at school/university. Students work individually, then check answers in pairs before checking with the class.

ANSWERS:

no; if people are sent to prison for minor crimes, they are more likely to commit serious crimes in the future; it's a good deterrent; the victim is forgotten

Language live, Writing, exercise 2: Alternative suggestion

Copy the text onto separate pieces of paper, one for each pair of students, and cut each one up into the five paragraphs. Students put the text in the correct order before answering the questions in the Students' Book.

3a Elicit the first answer as an example. Students work individually or in pairs before checking answers with the class.

ANSWERS:

1 e **2** d **3** a **4** b, c

b Go through the example with the class. Give students plenty of time to underline the phrases in each paragraph. Check answers with the class.

ANSWERS:

1 I strongly believe that ... ; I am therefore convinced that ...
2 However, in my opinion, ... ; Many people argue that ...
3 Firstly, ...
4 ... it is important to remember that ... ; For that reason, ... ; What is more, ... ; And, of course, ...

c Refer students back to the linking words they studied in exercise 1 on page 109. Students work individually, then check answers in pairs before checking answers with the class.

ANSWERS:

Paragraph a: However, and, because
Paragraph b: Firstly, as a result, For that reason
Paragraph c: What is more, and, For example, This means that
Paragraph d: However, also, And, of course,
Paragraph e: Despite this, therefore

4a Go through each of the statements and check understanding. Elicit a supporting argument for one of them as an example. Students work individually or in pairs, then check answers with the class.

ANSWERS:

1 + **2** – **3** – **4** +

b Give students plenty of time to think of more arguments. Circulate and help with vocabulary where necessary.

5 Circulate while students are writing their first drafts and help with ideas/vocabulary where necessary. When they have finished, get them to check their work using the checklist.

6 Put students in pairs to swap and read their essays. Emphasise that they shouldn't just look for language errors, but should suggest different ways of expressing their arguments and remind them of the phrases in exercise 3b. Students write their final drafts in class or for homework.

ADDITIONAL PRACTICE

Resource bank: Activity 11D *Wordspot:* do (Collocations with *do*)

Workbook: Language live: *Expressing and responding to opinions*, page 68; Writing: *Checking for mistakes*, page 69

Study, practice & remember

(PAGES 162–164)

See *Teaching tips: Using the Study, practice & remember sections*, page 25.

Practice 1

ANSWERS:

1

1 b **2** c **3** a **4** d

2

1 are allowed to **2** You should **3** Do I have to **4** You're not allowed to **5** Are you allowed to **6** you must/have to **7** You don't have to, you ought to **8** We are allowed to **9** We don't have to

Practice 2

ANSWERS:

1 As a result **2** Even though **3** also **4** Besides **5** In spite of this **6** what's more

Practice 3

ANSWERS:

1

1 We weren't allowed to take our jackets off.
2 I wasn't allowed to wear jeans at school.
3 We had to leave early.
4 We were allowed to invite who we wanted.
5 I didn't have to go to work.
6 We had to write an essay for homework.
7 Did you have to work on Saturdays?
8 Were you allowed to do that?

2

1 didn't have to **2** could **3** wasn't **4** couldn't **5** had to **6** had to

Remember these words

ANSWERS:

2

1 O 2 S 3 S 4 O 5 S 6 O 7 O

3

1 prisoner **2** criminal **3** burglar **4** robber **5** kidnapper **6** mugger

Study tips

If you do these exercises in class, you'll need to make sure students have access to monolingual dictionaries, either in book form or on the internet.

1 Go through the definition with the class and elicit the answer. Emphasise that the collocation does not always appear next to its 'partner' in the text.

ANSWER:

give

2 Go through the information with the class. Emphasise that when they look up words in dictionaries, looking for and recording collocations will also help them produce the words more naturally when they come to use them.

3 Students work individually to find the collocations, then check answers in pairs. Go through the answers with the class.

ANSWERS:

1 had **2** made **3** get **4** went **5** give **6** take

12 YOUR CHOICE

OVERVIEW

PAGES 116–117

Grammar: *could have, should have, would have*

Pronunciation: Past modals

Common European Framework: Students can explain why something is a problem, discuss what to do next, compare and contrast alternatives.

PAGES 118–119

Listening: The toughest decision of their lives

Grammar: Hypothetical situations in the past with *if*

Common European Framework: Students can understand the description of events, feelings and wishes; can convey information and ideas on abstract topics.

PAGES 120–121

Vocabulary: Problems and solutions

Reading: How to make decisions

Common European Framework: Students can read factual texts on subjects related to their interests; can express themselves on topics pertinent to their interests.

PAGES 122–123

Task: Discuss dilemmas

Common European Framework: Students can explain why something is a problem, discuss what to do next, compare and contrast alternatives; can give brief comments on the views of others.

PAGES 124–125

World culture: Life in a new country

Common European Framework: Students can understand most TV news and current affairs programmes; can give clear, detailed descriptions on a range of topics.

Language focus 1 (PAGES 116–117)

could have, should have, would have

See *Teaching tips: Using a discovery approach to grammar*, page 20.

WARM UP

Before class, write *stressful situations* in the middle of the board and draw a circle around it. Build a mind map with some or all of the following things: *getting stuck in traffic, dealing with bureaucracy, not getting enough sleep, being late for something, an exam or job interview, not having enough money*. Elicit any other situations that students find stressful and add them to the mind map. Students discuss which of the situations they find most stressful and how they try to deal with each one. In feedback, nominate students to share their ideas with the class.

1a Check understanding of *blow your top*. Go through the title and introduction with the class. Elicit their ideas and write them on the board.

b Check that students understand *feel nauseous* (/'nɔːziəs/) and *to storm out* (*of the house*). Students do the quiz individually, then check their answers on page 130.

c Students compare their profiles in pairs. In feedback, find out how many students agree with their profiles. Ask them to give examples of why they agree/disagree.

2 Introduce the activity by giving students an example of a problem you had recently and how you reacted. Give students a few minutes to think of a recent problem individually. If they are having trouble thinking of one, suggest some topics, e.g. *colleagues/classmates, transport, health, relationships*.

3 Do the first item as an example. Students work individually, then check in pairs. Check answers with the class.

ANSWERS:

1b I shouldn't have worked so hard recently.
2b I shouldn't have taken this job.
2d I should have given my point of view!
3c I could have died!
4b I wouldn't have walked out like that.
5a You couldn't have known it was a trick.
5c I wouldn't have stopped to help a stranger.

GRAMMAR

could have*, *should have*, *would have

Students work in pairs before checking answers with the class.

ANSWERS:

1 c 2 a 3 b

Focus students' attention back on sentences 1–3 and point out the constructions used in each case, including the negative forms:

- *could/should/would* + *have* + past participle
- *couldn't/shouldn't/wouldn't* + *have* + past participle

Point out that *would* can be contracted to *'d*. You may want to ask students to read Study 1 on page 165 for a more detailed explanation of *could have, should have, would have*.

PRONUNCIATION

See *Teaching tips: Helping students with pronunciation*, page 22.

1 **12.1** Point out the weak pronunciation of *have* and the vowel sound /ə/ in the modals, e.g. /'kʊdəv/, /'kʊdəntəv/. Drill the forms as isolated phrases, including the negative forms.

2 **12.2** Students listen and practise the phrases.

Potential problem with pronunciation

Students may find it difficult to produce or hear these forms naturally, as they may be used to the written forms. If so model the phrases yourself, slowly at first and gradually speeding up to normal speech.

PRACTICE

1 Students work in pairs. If necessary, refer them to the list of irregular verbs on page 175 to check any past participle forms.

ANSWERS:

1 could have **2** would have **3** couldn't have **4** wouldn't have
5 could/should have, would have **6** should have, could have
7 shouldn't have, could have **8** shouldn't have, would have

2a Check the meaning of *vase*. Students read the text, then answer the questions in pairs. Check answers with the class.

ANSWERS:

Someone was burgling their house in the night. She hit the burglar over the head with a vase.

b Students work individually or in pairs to write sentences. Circulate, supplying vocabulary before checking answers with the class.

3a Put students into pairs, A and B. Explain that they will read about different situations. Refer them to the relevant pages at the back of the book and give them five minutes to read the story and make notes of the main points. Circulate, explaining vocabulary if necessary.

b Do this as a speaking activity. Circulate and note down errors to focus on at the end of the activity and ensure that students are using weak forms of *have* and contractions where appropriate.

ADDITIONAL PRACTICE

Study, practice & remember: Practice 1

Workbook: Language focus 1: *could have, should have, would have*, pages 70–71; Pronunciation: *Past modal forms in connected speech*, page 72

Listening (PAGE 118)

WARM UP

Tell students about a long or difficult journey you have made. Include as much detail as possible, including where you were travelling from/to, the type of transport, who you were travelling with, why you were travelling and how long it took. Encourage students to ask you follow-up questions to find out more information. Give students a few minutes to think about a long or difficult journey they have made, then ask them to tell each other about it in pairs.

1 Focus students' attention on the photos and the headline of the story. Check the meaning of *to row*, and *shifts*. Students read the text, then discuss the questions as a class.

2 Go through the key words and check understanding. Get students to share their ideas with the class. Write their guesses on the board.

3 **12.3** Go through the questions so that students know what to listen for. Students listen, then check answers in pairs before checking with the class.

ANSWERS:

1 Andrew was very experienced and had won international competitions. Debra had only learned to row a year before.
2 Debra enjoyed it. Andrew suffered from acute anxiety and developed an irrational fear of the ocean.
3 The boat was caught in a violent storm. Andrew shook with fear and was unable to talk.

4 **12.4** Get students to discuss their ideas in pairs. Write their ideas on the board. Refer students to the questions before they listen to the next part. As you check answers, discuss which of their ideas were closest before going through the comprehension questions.

ANSWERS:

1 yes
2 collision with huge oil tankers; sharks; extreme weather conditions
3 Debra met a yacht and was given fresh bread, biscuits and ten minutes of conversation.
4 113 days
5 Journalists, TV cameras, her husband, a crowd of people
6 70 days
7 The Queen made Debra an MBE. Debra and Andrew divorced and she remarried. She has a successful career as a motivational speaker.

5 Students discuss the questions in small groups.

Language focus 2 (PAGE 119)

Hypothetical situations in the past with *if*

See *Teaching tips: Using a discovery approach to grammar*, page 20.

1 **12.5** Students match the sentence halves individually. When they are ready, play the recording for them to check their answers, pausing after each sentence.

ANSWERS:

1 d 2 c 3 a 4 e 5 b

2 Go through the example, then students work individually to underline verbs in the other sentences. Check answers with the class.

ANSWERS:

1 had known, wouldn't have entered
2 had stayed, would have got
3 had hit, would have sunk
4 had continued, might (still) be
5 hadn't had, wouldn't be

GRAMMAR

Hypothetical situations in the past with *if*

Grammar: language notes

Most classes will find this Grammar challenging, so it is advisable to work through it step by step as a class, rather than leaving students to work it out for themselves. We have dealt with 'mixed conditionals', as well as 'third conditionals' because in most real-life communicative situations these are found together. However, your students may not be familiar with 'mixed conditionals' and may find them difficult at first.

1 Remind students of the hypothetical possibilities with *if* on page 100. Discuss each question in turn as a class.

ANSWERS:

1 hypothetical 2 past; Past perfect (*had* + past participle)
3 past: a, c, d; present: b, e
a, c, d: *would* (*not*) + *have* + past participle; b: *would not* + infinitive; e: *might* + infinitive

2 Highlight both forms. First write up the following formula to summarise the 'third conditional':

past condition (*imaginary*) → *past result* (*imaginary*)

if + Past perfect + would/wouldn't + have + past participle

If he hadn't been bored (*then*), *he wouldn't have started dicing* (*then*).

Emphasise that it is not possible to use *would have* after *if* and that both *had* and *would* can be contracted to *'d*. Leave this summary on the board to contrast it with the 'mixed conditional':

past condition (*imaginary*) → *present/general result* (*imaginary*)

if + Past perfect + would/wouldn't + verb

If the book hadn't been successful (*then*), *he would still be a college professor.* (*now*)

Emphasise that the use of the verbs here is entirely logical. It may be useful to translate the 'mixed conditional' to make this clear. Students may ask you if they can mix the conditional the other way round (a present/general condition with a past result). This is also possible, for example:

If I didn't trust you (*now*), *I wouldn't have lent you my car yesterday.* (*then*)

Don't go into this unless students ask specifically. You may want to ask students to read Study 2 on page 166 for a more detailed explanation of hypothetical situations in the past with *if*.

Notes on the use of past tenses with hypothetical language

It can be useful to think of past tenses as 'distant' and present tenses as 'near'. In this way, there are three things which affect our choice of tense: time, register and reality.

- Time: we use past tenses to describe past actions because they are distant in time (*I crashed the car yesterday.*)
- Register: we communicate with people we see as distant by using past tenses to sound more formal (*I was wondering if you could tell me how to get there?*).
- Reality: we speak hypothetically by using past tenses to indicate distance in reality (*If I had arrived earlier, I would have seen her.*).

Hypothetical situations in the past with *if* are made up of two 'pasts' – one to express non-reality and one to express past time. Explaining this to your students with examples can help give them a better understanding of hypothetical language.

PRACTICE

If you think your students need more controlled practice before these exercises, they could do Practice 2 on page 166 first.

1 **12.6** Check the meaning of *company director, nanny, second best, to work out well*. Students listen before checking answers in pairs and then as a whole class.

ANSWERS:

Erin:

1 to give up her job and become a full-time mother **2** hated leaving her first baby with a nanny **3** has two children and less money

Kieron:

1 to give up his career as a football player and retrain as a coach
2 broke his leg when he was 19 and continued to have problems with it
3 is now a coach, but lost his dream

Margot:

1 to leave her family and friends and her job as a nurse to live in Greece **2** met Nikos on holiday and really liked him
3 runs a restaurant on a Greek island with Nikos

2a Students work individually or in pairs before checking answers as a class. Emphasise that answers will vary slightly if they use *might*.

ANSWERS:

1 hadn't had, would have continued
2 hadn't left, would have spent/would spend
3 would/might have, had stayed, wouldn't be
4 could/might have become, hadn't broken
5 had been able, wouldn't/might not have become
6 would/might be, had fulfilled
7 hadn't gone, wouldn't have met
8 would/might have forgotten, hadn't followed
9 hadn't married, would/might still be living
10 hadn't moved, would/might still be

b Students discuss in pairs. In feedback, nominate students to share their answers with the class and find out if others agree.

3a Give one or two personal examples of your own, before getting students to write their sentences individually. Circulate, monitoring and supplying vocabulary.

b Go through the examples with the class. Encourage students to ask follow-up questions.

Language focus 2, Practice, exercise 3: Alternative suggestion

Before class, write the sentence starters from exercise 3a at the top of blank pieces of paper and display them around the room. Ask students to walk around and add their endings to each piece of paper and read what other students have written. When they have finished, put students in small groups and give one of the papers to each group. Ask them to correct any mistakes they can find and circulate and help them where necessary.

ADDITIONAL PRACTICE

Resource bank: Activity 12A *Suzie's story* (Hypothetical situations in the past with *if* and *shouldn't have*)

Study, practice & remember: Practice 2

Workbook: Language focus 2: *Imaginary situations in the past with if*, pages 72–73

Vocabulary (PAGE 120)

Problems and solutions

See *Teaching tips: Working with lexis*, page 21.

1 Point out that the sentences tell the same story, but that they are in the wrong order. Students should first check the words in bold, then order the sentences in pairs. Check answers with the class, going over language points relating to phrasal verbs. Drill both as isolated phrases and as longer sentences.

ANSWERS:

c 1 **a** 2 **g** 3 **d** 4 **h** 5 **b** 6 **f** 7 **e** 8

Vocabulary, exercise 1: Alternative suggestion

Do this as a 'disappearing story' in the following way:

- As you check the order of the story, write it out on the board.
- Tell students to close their books and get a student to read the story aloud from the board, correcting pronunciation as necessary.
- Rub out one or two of the phrases in bold in exercise 1, replacing them with gaps.
- Get another student to read the story aloud, filling in the gaps as necessary.
- Repeat the process, removing one or two phrases each time, until all the target phrases are replaced by gaps. (As the reading-aloud stage gets more difficult, it may be necessary to ask other students to help, to keep up the pace.)
- Finally, get students to write out the story from the remaining prompts. Alternatively, they could write a more complete story, explaining what the problem was, either in class or for homework.

2 Students work in pairs to match phrases and definitions.

ANSWERS:

1 go away **2** didn't have a care in the world **3** sort the problem out **4** talk it over **5** ignore **6** make a decision **7** have a problem with **8** sympathetic **9** concerns **10** trust your intuition **11** lose sleep over it

3a Elicit students' ideas as to what the problem was in exercise 1. Go through the ideas in the list and see if any of their ideas were mentioned, then put students into pairs to choose a problem from the list or the board to write about.

b Go through the example with the class. Circulate and help with vocabulary where necessary, writing any new words/phrases on the board. If your students have problems coming up with ideas, put up the following prompts:

He saw his nephew hanging around with some bad people and didn't know whether to tell his sister.

He was once arrested for shoplifting.

His debts were getting worse and worse, but he couldn't stop spending money.

He was terribly in love with his boss, a married woman ten years older than himself.

4 Students take it in turns to read out their stories, while other students listen and choose their favourite one.

Vocabulary, exercise 4: Alternative suggestion

When students have written their stories in exercise 4, ask them to choose six key moments in the story and take a photo of each other acting out that moment, then send them to you. Before the next class, print out the 'photostories' and give them back to students. They then swap with another group and guess what happened in the story from the photos, before checking with the group who wrote the story. As a follow up, ask students to write captions under each photo and display them round the class for others to read.

ADDITIONAL PRACTICE

Resource bank: Activity 12B *No problem!* (Vocabulary extension: problems and solutions)

Workbook: Vocabulary: *Problems and solutions*, page 73

Reading (PAGES 120–121)

1 Introduce the topic by telling students about something you find difficult and how you usually decide. Students discuss the questions in small groups.

2 Focus attention on the photos and elicit what type of decision-making is shown in each. Check understanding of *low mileage* and *jelly beans*. Students read the text, then answer the questions in pairs. Check answers with the class.

ANSWERS:

1 which used car to buy
2 She can't make a decision.
3 a 2 **b** 1 **c** 3

3 Students work individually, then check answers in pairs before checking with the class.

ANSWERS:

1 a black car **b** red car **c** blue car
2 a intuitive **b** rational **c** fatalistic
3 a Goizueta **b** Rhinehart
4 Goizueta changed the taste of Coca-Cola. People were emotionally attached to the old drink. Rhinehart offered two nurses a lift in his car. He married one of the nurses.

4 Students discuss the questions in small groups.

Task (PAGES 122–123)

Discuss dilemmas

See *Teaching tips: Making tasks work*, page 23.

Preparation

Reading

1a Discuss the questions as a class.

b Students just read the three titles and predict the contents of each letter in small groups. Write students' predictions on the board.

c Students read the texts then check answers in pairs before checking answers with the class.

2a Put students in groups of three, but ask them to work individually to read their text and make notes of their answers.

b Get students to close their books and summarise each problem.

ANSWERS:

1 Should I choose the job or my girlfriend?

1 Larry, Vanessa, Vanessa's parents, Larry's friends **2** Larry has asked his girlfriend Vanessa to marry him and has accepted a new job 300 miles away. **3** Larry was confused about whether to take the great new job or split up with the love of his life; he was worried in case he never met anyone else like her again.

2 Professional football or accountancy?

1 Oscar, his parents **2** Oscar had a trial with a local football club when he was 15. He has now been accepted on an accountancy course at university. **3** Oscar was confused because he thought he was good enough to play football for his club and his country, but his parents wanted him to go to university. He was worried about making the wrong choice.

3 It's my mother-in-law or me!

1 Astrid, her husband, her father-in-law, her mother-in-law, her two children **2** Astrid has been married to her husband for ten years and has had two children. She has tried to help her mother-in-law as much as possible when her husband died. She has told her husband that they have to find a care home for his mother or else she will leave him. **3** Astrid was finding it difficult to cope with the situation and had told her husband to choose between her and his mother. She was worried because her husband wouldn't discuss it with her.

Task (PAGE 122)

Speaking

1 Give students ten to fifteen minutes to work individually and brainstorm a list of options for each problem. Refer them to the Useful language box, sections a–c.

2a Put students into small groups. Encourage students to persuade each other of their point of view if there are differences of opinion, but do not insist that they reach a common solution if this is not possible. Circulate, supplying vocabulary. Monitor and note down errors and useful language for correction and analysis later on.

b Give students a few minutes to prepare what they will report to the class. Tell them to list the possible solutions they came up with before saying what they think the person should do. Collect errors and useful language as above.

3 Students turn to page 131 to read what the people did, then discuss the questions in groups. In feedback, find out if anyone had the same ideas.

Task: Alternative suggestions

a If you want to make the task shorter or split it over two lessons, do one of the following:

- Give students a list of difficult vocabulary from the texts to check in dictionaries before the lesson.
- Students read the problem letters for homework. Check comprehension before going on to Task: Speaking. (This homework could be combined with the vocabulary work above.)
- Do Preparation: Reading in one lesson and Task: Speaking in the next lesson. This would give students plenty of time to think about solutions and how to express them in English. Start the second lesson with a brief opportunity for students to ask you about vocabulary, etc.
- Just look at one of the problems in Preparation: Reading. These problems have been designed to appeal to a range of ages, but you could omit those that you think your students will have problems relating to.

b If you have a large class, in Task: Speaking, exercise 2b, ask one group to volunteer to list their ideas for each problem. Before they give their opinion, ask the other groups if they came up with any other possible solutions. After the nominated group has given their opinion, ask the other groups to say what solution they thought was the best.

Share your task

Some additional ideas could include:

- Students make a talk show TV/radio programme. Students choose one of their group members to play the role of the person with one of the problems from the task. Then prepare a programme where they tell their problem to an 'audience' (the other members of the group), who give them advice. Feed in some phrases for asking for/giving advice, for example: *I've got a (bit of a/terrible) problem … ; I just don't know what to do. What do you think should do? Perhaps you should … ; Have you thought about … ? You should definitely … ; Try not to worry so much … .* Students then film/record the programme, then show it to the class, who decide if they agree with the advice given.
- Students film/record themselves giving advice for each problem, then show it to the class, who decide if they agree.

Follow-up (PAGE 123)

Writing

1 Give students a few minutes to read through the options and decide which one they would like to do. Students work individually or in pairs. Give them plenty of time to do their piece of writing. Circulate, supplying vocabulary they need and correcting where necessary. When they have finished, get some/all of the students to read out their letters or act out their scenes. If there is time, follow this up with a correction slot. Students could write a more 'polished' version for homework, incorporating the corrections you have gone over in class.

ADDITIONAL PRACTICE

Resource bank: Activity 12C *Wordspot:* think (Collocations with *think*)

Workbook: Writing: *A letter to sort out a problem*, page 75

World culture (PAGES 124–125)

Life in a new country

Culture notes

UK: The United Kingdom is made up of Great Britain (which in turn is made up of England, Scotland and Wales) and Northern Ireland. It comprises an area of 243,610 km², and has a population of 63 million and is situated in the north of Europe. It has a constitutional Monarchy and a parliamentary democracy, the head of government being the prime minister. The capital city is London, which dates back to the Romans, who referred to it as *Londinium*, and the official language is English. It has a market economy, which is ranked the sixth largest in the world. It has a varied geography, with mountains in the north and lower lands in the south, and its coastline is 17,820 km long. The UK has a temperate climate, which is very changeable, and it can be difficult to predict what the weather will be like from one day to the next.

New Zealand: New Zealand is an island country made up of two main islands in the South West Pacific, with a population of only 4.7 million and an area of 268,676 km². Because of its remote location, it was one of the last lands to be settled by humans and was originally settled by the Polynesians around AD1250–1300, who developed a unique *Maori* culture. Europeans made contact in 1642. The capital city is Wellington and Queen Elizabeth II is the head of state, though the country is governed by a prime minister. The official languages are English and Maori, and the climate is mild, with above-average rainfall, but extended periods of sun. The country boasts stunning scenery, including mountains, lakes, rivers and beaches, and has been used as the backdrop for films such as *The Lord of the Rings*.

Find out first (PAGE 124)

1 Books closed. Write *London* and *New Zealand* on the board and elicit things that students associate with each place, building two mind maps on the board. Students open their books and look at the photos, then discuss the questions in pairs. In feedback, nominate students to share their ideas with the class.

2a Students discuss what they know in pairs. Elicit some of their ideas, but don't give any answers yet.

b Students research online, then compare information in pairs. Check answers with the class and feed in information from the Culture notes.

ANSWERS:

	New Zealand	UK
Population	4.7 million	63 million
Area	268,676 km²	243,610 km²
Capital	Wellington	London
Official language(s)	English, Maori	English
Climate	mild temperatures, moderately high rainfall, many hours of sunshine throught most of country	varied climate (We never know what the weather will be like from one day to the next.)
Scenery/ landscape	stunning mountains, lakes, rivers, bush, beaches	varied

Find out first, exercise 1c: Alternative suggestion

Put students in pairs. One student researches the UK and the other researches New Zealand. When they have finished, students tell their partner what they found out and complete the table.

View (PAGE 124)

3a Give students time to read the definitions in the glossary, then be ready to answer any questions with further examples/explanations if necessary. Check the pronunciation of *outdoor pursuits* /ˈaʊtdɔːpəˈsjuːts/.

b Go through the topics with the class and check students understand what to watch for. Play the first part of the video for students to watch and make notes.

c Students watch the video again and complete their notes before checking in pairs. Check answers with the class.

ANSWERS:

1 They live outside London. Imogen works as a language teacher and Charile works as a recruitment consultant. **2** relaxed, outdoor lifestyle **3** Imogen's family live in New Zealand. Charlie's live in Scotland. **4** Recruitment consultants can earn a good salary.
Things that attract them: Imogen: outdoor lifestyle, weather, being able to do outdoor sports, being able to teach, family already lives there; Charlie: career prospects, good salary
Things that do not attract them: Charlie: outdoor lifestyle – loves the city; fact that parents live in Scotland

4a Review the reasons for and against moving, then elicit via a show of hands which country the students think the couple will choose. Play the second part of the video for students to check.

ANSWER:

the couple choose to stay in the UK

b Students discuss the questions in groups. In feedback, nominate a student from each group to share their ideas with the class.

World view (PAGE 125)

See *Teaching tips: Using the video material in the classroom*, page 24.

5 Go through the questions with the class and check students understand what to watch for. Play the DVD for students to answer the questions, then check in pairs. Play the DVD a second time if necessary, then check answers with the class.

ANSWERS:

Anna
1 Germany
2 UK (London), because husband got a job there
3 diverse city, with museums, galleries, etc.;
4 people often move away after short time when you've just got to know them

Carol
1 Minnesota, USA
2 China, to study and then to teach
3 food, people, culture, language
4 not the place for a foreigner to have a family

Denise
1 Canada
2 North Korea, wanted to experience living in a different culture
3 life-changing to see a different way of living
4 being away from friends and family, language barrier

Bethan
1 UK
2 Italy, as part of university degree
3 learning a new language
4 being away from her family

6 Students discuss the questions in groups before sharing their ideas with the class.

Find out more (PAGE 125)

7a Discuss the questions as a class and elicit students' reasons for their opinions.

b Students research the questions individually, then compare what they found out in pairs. Circulate and help with vocabulary where necessary. Ask students to share their answers with the class and write them on the board.

Write up your research

8 Students write their paragraphs individually, using the prompts to help them. Circulate and help where necessary. When they have finished, students swap paragraphs with another student and read. Elicit any interesting information that students found out.

Students can now do Unit test 6 and the End of course test on the Teacher's Resource Disc.

Study, practice & remember (PAGES 165–167)

See *Teaching tips: Using the Study, practice & remember sections*, page 25.

Practice 1

ANSWERS:

1
1 should have taken **2** could have fallen
3 wouldn't have enjoyed **4** shouldn't have opened
5 could have been worse **6** would have cost

2
1 I wouldn't have left her all alone.
2 I was so happy, I could have kissed everyone.
3 I should have bought those shoes.
4 They talked so much they could have missed the last train.
5 Why didn't they buy that house? I think it would have been a good idea.
6 I couldn't have helped him.
7 They shouldn't have started a business together.

3
1a I wouldn't have done that.
1b They could have been dangerous.
1c She shouldn't have stopped.
2a I would have said no.
2b It could have been a bomb.
2c He should have said no.
3a She shouldn't have told the stranger her address.
3b The stranger could have been dangerous.
3c She should have ended the conversation.

Practice 2

ANSWERS:

1

1 If you'd been more careful, you wouldn't have lost it.
2 If I'd passed that exam, I could have gone to university.
3 I would have been embarrassed if it had happened to me.
4 If you hadn't forgotten your passport, we'd be there now.
5 I wouldn't have started if I'd known how long it would take.
6 If Rick hadn't stayed in the USA, he wouldn't have met Mia.

2

1 If I hadn't felt ill, I would have gone to work.
2 If my girlfriend hadn't gone out without me, she wouldn't have met another guy.
3 If he hadn't checked his emails in the bath, his computer wouldn't have got wet and broken.
4 If she had learnt from her mistakes, she wouldn't have done the same thing again.
5 If a storm hadn't damaged the plane, they wouldn't have made an emergency landing.
6 If we hadn't listened to her advice, we wouldn't have made the right decision.
7 If I hadn't answered the phone while driving, I wouldn't have crashed the car.
8 If my family hadn't moved house, I wouldn't have had to change school.
9 If it hadn't rained, we would have had a barbecue.
10 If he hadn't lost his job, he wouldn't have had to sell his sports car.

3

SUGGESTED ANSWERS:

1 If I'd learnt English as a child, I wouldn't be here now.
2 If I'd invested all my money in Google, I'd be rich now.
3 If I hadn't learnt to read as a child, life would be very difficult now.
4 If I had felt ill this morning, I would still be in bed now.
5 If I hadn't stayed out so late last night, I wouldn't feel so tired now.
6 If I had thought about the decision more, I wouldn't regret it now.

Remember these words

ANSWERS:

1

1 c 2 a 3 b 4 c 5 a 6 a 7 b

2

1 D 2 D 3 S 4 S 5 S

Study tips

If your class are taking an end-of-course test, then do these exercises a week or two in advance so they can put the advice into practice.

1 Give students a minute to choose their statement, then discuss answers with the class. Encourage students to give reasons for their choice.

2 Students work individually to tick the techniques they use, then compare answers in pairs.

3 Students underline the techniques they would like to try, then compare answers in pairs.

Pearson Education Limited
Edinburgh Gate
Harlow
Essex CM20 2JE
England
and Associated Companies throughout the world.

www.pearsonelt.com

First published 2013
Fifth impression 2017
ISBN: 978-1-4479-3757-9

Set in Bliss Light 8.5pt/10.5pt
Printed by Ashford Colour Press Ltd

Cover images: *Front:* Shutterstock.com: Rodho tr

Illustrated by: Pavely Arts, Kathy Baxendale,
Kevin Hopgood (Beehive Illustration),
Graham Humphreys/The Art Market, Ed McLachlan,
Graham Smith/The Art Market.